America and Its Sources

A Guided Journey through Key Documents,
1865-present

Edited by
Erin L. Conlin and Stephan Schaffrath

America and Its Sources: A Guided Journey through Key Documents, 1865-present

© 2019 Schlager Group Inc.

Editors in Chief: Erin L. Conlin and Stephan Schaffrath (Indiana University of Pennsylvania)

For Schlager Group:

Vice President, Editorial: Sarah Robertson
Vice President, Operations and Strategy: Benjamin Painter
Publisher: Neil Schlager

ISBN: 9781935306696

eISBN: 9781935306375

Schlager Group Inc.
1111 W. Mockingbird Lane, Suite 735
Dallas, TX 75247
(888)-416-5727

Contents

About the Editors

Erin L. Conlin (PhD, University of Florida, 2014) is an assistant professor of history at Indiana University of Pennsylvania (IUP). She specializes in public, oral, and 20th-century U.S. History. She regularly teaches courses in these areas and is actively developing the IUP Oral History Program. Her research examines the evolution of Florida's modern farm labor system and its heavy reliance on non-citizen workers.

Stephan Schaffrath (PhD, Indiana University of Pennsylvania, 2004) is developmental instructor in the Department of Developmental Studies at IUP. For most of the last twenty-some years, he has been working with first-year college students to prepare them in literacy education through composition, language, literature, reading, academic acclimation, learning skills, and career exploration courses. With a Certificate in Developmental Education from the Kellogg Institute and a PhD from IUP's Literature and Criticism program, Stephan is an ardent advocate for making even the most complex texts accessible to all students.

Acknowledgments

John P. Davis: "A Black Inventory of the New Deal": Reprinted from *The Crisis,* May 1935. Reprinted courtesy of the Crisis Publishing Co., Inc., the publisher of the magazine of the National Association of the Advancement of Colored People.

Advertisements from the 1950s and 1960s: Magazine advertisement for Hoover Vaccuums from the 1950s and advertisement for Alcoa Aluminum. Both: © The Advertising Archives/Bridgeman Images. 1935 advertisement for Elliott's Paint and Varnish: © Pictures from History/Bridgeman Images).

Martin Luther King, Jr: "Letter from Birmingham Jail": Reprinted by arrangement with The Heirs to the Estate of Martin Luther King Jr., c/o Writers House as agent for the proprietor New York, NY. Copyright © 1963 Dr. Martin Luther King Jr.; Copyright © renewed 1991 Coretta Scott King.

Betty Friedan: The Feminine Mystique: "The Problem That Has No Name", from *The Feminine Mystique* by Betty Friedan. Copyright © 1983, 1974, 1973, 1963 by Betty Friedan. Used by permission of W.W. Norton & Company, Inc.

Martin Luther King, Jr.: "Beyond Vietnam: A Time to Break Silence": Reprinted by arrangement with The Heirs to the Estate of Martin Luther King Jr., c/o Writers House as agent for the proprietor New York, NY. Copyright © 1967 Dr. Martin Luther King Jr.; Copyright © renewed 1995 Coretta Scott King.

Gay Liberation Front: Program Platform Statement: University of Washington Libraries, Special Collections, PNW04837.

Barry Goldwater: Acceptance Speech for the Presidential Nomination of the Republican Party: Reprinted by permission of the Arizona Historical Foundation.

Jerry Falwell: "Listen America": Excerpt(s) from *Listen, America!* by Jerry Falwell, copyright © 1980 by Jerry Falwell. Used by permission of Doubleday, an imprint of the Knopf Doubleday Publishing Group, a division of Penguin Random House LLC. All rights reserved.

Bill Tolan: "In Desperate 1983, There Was Nowhere for Pittsburgh's Economy to Go but Up: A Tide of Change": Copyright © *Pittsburgh Post-Gazette,* 2018, all rights reserved. Reprinted with permission.

The publisher and editors are grateful to the following instructors for reviewing this publication:

Katrina A Sinclair, Pennsylvania College of Technology

Derek Kutzer, San Antonio College

Jeffrey Parker, Clackamas Community College

Jonathan Rees, Colorado State University - Pueblo

Elias Paulk, North Florida Community College

Kelsey Walker, University of North Carolina, Greensboro

William Wantland, Mount Vernon Nazarene University

Introduction

History tells a story. This sourcebook is designed to help students develop their critical-reading competencies while simultaneously introducing students to the nation's story through the words of people who shaped and experienced the nation's history. It is a survey of U.S. history since the Civil War, and it intentionally views that history through the lenses of race, gender, and labor since those are facets of life that affect nearly all people and are thus useful tools of analysis through which to examine contemporary America.

We designed the sourcebook to include fourteen units as opposed to fifteen or sixteen, in order to give instructors greater flexibility over the course of a semester rather than feeling like they need to cover one unit per week. Some units include a variety of topics and themes in order to illustrate major points without getting bogged down in too much detail. For example, the first unit includes primary sources that span more than 200 years. The purpose is to remind students of the nation's labor origins as it transitioned from indentured to enslaved labor. The subsequent thirteen units take a thematic and chronological approach, fleshing out important historical moments as well as important concepts like identity, citizenship, and democracy. Some topics, like the civil rights movement, span two units since the events of the 1950s, 60s and 70s caused such a profound shift in American society. This sourcebook is not designed to be a comprehensive account of every facet of U.S. history from the Civil War to the present. Rather, it seeks to introduce students to a nuanced narrative of American history that highlights major themes while also introducing them to new voices and ideas that may be less familiar to them from their previous history courses.

Many students, even at the college level, struggle with reading proficiency and comprehension. This book is intentionally designed to meet the needs of instructors who want their students to work with primary sources but recognize that many college students (especially those in their first year) benefit from guidance to understand and critically evaluate information from the readings and apply new knowledge they are developing in the course across topics and periods of time. Primary sources can be particularly challenging for students because these sources often use unfamiliar language and require students to understand the historical context in which sources were produced in order to fully appreciate their meaning and significance. This sourcebook aims to support student reading and learning in several ways.

Each unit of the sourcebook consists of an introduction, five primary source documents, and a unit review. There are three unit questions posed at the beginning and end of each unit. These questions are designed to guide students' reading throughout the unit. They encourage students to think critically about the material by asking them to apply and evalute knowledge they learned from previous units in order to establish connections, draw conclusions, and make predictions. They also frequently contain note-taking tips and directions so that students will produce thorough, useful notes to review at the end of a unit.

The five primary source readings in each unit follow a similar, highly structured format. To facilitate improved reading competencies and strengthen historical understanding, each primary source reading provides historical context as well as guiding questions designed to facilitate students' engagement with the material, prompting them to form their own perspective. The "Historical Context" section is aimed at providing relevant information about the document itself, the author, the period and circumstances in which it was produced, and/or how a source relates to other events, readings, and themes throughout the sourcebook. As with the unit questions, there are three "Guiding Questions" for each source. It is often a struggle to get students to read course material, much less retain the content so that they are prepared to critically engage with it. The Guiding Reading Questions, then, are designed to improve basic reading comprehension. They help students take notes on what they read, flesh out major ideas, and identify key supporting details. While some questions engage higher order thinking skills like making comparisons, drawing conclusions based on previous knowledge, making predictions about the future based on what they have learned, or evaluating or analyzing information, the questions are generally designed to help students breakdown a reading so that at the end they can explain what the reading was about and what important ideas it helps illustrate in relation to a given unit. Once students master a basic understanding of the primary sources, they will be better equipped to critically analyze the material during class discussions, activities, and assignments.

The primary sources in each unit have been carefully edited to limit them to an average of 500 words per document, in order to provide students with enough material to work with as they analyze a source but not so much that they get overwhelmed and quit reading. Some primary sources exceed 500 words, but no unit exceeds 2,500 words of primary source content in total. Where sources have been edited for length, we have included ellipses to indicate places where the original material has been excised.

We would like to extend our gratitude to the scholars who reviewed this sourcebook and provided feedback that helped us alter and improve the final version. We welcome any additional feedback about this sourcebook. If you would like to contact us, please do so via the publisher:

Schlager Group / Milestone Documents
Attn: Erin L. Conlin and Stephan Schaffrath
1111 W. Mockingbird Ln. STE 735
Dallas, TX 75247
info@MilestoneDocuments.com

Erin L. Conlin and Stephan Schaffrath
July, 2019

How to Read Primary Sources

Eric Cunningham, Gonzaga University

The Challenge of Primary Sources

Reading primary sources always presents a challenge because even though they are the most important of all historical texts, primary sources are not always the easiest documents for students to read or understand. Most of us get our first formal exposure to history from secondary sources, such as school textbooks or historical monographs, or even from tertiary sources, such as encyclopedias, online reference sites, or commercial study guides like CliffsNotes or SparkNotes. Because we are used to reading history as it is presented to us by historians, we are also used to having the background and the significance of historical events explained to us in a readable easy-to-consume fashion. When we take up the challenge of reading primary sources, we become historians ourselves, and it falls to us to figure out what the documents mean, how they were generated, and why they are important.

As we read them, we need to keep a series of questions in mind. Initially, these questions may be considered "what, when, and why does it matter?" This is the first pass of interpretation and it consists of being able to state:

• the substance of the document,

• the historical circumstances and contexts of the document, and

• the historical significance of the document.

In determining the historical significance of the document, we are taken to a second level of questions:

• Who wrote (drew, painted, photographed, or filmed) it?

• Can we tell the author's purpose in producing the source?

• Can we determine the positions the author takes and figure out the assumptions upon which the author bases his or her positions?

• Are there any biases or inclinations that we can detect in the author's thinking that may not be openly stated?

• What is the historical context of the source? In other words, what were the historical conditions that led to the production and initial reception of this source?

• Does the source stand alone or does it belong to a genre of similar sources?

• How persuasive or credible is the source? We can base this judgment on the author's own authority, the effectiveness of his or her presentation and the quality of the content.

• What influence has the source had upon history? Has its significance changed over time?

This is a lot more than most of us think about when watching the History Channel or reading the works of a popular historical novelist, but these kinds of questions about primary sources are the means by which histories are written and our civilization's memory is preserved. It is very serious business.

Determining the Difference between Primary, Secondary, and Tertiary Sources

To illustrate the difference between these three kinds of historical documents let's take a real-world example. We'll start with a primary source document: Abraham Lincoln's Gettysburg Address of November 19, 1863. We know this is a primary source because it was directly produced by Abraham Lincoln, a well-known historical figure. Primary sources are first-hand sources and are important to historians not because of what they say about history, but because of what they indicate about the times in which they were written and about the people who produced them. All letters, memos, diaries, speeches, essays, sketches, and directives produced by historical agents fall under the category of primary sources. They do not necessarily narrate the history of anything, but they are real-time records of authentic historical events.

The Gettysburg Address poses a few interesting documentation challenges, as there are five handwritten copies of the address, and the newspapers of Lincoln's day printed slightly different versions of his remarks in the days following the actual speech. Lincoln gave copies away to his closest confidants, and they differ from one another in small ways. Nevertheless, there is only one signed copy — the so-called "Bliss copy" (the one we use) — that serves as the "official" version for historians. Determining which, if any of these handwritten versions is the exact original copy of the "real" Gettysburg Address might be an interesting problem for antiquarians or archivists, but the academic historian's concerns with the document are different. Historians accept that there are five "originals" and look to the historical context of the address to learn the extent of its meaning.

What can historians learn from the Gettysburg Address? They can use it as a primary source to gain insights into Lincoln's character and into his views on the importance of American democracy to the history of the world. First, the address gives an indication of Lincoln's knowledge of and respect for classical civilization. Several historians have pointed out formal and rhetorical similarities between the address and the Funeral Oration of Pericles. In noticing Lincoln's purposeful appropriation of stylistic elements of a memorial speech from the democracy of ancient Athens, they can recognize the degree to which Lincoln saw the American civil war as a means of preserving democracy as a legacy of world civilization. They can also ascertain that Lincoln was a humble man whose remarks took only about two minutes to recite — in comparison with the two-hour speech given by Edward Everett earlier that day. When Lincoln said, "The world will little note, nor long remember what we say here," he could not have known that his address would become one of the most remembered orations in history. In its short, expressive entirety, the Gettysburg Address is a primary source that shows us the depth of Abraham Lincoln's awareness of the world-historical importance of democracy as well as his sincere belief in America's role in preserving it.

Within days of the address, newspaper reporters and diplomats weighed in on the address. In these secondary sources, Lincoln's political enemies generally criticized it as a shallow and unimpressive speech, while his political supporters hailed it as a concise and eloquent summation of the principles of democracy. With the victory of the Union forces in 1865, the Gettysburg Address became an essential text of Civil War history and part of the canon of the literature of democracy. Accordingly, it has been examined, contextualized, and praised in countless other secondary sources describing military history, political history, oratory, and Lincoln's life, letters, and philosophy.

It should be noted that these particular secondary sources, that is, the editorials and commentaries responding to the Gettysburg Address, could also serve as primary sources for historians doing research, for example, on the political climate of the United States during the Civil War. In this case, the journalist or commentator is the historical agent producing the source to be studied. For this reason, newspaper articles are generally valuable primary sources, but the good student will have to distinguish between what a journalist writes about a policy or a speech and what the policy or speech (the original primary source) actually says. The questions the student must always ask are "Who wrote the source and for what purpose?"*

An entire library could be filled with the tertiary sources that deal with the Gettysburg Address — from history textbooks to encyclopedia entries to online source entries (including this short article). The speech is regularly referenced as one of the great moments of the civil war and a defining moment in the Lincoln presidency. For the serious student of history, secondary and tertiary sources, while they are important for understanding the broad narratives of the past, are no substitute for the "raw" immediacy of the primary source.

It is worth noting that collections, anthologies, and online databases represent an interesting intersection of primary, secondary, and tertiary literature. A prudent student of history will ask why certain primary sources have been selected for inclusion in a collection while countless others have not. Choices made by historians and editors as to "what matters" come to form a significant part of our historical knowledge; fortunately, the skills acquired in reading these selected sources will serve students well when they engage in their own research and come across entirely new materials on their own. As you analyze primary sources, asking and answering the questions posed earlier, you may find yourself needing to consult secondary and tertiary sources. Strive both to become aware of how important interpretation of all documents is to the study of history and to understand the necessity of close and careful reading of primary sources.

*It should be noted further that even tertiary sources such as textbooks and encyclopedia articles can be used as primary sources in certain cases. For example, if a historian were doing research on educational practices or school systems in colonial America, he could look to textbooks as obvious primary sources, as they would give the most immediate evidence of what students were learning in schools. Encyclopedia articles have often been used as primary sources by intellectual, cultural, or social historians because they give evidence of the quality of knowledge that was considered standard by the educated people in a given period.

1.1: Early America and the Civil War

Overview

This course begins around the Civil War and Reconstruction, but it's important to understand how those events came about. The five readings in this unit span over 200 years of U.S. history (from 1623 to 1865). They reveal what life was like for early Americans, both white indentured servants (Richard Frethorne) and enslaved Africans and African Americans (Virginia Acts, *Dred Scott v. Sanford*). They also illustrate the impact of slavery on the nation (South Carolina's Declaration of the Causes of Secession and Abraham Lincoln's Second Inaugural Address). Read together, these sources should help you think about how slavery and its legacy have shaped the nation and created ongoing challenges for America.

Before you read the actual documents, create a timeline for these documents. Then think about other things that happened around that time. Above the timeline, write things you do know (or think you know with a question mark) about that time period (anywhere in the world). Underneath the timeline, write things you would like to know. Your timeline should look like a fishbone when it's done. The messier, the better.

Unit Questions

1. How comfortable do you feel with the language? Rate it between "not at all comfortable" to "very comfortable." How different is it from the dialects (kinds) of English that you use every day? How much time will it take to look up words that you are not sure about?

2. How did individual colonies/states and the federal government create and uphold the institution of slavery over time? Use specific examples from multiple readings to support your argument.

3. What do the documents show us about the emerging relationship between race and citizenship in America? How did this create long-term problems for the nation?

1.2: Richard Frethorne: Letter to His Parents (1623)

Historical Context

People arrived in America under a variety of circumstances. Some colonists were wealthier individuals looking to invest in England's newest territories. Many more were impoverished people looking for a better life in the New World. And thousands of people were kidnapped, enslaved, and forced to come to America.

Individuals who could not afford to pay for their travel often became "indentured servants." They signed a contract, or "indenture," in which they agreed to serve the master who paid for their ship passage. Indentures established specific conditions of employment. Typically, an indenture lasted four to seven years. It included ship passage to the colony as well as shelter, clothing, and food during the contract period. Upon completion of the contract, the indentured person would receive "freedom dues." The conditions varied, but sometimes this included additional food and clothing, land, and a firearm. As you'll see from the reading, however, a contract did not guarantee fair treatment.

Guiding Questions

As you read the document from indentured servant Richard Frethorne, take notes and answer the following questions:

1. What does Frethorne's letter reveal about his living conditions in America as an indentured servant? Make a list of problems that Frethorne explains. What words would you use to describe his situation?

2. Why was Frethorne writing to his parents?

3. Compare Frethorne's situation four centuries ago to people's situations today. Do you know of people who are in a similar situation to Frethorne? (Consider access to food, freedom, safety, etc.)

Loving and Kind Father and Mother:

My most humble duty remembered to you, hoping in god of your good health, as I myself am at the making hereof. This is to let you understand that I your child am in a most heavy case by reason of the country, [which] is such that it causeth much sickness, [such] as the scurvy and the bloody flux and diverse other diseases, which maketh the body very poor and weak. And when we are sick there is nothing to comfort us; for since I came out of the ship I never ate anything but peas, and loblollie (that is, water gruel). As for deer or venison I never saw any since I came into this land. There is indeed some fowl, but we are not allowed to go and get it, but must work hard both early and late for a mess of water gruel and a mouthful of bread and beef. A mouthful of bread for a penny loaf must serve for four men which is most pitiful. . . .

. . . We live in fear of the enemy every hour, yet we have had a combat with them on the Sunday before Shrovetide, and we took two alive and made slaves of them. But it was by policy, for we are in great danger; for our plantation is very weak by reason of the death and sickness of our company. For we came but twenty for the merchants, and they are half dead just; and we look every hour when two more should go. . . . And the nighest help that we have is ten mile of us, and when the rogues overcame this place [the] last [time] they slew 80 persons. . . .

. . . I have nothing to comfort me, nor is there nothing to be gotten here but sickness and death, except [in the event] that one had money to lay out in some things for profit. But I have nothing at all no, not a shirt to my back but two rags (2), nor clothes but one poor suit, nor but one pair of shoes, but one pair of stockings, but one cap, [and] but two bands [collars]. My cloak is stolen by one of my fellows, and to his dying hour [he] would not tell me what he did with it; but some of my fellows saw him have butter and beef out of a ship, which my cloak, I doubt [not], paid for. . . .

. . . And indeed so I find it now, to my great grief and misery; and [I] saith that if you love me you will redeem me suddenly, for which I do entreat and beg. And if you cannot get the merchants to redeem me for some little money, then for God's sake get a gathering or entreat some good folks to lay out some little sum of money in meal and cheese and butter and beef. Any eating meat will yield great profit. . . . But if you send cheese, you must have a care how you pack it in barrels; and you must put cooper's chips between every cheese, or else the heat of the hold will rot them. . . .

ROT
RICHARD FRETHORNE,
MARTIN'S HUNDRED

1.3: Virginia Slave Acts (1660s)

Historical Context

The excerpts below come from two different acts (pieces of legislation) created by the Virginia Colony, which was ruled by England. At this point in time, England did not practice slavery, therefore it had no laws to govern how a slave system operated. Additionally, following in the tradition of many European nations, England embraced a patriarchal system, meaning a person's inheritance and social status passed through the males of the family (typically from father to son).

Guiding Questions

1. Make a diagram or flowchart that explains the fate of a people who are of mixed race. Is there a legal way out of slavery for descendants of people who were brought/trafficked from Africa as slaves according to these legal documents?

2. Make a prediction: How do you think these colonial policies break with traditional English policies?

3. What do the acts reveal about Virginia's strategy for creating a slave society?

Document Text

Virginia's Act XII: Negro Women's Children to Serve according to the Condition of the Mother (1662)

Whereas some doubts have arisen whether children got by any Englishman upon a negro woman should be slave or free, *Be it therefore enacted and declared by this present grand assembly,* that all children borne in this country shall be held bond or free only according to the condition of the mother, *And* that if any christian shall commit fornication with a negro man or woman, he or she so offending shall pay double the fines imposed by the former act.

Virginia's Act III: Baptism Does Not Exempt Slaves from Bondage (1667)

Whereas some doubts have arisen whether children that are slaves by birth, and by the charity and piety of their owners made partakers of the blessed sacrament of baptism, should by virtue of their baptism be made free; It is enacted and declared by this grand assembly, and the authority thereof, that the conferring of baptism doth not alter the condition of the person as to his bondage or freedom; that diverse masters, freed from this doubt, may more carefully endeavor the propagation of Christianity by permitting children, though slaves, or those of greater growth if capable to be admitted to that sacrament.

1.4: *Dred Scott v. Sanford* (1857)

Note: court case names are always italicized.

Historical Context

The Supreme Court is an appeals court and is the "highest court" in the country. The Court most often hears cases when one of the parties involved in the case is unhappy with the lower court's ruling and appeals the case for review. The Court's main job is to determine if the lower court's ruling adheres to, or violates, the Constitution of the United States. Often, the decisions made by the Court are binding and set precedent for future rulings. That is why the Court's conclusions have far reaching consequences for the nation and the people who live in it.

Guiding Questions

1. Summarize in your own words the first paragraph of these excerpts. What is the main question the Court is trying to answer?

2. Dred Scott, an enslaved man, sued for his freedom (and that of his family) after his owner moved them from the slave-holding state of Missouri to the free state of Illinois. On what grounds did the Supreme Court reject Scott's claim to freedom?

3. Why is the *Dred Scott* case considered one of the worst U.S. Supreme Court rulings? Identify specific reasons or language from the document to support your argument.

Document Text

Mr. Chief Justice Taney delivered the opinion of the court (excerpts).

... The question is simply this: Can a negro, whose ancestors were imported into this country, and sold as slaves, become a member of the political community ... and as such become entitled to all the rights, and privileges, and immunities, guaranteed by that instrument to the citizen? One of which rights is the privilege of suing in a court of the United States in the cases specified in the Constitution. ...

... The words "people of the United States" and "citizens" are synonymous terms, and mean the same thing. . . . The question before us is, whether the class of persons described in the plea in abatement [people of enslaved African descent] compose a portion of this people, and are constituent members of this sovereignty? We think they are not, and that they are not included, and were not intended to be included, under the word "citizens" in the Constitution, and can therefore claim none of the rights and privileges which that instrument provides for and secures to citizens of the United States. On the contrary, they were at that time considered as a subordinate and inferior class of beings, who had been subjugated by the dominant race, and, whether emancipated or not, yet remained subject to their authority, and had no rights or privileges but such as those who held the power and the Government might choose to grant them. . . .

. . . They had for more than a century before been regarded as beings of an inferior order, and altogether unfit to associate with the white race, either in social or political relations; and so far inferior, that they had no rights which the white man was bound to respect; and that the negro might justly and lawfully be reduced to slavery for his benefit. He was bought and sold, and treated as an ordinary article of merchandise and traffic, whenever a profit could be made by it.

This state of public opinion had undergone no change when the Constitution was adopted, as is equally evident from its provisions and language. . . .

. . . And if the Constitution recognises the right of property of the master in a slave, and makes no distinction between that description of property and other property owned by a citizen. . . .

Upon these considerations, it is the opinion of the court that the act of Congress which prohibited a citizen from holding and owning property of this kind in the territory of the United States north of the line therein mentioned, is not warranted by the Constitution, and is therefore void; and that neither Dred Scott himself, nor any of his family, were made free by being carried into this territory [Illinois]; even if they had been carried there by the owner, with the intention of becoming a permanent resident. . . .

. . . It is now firmly settled by the decisions of the highest court in the State, that Scott and his family upon their return [to Missouri from Illinois] were not free, but were, by the laws of Missouri, the property of the defendant; and that the Circuit Court of the United States had no jurisdiction, when, by the laws of the State, the plaintiff was a slave, and not a citizen. . . .

1.5: South Carolina Declaration of Causes of Secession (1860)

Historical Context

"Secession" means to withdraw from a larger entity. (The verb is "to secede.") In this document, the state of South Carolina is explaining why it plans to secede, or withdraw, from the Union [the United States of America].

Guiding Questions

1. This document contains some rather legalistic language. Start out your reading with a quick pre-read or skim-read that gives you a sense of what this document is about. Rate the difficulty of this text. Did you come across challenging terminology in your skim-read? Try to use context clues to figure out what the terms mean. Then look up words that you need for comprehension of the document. Add these words and definitions to your notes.

2. Many people like to say the Civil War was about "states' rights" rather than about slavery. What evidence does South Carolina's "Declaration of Causes of Secession" provide to show the pivotal role slavery played in the state's decision to leave the United States? Identify all of the ways in which slavery, and the issues relating to it, are addressed in this document.

3. Why did South Carolina see Abraham Lincoln's election to the presidency as a threat to the state? Provide specific evidence or examples from the document.

Document Text

December 24, 1860

. . . The Constitution of the United States, in its fourth Article, provides as follows: "No person held to service or labor in one State, under the laws thereof, escaping into another, shall, in consequence of any law or regulation therein, be discharged from such service or labor, but shall be delivered up, on claim of the party to whom such service or labor may be due."

. . . The General Government, as the common agent, passed laws to carry into effect these stipulations of the States. For many years these laws were executed. But an increasing hostility on the part of the non-slaveholding States to the institution of slavery, has led to a disregard of their obligations ... [non-slaveholding states] have enacted laws which either nullify the Acts of Congress or render useless any attempt to execute them. ... Thus the constituted compact has been deliberately broken and disregarded by the non-slaveholding States, and the consequence follows that South Carolina is released from her obligation. ...

... The right of property in slaves was recognized by giving to free persons distinct political rights, by giving them the right to represent, and burthening them with direct taxes for three-fifths of their slaves; by authorizing the importation of slaves for twenty years; and by stipulating for the rendition of fugitives from labor. ... Those [non-slaveholding] States have assume the right of deciding upon the propriety of our domestic institutions; and have denied the rights of property established in fifteen of the States and recognized by the Constitution; they have denounced as sinful the institution of slavery .... They have encouraged and assisted thousands of our slaves to leave their homes; and those who remain, have been incited by emissaries, books and pictures to servile insurrection. ...

... A geographical line has been drawn across the Union, and all the States north of that line have united in the election of a man to the high office of President of the United States, whose opinions and purposes are hostile to slavery. He is to be entrusted with the administration of the common Government, because he has declared that that "Government cannot endure permanently half slave, half free," and that the public mind must rest in the belief that slavery is in the course of ultimate extinction.

This sectional combination for the submersion of the Constitution, has been aided in some of the States by elevating to citizenship, persons who, by the supreme law of the land, are incapable of becoming citizens; and their votes have been used to inaugurate a new policy, hostile to the South, and destructive of its beliefs and safety.

On the 4th day of March next, this party [Republican] will take possession of the Government. It has announced that the South shall be excluded from the common territory, that the judicial tribunals shall be made sectional, and that a war must be waged against slavery until it shall cease throughout the United States.

The guaranties of the Constitution will then no longer exist; the equal rights of the States will be lost. The slaveholding States will no longer have the power of self-government, or self-protection, and the Federal Government will have become their enemy. ...

. . . We, therefore, the People of South Carolina . . . have solemnly declared that the Union heretofore existing between this State and the other States of North America, is dissolved, and that the State of South Carolina has resumed her position among the nations of the world, as a separate and independent State.

Adopted December 24, 1860

1.6: Abraham Lincoln: Second Inaugural Address (1865)

Historical Context

Abraham Lincoln first took office in 1861. He was re-elected, and then assassinated, in 1865. Consequently, his entire presidency was defined by tension and war.

A president's "inaugural address" is the speech given when he takes office. It is written to be verbally recited. With that in mind, you may want to read this document out loud so you can better understand the language and cadence.

Guiding Questions

1. After reading this document, think about why Lincoln uses this type of language! How would you characterize his way and style of discussing a defining event such as a civil war that cost many lives and destroyed many more? What sort of style of speech would you use if you were in his shoes?

2. According to Lincoln, what was slavery's role in the Civil War?

3. How would you characterize Lincoln's attitude towards the South? How might this have affected reunification when the war eventually ended, had Lincoln lived?

Document Text

March 4, 1865

Fellow Countrymen:

At this second appearing to take the oath of the presidential office, there is less occasion for an extended address than there was at the first. . . .

On the occasion corresponding to this four years ago, all thoughts were anxiously directed to an impending civil-war. All dreaded it—all sought to avert it. While the inaugural address was being delivered from this place, devoted altogether to *saving* the Union without war, insurgent agents were in the city seeking to *destroy* it without war—seeking to dissol[v]e the Union, and divide effects, by negotiation. Both parties deprecated war; but one of them would *make* war rather than let the nation survive; and the other would *accept* war rather than let it perish. And the war came.

One eighth of the whole population were colored slaves, not distributed generally over the Union, but localized in the southern part of it. These slaves constituted a peculiar and powerful interest. All knew that this interest was, somehow, the cause of the war. To strengthen, perpetuate, and extend this interest was the object for which the insurgents would rend the Union, even by war; while the government claimed no right to do more than to restrict the territorial enlargement of it. . . .

. . . Both read the same Bible, and pray to the same God; and each invokes His aid against the other. . . . The prayers of both could not be answered; that of neither has been answered fully. . . . If we shall suppose that American Slavery is one of those offences which, in the providence of God, must needs come, but which, having continued through His appointed time, He now wills to remove, and that He gives to both North and South, this terrible war, as the woe due to those by whom the offence came, shall we discern therein any departure from those divine attributes which the believers in a Living God always ascribe to Him? Fondly do we hope—fervently do we prayóthat this mighty scourge of war may speedily pass away. Yet, if God wills that it contin- ue, until all the wealth piled by the bond-man's two hundred and fifty years of unrequited toil shall be sunk, and until every drop of blood drawn with the lash, shall be paid by another drawn with the sword, as was said three thou- sand years ago, so still it must be said "the judgments of the Lord, are true and righteous altogether."

With malice toward none; with charity for all; with firmness in the right, as God gives us to see the right, let us strive on to finish the work we are in; to bind up the nation's wounds; to care for him who shall have borne the battle, and for his widow, and his orphan—to do all which may achieve and cherish a just, and a lasting peace, among ourselves, and with all nations.

1.7: Unit 1 Review

Now that you have finished reading all of the documents in this unit, take a moment to think about how they fit together. Review your documents from each document and add any relevant information to the unit questions (first presented in the Unit Overview).

1. How comfortable do you feel with the language? Rate it between "not at all comfortable" to "very comfortable." How different is it from the dialects (kinds) of English that you use every day? How much time DID it take to look up words that you are not sure about?

2. How did individual colonies/states and the federal government create and uphold the institution of slavery over time? Use specific examples from multiple readings to support your argument.

3. What do the documents show us about the emerging relationship between race and citizenship in America? How did this create long-term problems for the nation?

You should now be able to see how issues of labor, race, identity, and access to rights shaped early America. This will be a pattern you'll see throughout the course.

Make a Prediction

The next unit is "Reconstruction and Redemption." What kinds of challenges do you think the nation will face as it attempts to reunite the country and rebuild the South after the Civil War?

2.1: Reconstruction and Redemption

Overview

The last unit introduced you to the role of slavery in American history and asked you to think about how that institution's legacy created long-lasting challenges for the nation. This unit consists of two main concepts, "Reconstruction" and "Redemption."

"Reconstruction" refers to the period from the end of the Civil War (1865) through the Compromise of 1877. (The Compromise of 1877 allowed the North to retain control of the presidency, but it effectively ended its influence in the South by removing federal troops that had been placed there to enforce national laws.) "Redemption" overlaps with this period and is generally considered to begin about 1873 and continues throughout the early nineteenth century.

Both the nation and the South needed reconstructing after the war. The federal government eventually allowed all the former Confederate states to rejoin the union and began the slow process of rebuilding the South. The South's infrastructure, economy, politics, and society all needed reconstructing. The central question that emerged was, what would a New South look like? This unit focuses on answering that question from an economic and sociopolitical (social + political) perspective that includes both people's everyday challenges as well as the political decisions made by the various state and federal branches of government.

White southerners and African Americans and their allies (usually northerners) had very different ideas about what the post-war South should look like. While African Americans and their allies sought to protect the rights of black Americans, southern whites often fought to maintain the status quo. Those who hoped to "redeem" the South to its "former glory" were called Redeemers. Their attempts to return the South to its pre-war practices, where white supremacy ruled, is called "Redemption." The legacy of their ideas, and their successes in maintaining white supremacy, persisted well into the twentieth century and created problems that the country is still grappling with today.

As you read the documents in this unit, think about what they have in common and how they conflict. Use the documents and these questions to tell the story of what happened in the South during Reconstruction and Redemption.

1. What kinds of civil rights did African Americans successfully secure in the post-war period?

2. How were African Americans' rights circumscribed, or limited by others, during this same period?

3. Make a prediction. Based on what you learned in this unit, why do you think racial issues will end up defining much of twentieth-century America and continue to be problematic today?

Grammar Tip! Words and phrases like "the Civil War," "the South," "Reconstruction," and "Redemption" are names (i.e. proper nouns); therefore, they must be capitalized.

2.2: The "Civil War Amendments": Excerpts from the Thirteenth, Fourteenth, and Fifteenth Amendments to the Constitution

Historical Context

When the Civil War ended, Republicans in Congress sought to reunite the country and secure the rights of the newly freed African Americans. As you read, make a three-column chart to map the key facets of each act. Answer these guiding questions in your chart.

Guiding Questions

1. What does each amendment establish in regards to African American civil rights?

2. Under what conditions could slavery or involuntary servitude continue, even after passage of the Thirteenth Amendment?

3. Why do you think Congress had to pass three different amendments over five years to protect African American civil rights?

Document Text

Thirteenth Amendment to the U.S. Constitution (1865)

Section 1. Neither slavery nor involuntary servitude, except as a punishment for crime whereof the party shall have been duly convicted, shall exist within the United States, or any place subject to their jurisdiction. . . .

Fourteenth Amendment to the U.S. Constitution (1868)

Section 1. All persons born or naturalized in the United States, and subject to the jurisdiction thereof, are citizens of the United States and of the State wherein they reside. No State shall make or enforce any law which shall abridge the privileges or immunities of citizens of the United States; nor shall any State deprive any person of life, liberty, or property, without due process of law; nor deny to any person within its jurisdiction the equal protection of the laws. . . .

Fifteenth Amendment to the Constitution (1870)

Section 1. The right of citizens of the United States to vote shall not be denied or abridged by the United States or by any State on account of race, color, or previous condition of servitude. . . .

2.3: Black Code of Mississippi (1865)

Historical Context

In the days of slavery, southern states created Slave Codes, or laws explicitly designed to control the lives, labor, and behavior of enslaved people. When slavery ended with the Thirteenth Amendment, southerners feared that African Americans would refuse to work or act in the same way they had been forced to during the days of slavery. Consequently, many southern states started passing Black Codes. While in some cases those codes granted genuine legal rights, like the opportunity for formerly enslaved married couples to have their marriage recognized before the law, the Black Codes were ultimately designed to punish and control local black populations. Keep this in mind as you read the following excerpts from the Black Code of Mississippi.

Guiding Questions

1. As you read these excerpts of Mississippi's post-war state laws, make connections with the excerpts of the Civil War Amendments. Be ready to provide at least one example where these amendments to the U.S. Constitution conflict or seem to conflict with Mississippi state law.

2. What facets of life do the selected sections of the Black Code of Mississippi try to regulate? Identify specific examples from the document to support your argument. Why were white people often penalized more harshly for violating certain laws?

3. What is a "vagrant" and how were vagrancy statutes used to control local black populations?

A note on terminology: "Mulatto" was a historical term used to describe people of mixed race ancestry.

Document Text

An Act to Confer Civil Rights on Freedmen, and for other Purposes

... **Section 3.** .... [I]t shall not be lawful for any freedman, free negro or mulatto to intermarry with any white person; nor for any person to intermarry with any freedman, free negro or mulatto; and any person who shall so intermarry shall be deemed guilty of felony, and on conviction thereof shall be confined in the State penitentiary for life; and those shall be deemed freedmen, free negroes and mulattoes who are of pure negro blood, and those descended from a negro to the third generation, inclusive, though one ancestor in each generation may have been a white person. . . .

. . . **Section 5.** Every freedman, free negro and mulatto shall, on the second Monday of January, one thousand eight hundred and sixty-six, and annually thereafter, have a lawful home or employment, and shall have written evidence. . . .

Section 6. All contracts for labor made with freedmen, free negroes and mulattoes for a longer period than one month shall be in writing, and . . . if the laborer shall quit the service of the employer before the expiration of his term of service, without good cause, he shall forfeit his wages for that year up to the time of quitting. . . .

An Act to Amend the Vagrant Laws of the State

Section 1. All rogues and vagabonds, idle and dissipated persons, beggars, jugglers, or persons practicing unlawful games or plays, runaways, common drunkards, common night-walkers, pilferers, lewd, wanton, or lascivious persons, in speech or behavior, common railers and brawlers, persons who neglect their calling or employment, misspend what they earn, or do not provide for the support of themselves or their families, or dependents, and all other idle and disorderly persons, including all who neglect all lawful business, habitually misspend their time by frequenting houses of ill-fame, gaming-houses, or tippling shops, shall be deemed and considered vagrants, under the provisions of this act, and upon conviction thereof shall be fined not exceeding one hundred dollars, with all accruing costs, and be imprisoned, at the discretion of the court, not exceeding ten days.

Section 2. All freedmen, free negroes and mulattoes in this State, over the age of eighteen years, found on the second Monday in January, 1866, or thereafter, with no lawful employment or business, or found unlawful assembling themselves together, either in the day or night time, and all white persons assembling themselves with freedmen, free negroes or mulattoes, or usually associating with freedmen, free negroes or mulattoes, on terms of equality, or living in adultery or fornication with a freed woman, freed negro or mulatto, shall be deemed vagrants, and on conviction thereof shall be fined in a sum not exceeding, in the case of a freedman, free negro or mulatto, fifty dollars, and a white man two hundred dollars, and imprisonment at the discretion of the court, the free negro not exceeding ten days, and the white man not exceeding six months.

Section 3. All justices of the peace, mayors, and aldermen . . . shall have jurisdiction to try all questions of vagrancy . . . to have said party or parties arrested, and brought before them, and immediately investigate said charge, and, on conviction, punish said party or parties, as provided for herein. And it is hereby made the duty of all sheriffs, constables, town constables, and all such like officers, and city marshals, to report to some officer having jurisdiction all violations of any of the provisions of this act, and in case any officer shall fail or neglect any duty herein it shall be the duty of the county court to fine said officer, upon conviction, not exceeding one hundred dollars, to be paid into the county treasury for county purposes. . . .

. . . **Section 5.** . . . [I]n case of any freedman, free negro or mulatto shall fail . . . to pay [their fines]. . . it shall be. . . the duty of the sheriff . . . to hire out said freedman, free negro or mulatto, to any person who will, for the shortest period of service, pay said fine and forfeiture and all costs . . . the employer shall be entitled to deduct and retain the amount so paid from the wages of such freedman, free negro or mulatto. . . .

2.4: Organization and Principles of the Ku Klux Klan (1869)

Historical Context

This document and the one that follows are closely related. Read the titles carefully, as they clearly indicate the purpose each document serves. This selection focuses mainly on the KKK's purported "principles." Consider the difference in tone between the "Organization and Principles" and the "Initiation Charge." As you read, take notes as directed.

Guiding Questions

1. Next to each paragraph, write a brief summary of the content and add a comment about what this means.

2. In a few sentences, discuss whether this sounds as if it were written specifically for the KKK or whether it could fit a number of different organizations. For instance, the KKK refers to itself as an "Order" instead of an association or organization. In addition, they see themselves as an "institution of chivalry." Use these or other examples to make your case.

3. Based on your knowledge of the period and the goals and actions of the Ku Klux Klan, how does the Klan's language in the document conflict with its actual intent and twist positive characteristics and goals into violent and racist actions and attitudes? Identify specific examples from the text and try to provide an example of how the Klan may use this language to justify its actions.

Document Text

Appellation

This organization shall be styled and denominated the Order of the ——We, the Order of the——, reverentially acknowledge the majesty and supremacy of the Divine Being and recognize the goodness and providence of the same. And we recognize our relation to the United States government, the supremacy of the Constitution, the constitutional laws thereof, and the Union of states thereunder.

Character and Objects of the Order

This is an institution of chivalry, humanity, mercy, and patriotism; embodying in its genius and its principles all that is chivalric in conduct, noble in sentiment, generous in manhood, and patriotic in purpose; its peculiar objects being:

First: To protect the weak, the innocent, and the defenseless from the indignities, wrongs, and outrages of the lawless, the violent, and the brutal; to relieve the injured and oppressed; to succor the suffering and unfortunate, and especially the widows and orphans of Confederate soldiers.

Second: To protect and defend the Constitution of the United States, and all laws passed in conformity thereto, and to protect the states and the people thereof from all invasion from any source whatever.

Third: To aid and assist in the execution of all constitutional laws, and to protect the people from unlawful seizure and from trial, except by their peers in conformity to the laws of the land.

2.5: Initiation Charge of the Ku Klux Klan (1869)

Historical Context

You may have been surprised reading the Principles of the KKK that it sounded like a rational and civic-minded organization. Do not be fooled—members joining the group knew exactly what they were signing up for, as demonstrated in the text of the Initiation Charge.

Guiding Questions

1. As you read this document, in your notes write a very brief summary for each paragraph. This does not have to be in complete sentences. But make sure you get a sense of what each paragraph says and what its purpose is. Then answer the questions below.

2. What is an "initiation charge"? How does this document compare to the principles stated in the "Organization and Principles" document?

3. On what grounds does the KKK claim to have racial superiority and how does it plan to protect that status?

Document Text

Brothers:

. . . As you may have already gathered . . . our main and fundamental object is the MAINTENANCE OF THE SUPREMACY OF THE WHITE RACE in this Republic. History and physiology teach us that we belong to a race which nature has endowed with an evident superiority over all other races, and that the Maker, in thus elevating us above the common standard of human creation, has intended to give us over inferior races a dominion from which no human laws can permanently derogate. . . .

Convinced that we are of these elements of natural ethics, we know, besides, that the government of our Republic was established by white men, for white men alone, and that it never was in contemplation of its founders that it should fall into the hands of an inferior and degraded race. We hold, therefore, that any attempt to wrest from the white race the management of its affairs in order to transfer it to the control of the black population, is an invasion of the sacred prerogatives vouchsafed to us by the Constitution, and a violation of the laws established by God himself. . . .

It, then, becomes our solemn duty, as white men,. . . to maintain, in this Republic, the supremacy of the Caucasian race, and restraint the black or African race to that condition of social and political inferiority for which God has destined it. This is the object for which our Order was instituted; and, in carrying it out, we intend to infringe no laws, to violate no rights, and to resort to no forcible means, except for purposes of legitimate and necessary defense.

As an essential condition of success, this Order proscribes absolutely all social equality between the races. If we were to admit persons of African race on the same level with ourselves . . . it would be a virtual recognition of *status,* after which we could not consistently deny them an equal share in the administration of our public affairs. . . .

There is another reason, Brothers, for which we condemn this social equality. Its toleration would soon be a fruitful source of intermarriages between individuals of the two races; and the result of this *miscegenation* would be gradual amalgamation and the production of a degenerate and bastard offspring. . . . We must maintain the purity of the white blood, if we would preserve for it that natural superiority with which God has ennobled it.

. . . Our statutes make us bound to respect sedulously the rights of the colored inhabitants of this Republic, and in every instance, to give them whatever lawfully belongs to them. It is an act of simple justice not to deny them any of the privileges to which they are legitimately entitled; and we cannot better show the inherent superiority of our race than by dealing with them in that spirit of firmness, liberality and impartiality which characterizes all superior organizations. . . .

2.6: Richard Harvey Cain: "All That We Ask Is Equal Laws, Equal Legislation, and Equal Rights" (1874)

Historical Context

Cain was a free-born African American who moved to South Carolina as a minister following the Civil War. He became active in local politics and was elected to the U.S. House of Representatives in 1872. He was a vocal proponent of African American civil rights. The excerpt here is a speech arguing in support of a civil rights bill before Congress.

Guiding Questions

1. This document contains a lot of examples of civil rights. In your notes, you should list these examples and annotate them with a few words regarding their significance.

2. Why, according to Cain, were some people opposed to granting African Americans certain civil rights?

3. Why does Cain argue that African Americans are entitled to full civil rights?

Document Text

. . . If four, or nearly five, million people have been lifted from the thralldom of slavery and made free; if the Government by its amendments to the Constitution has guaranteed to them all rights and immunities, as to other citizens, they must necessarily therefore carry along with them all the privileges enjoyed by all other citizens of the Republic.

Sir, the gentleman from North Carolina [Mr. Vance] who spoke on the question stated some objections, to which I desire to address a few words of reply. He said it would enforce social rights, and therefore would be detrimental to the interests of both the whites and the blacks of the country. . . .

. . . Sir, social equality is a right which every man, every woman, and every class of persons have within their own control. They have a right to form their own acquaintances, to establish their own social relationships. Its establishment and regulation is not within the province of legislation. No laws enacted by legislators can compel social equality. . . .

. . . [T]he gentleman states that in the State of North Carolina the colored people . . . have all the rights and all the immunities accorded to any other class of citizens of the United States. Now, it may not have come under his observation, but it has under mine, that such really is not the case; and the reason why I know and feel it more than he does is because my face is painted black and his is painted white. . . . Coming here last week . . . there was objection on the part of the railroad people to our eating our meals in the cars, because they said we were putting on airs. They refused us in the restaurant, and then did not desire that we should eat our meals in the cars, although we paid for them. . . .

. . . [S]outhern friends, or a certain class of them, always bring back this old ghost of prejudice and of antagonism. There was a time, not very far distant in the past, when this antagonism was not recognized, when a feeling of fraternization between the white and the colored races existed. . . . But since our emancipation . . . this bugbear is brought up against us again. Sir, the progress of the age demands that the colored man of this country shall be lifted by law into the enjoyment of every right, and that every appliance which is accorded to the German, to the Irishman, to the Englishman, and every foreigner, shall be given to him; and I shall give some reasons why I demand this in the name of justice. . . .

. . . [W]e have been identified with the interests of this country from its very foundation. The cotton crop of this country has been raised and its rice-fields have been tilled by the hands of our race. . . . This was done in the time of slavery. . . . if we have sweated and toiled to build up the prosperity of the whole country by the productions of our labor, I submit, now that the war has made a change, now that we are free . . . we should come in and enjoy to the fullest extent our freedom and liberty.

A word now as to the question of education. . . . It is against discrimination in this particular that we complain. . . .

The gentleman from North Carolina [Mr. Vance] also says that the colored men should not come here begging at the doors of Congress for their rights. I agree with him. I want to say that we do not come here begging for our rights. We come here clothed in the garb of American citizenship. We come demanding our rights in the name of justice. We come, with no arrogance on our part, asking that this great nation, which laid the foundations of civilization and progress more deeply and more securely than any other nation on the face of the earth, guarantee us protection from outrage. We come here, five millions of people—more than composed this whole nation when it had its great tea-party in Boston Harbor, and demanded its rights at the point of the bayonet—asking that unjust discriminations against us be forbidden. We come here in the name of justice, equity, and law, in the name of our children, in the name of our country, petitioning for our rights. . . .

. . . The gentleman from North Carolina has said he desires to have forever buried the memory of the recent war. I agree with him. . . . I have voted in this House with a free heart to declare universal amnesty. . . . Amnesty and civil rights should go together. . . .

2.7: Unit 2 Review

The Ku Klux Klan (KKK) is one of America's first and most violent hate groups. It perpetuated acts of terror against many people, most specifically African Americans. The Klan originally emerged in southern states immediately after the Civil War. Members of the Klan sought to limit the influence of Republicans in Congress, since Republicans were passing legislation designed to improve black Americans' access to equal rights and opportunities. Congress passed legislation to try and stamp out the organization. Klan membership did in fact decline toward the end of the nineteenth century, but that was not really a result of congressional action. Rather, the racist ideas promoted by the KKK had moved to the mainstream by that point and were largely adopted by the southern Democratic Party. With the firm establishment of Jim Crow segregation throughout the South, the KKK was less necessary. As a result, even though membership in the Klan declined, white supremacy flourished.

The Klan reappeared forcefully in the 1920s, in response to fears about a rapidly changing society. As we'll see in future units, America underwent profound changes in the early part of the twentieth century. Industrialization led to significant increases in immigration from southern and eastern Europe. African Americans fighting to defend democracy during World War I returned demanding better treatment. In the 1920s black culture flourished in areas like New York City's Harlem and gained more popularity with white audiences. However, this increased visibility was met with hostility by significant swaths of white America. The KKK represented the most extreme response. Many Klan members used white supremacy and nativism to justify horrific acts of violence, like lynchings.

By the 1920s, the expanded anti-black, anti-Catholic, anti-Jewish, anti-immigrant, anti-communist, and anti-socialist KKK captivated the imagination and interest of thousands of white Americans. Capitalizing on the release of the film *Birth of a Nation,* which played on common racial tropes and stereotypes, the KKK recruited larger numbers of Americans across the country to join its cause. In fact, it first re-appeared in the midwestern state of Indiana, not in the Deep South as one might expect. It's also important to note that women joined the Klan in record numbers in the 1920s. They masked white supremacist agendas by advocating for social reforms and—like their male counterparts—promoting a white, Protestant "American" identity.

The speech by Richard Harvey Cain shows us that African Americans were unwilling to sit by while their rights were ignored or degraded to a second-class status. If you juxtapose his position with that of the KKK, you can see why the country—and the South in particular—faced severe challenges.

At the start of the unit, we asked you three questions:

1. What kinds of civil rights did African Americans successfully secure in the post-war period?

2. How were African Americans' rights circumscribed, or limited by others, during this same period?

3. Make a prediction. Based on what you learned in this unit, why do you think racial issues will end up defining much of twentieth-century America and continue to be problematic today?

Based on what you learned in the readings, how would you now answer these questions? As we continue our journey through U.S. history, think about American identity and access to rights and opportunities. In the next unit, you will see America grappling with issues of expansion and how to define itself and its citizenry.

3.1: Westward Expansion and American Identity

Overview

The readings in this unit address two different, yet related, aspects of U.S. history—western expansion and American identity. Although each topic can be studied individually, when read together they illustrate how "Americans" perceived of themselves and the land they inhabited.

Expansion

Nineteenth-century Americans employed the term *Manifest Destiny* to capture their belief that Americans were "destined" to expand the United States from coast to coast. Many Americans believed it was their right and obligation to spread American culture and Christianity throughout the continent. By the late 1890s they had achieved this goal, but it came at a great cost to native populations inhabiting western lands. As America moved into the twentieth century, it looked to expand its influence beyond the continental United States.

Historian Frederick Jackson Turner developed the so-called Frontier Thesis in 1893, in response to the 1890 census. The census appeared to show that there were no more large tracts of unsettled land left in the United States. Therefore, there was no more American "frontier." In the document "The Significance of the Frontier in American History," Turner outlines the various ways in which the frontier shaped the nation and its people. The excerpt highlights the positive impacts settlement had on the United States in building a new nation and a new national identity. The excerpt, however, does not address the conflicts that also emerged as a result of American expansion. As several of the other readings demonstrate, American settlers were not moving into uninhabited lands. Their encounters with and treatment of Native Americans show readers today how they viewed native populations.

The Dawes Severalty Act shows how the law, although somewhat well intentioned, severely limited and sometimes eradicated native people's lives and identities. Coupled with the eyewitness accounts of the Wounded Knee Massacre, we see the brutality inflicted upon native populations by the American government and military in western territories. Native Americans' experiences show us that even though they were "American" in the deepest sense of the word, they existed outside the boundaries and protections of citizenship.

By the turn of the twentieth century (the start of the 1900s), America was well on its way to becoming an industrial powerhouse. With the frontier "closed," Americans looked abroad. They began to question their role in international affairs and asked what the United States should do to ensure its physical and economic success and safety. In 1898 the United States engaged in the Spanish-American War. At the end of that conflict and the Philippine-American War that immediately followed it, the United States gained territories around the world formerly controlled by Spain including Puerto Rico, Guam, and the Philippines. Shortly after these conflicts, the United States also took over building the Panama Canal. The canal significantly reduced travel time to Asia. This opened up new trading and military opportunities. As the United States expanded its reach in the world, it also embraced the idea of "civilizing missions." Many people in the United States and Western Europe had long believed that Western culture was superior to those of others around the world. America's international expansion increased after the frontier closed, but questions about American identity persisted at home.

Identity

At the same time that America sought to expand its physical boundaries, it also grappled with questions about the nation's, and its people's, identity. *Identity* is the term we use to describe the attributes associated with a particular group. When we talk about a nation, typically we associate the term *identity* with citizenship. Remember that these readings follow on the heels of Unit 2 ("Reconstruction and Redemption"), where we discussed two main ideas competing in the South. One philosophy held that African Americans should be fully integrated as equal members into American society (promoted by Radical Republicans throughout Reconstruction). The other idea, promoted by Redemptionists, was that white supremacy should rule the South and African Americans should be held permanently in a position of second-class citizenship based on their racial identity.

Frederick Jackson Turner argued that the frontier helped create a new American identity. As colonists moved further inland, they shed their English identity and adopted new practices and cultural markers from their immigrant neighbors. This change, however, was not a seamless process. Some immigrants were more welcome than others. As the first reading in this unit illustrates, Chinese immigrants were not welcomed as warmly in America as their colonial Scotch-Irish settlers. Keeping this in mind, think about how groups like Native Americans and Chinese Americans further challenged ideas about American identity.

As you read, then, you should ask yourself: Who is considered "American" and who is not in these documents? Why? Based on what you've learned so far, it should come as no surprise that some people were seen as full American citizens, while others were seen as unfit for American citizenship. Consider who was included and excluded from the full benefits of American citizenship as you read the Dawes Severalty Act, the letter from Wong Ar Chong, and the Supreme Court case *Plessy v. Ferguson*.

1. How would you characterize American identity **historically**? How would you describe American identity **today**? Draw a two-column comparison chart, listing historical American identity traits in one category and modern traits in another. How are the lists similar and different?

2. How did the nation's physical expansion intensify questions about American identity and citizenship? Before you answer this question, draw a simple map of today's United States. Then mark areas that you know were inhabited by many people that were not always considered "real" Americans in the past. Add notes to this map as you read these documents and learn more about these groups.

3. How can an individual or a nation's economic status affect their ability to access full rights or fair treatment by their own country or a neighboring country? Where do you see an example of this both historically and today?

3.2: Letter from Wong Ar Chong (1879)

Historical Context

Very large numbers of Chinese immigrants began coming to America, via California, during the Gold Rush of the 1840s and the transcontinental railroad construction in the 1860s. While they regularly faced discrimination, conditions for these immigrants deteriorated as time went on.

Chinese-American merchant Wong Ar Chong wrote the following letter in 1879 to activist and longtime abolitionist William Lloyd Garrison. He wrote during an era of increasing anti-Chinese and Chinese American sentiment. Americans' nativist and racist attitudes manifested themselves in a variety of ways throughout the late nineteenth and early twentieth centuries, culminating in the passage of the 1882 Chinese Exclusion Act. As the name indicates, that law banned Chinese laborers from migrating to the United States and Chinese nationals in America from becoming American citizens.

Guiding Questions

1. What prompted Wong to write this letter?

2. On what grounds does Wong argue on behalf of Chinese immigrants?

3. Make a list of recent immigrant groups to the United States that you are aware of and think about what people generally say about them. What are people saying now about immigrants and how does this compare to the claims Wong says people are making about Chinese immigrants in 1879?

Document Text

Fri Feb 28th 1879

In your Declaration of Independence it is asserted that all men are born free and equal . . . but I fear there is a backward step being taken by the government.

The able Senator from Maine . . . says the Chinese must go, and gives his reasons. . . . . I claim for my countrymen the right to come to this country as long as other foreigners do. If they make themselves a nuisance, establish proper health laws and enforce them, and if they don't like them let them go back home again, but they must conform to American ideas of law and order if they wish to stay. . . .

The Honorable Senator calls us heathens, but . . .look at the records of fire in Chicago and yellow fever in New Orleans, and he will find Chinamen giving as much, according to their means, as any other people. . . .

. . . He says that China people pay no taxes in this country, but I think if he will take the pains to look into the matter he will find that they pay as much taxes in California as any other foreigners. . . .

He says that China people are not healthy, do not keep their places of habitation as clean as other people, that they smell badly, &c., &c. I could mention several other nationalities, each having its own particular smell. Also that no decent China women come here, that they are mostly prostitutes, but do not the women of other nations furnish a goodly number of prostitutes.My idea is that if the Chinese are allowed to come to this country and enjoy the same privileges as the people from any other foreign land, they will educate themselves and conform to your laws and manners, and become as good citizens as any other race. The Chinese people are willing to work, they mind their own business, and do not get drunk, and why is it they have not as much right to come here, and in as large numbers as any other foreign people. . . .

. . . You go against the principles of George Washington, you go against the American flag, and you act in conflict with Christian charity and principle. . . .

. . . As it stands now, it is 5000 Caucassians [sic] to 1 Mongolian, yet you charge the Chinamen when robbing you of work. I ask God to forbid that Senator Blaine should fear the odds of 1 to 5000. . . .

Yours respectfully,

Wong Ar Chong

3.3: Dawes Severalty Act (1887)

Historical Context

American settlers continued moving westward throughout the mid-to late-19th century. Native Americans were forced onto smaller and smaller reservations in order to free up more land for settlers to farm and exploit natural resources. President Grover Cleveland signed the Dawes Severalty Act in an attempt to assimilate Native Americans into mainstream American culture.

Assimilation is the process by which an outsider becomes part of a group by adopting values, behaviors, and practices associated with the group. More often than not, individuals or minority communities are forced to assimilate to the dominant group's cultural norms and practices. In the context of U.S. history, this assimilation process is often referred to as "Americanization" and is often linked to access to citizenship.

Guiding Questions

1. Under this act, the U.S. government divided and distributed community-owned land to individual tribe members. (Usually this decision was made by the U.S. government, and tribes did not have the opportunity to refuse.) Considering the way of life most Native Americans led, what impact might this have on tribes? And what happened to the remaining lands not divided among individual tribe members?

2. How was this law designed to assimilate Native Americans? Another way of asking this is, how could a Native American become an American citizen? And, what does this say about how the U.S. government in the 19th Century viewed Native Americans?

3. What impact do you think the Dawes Severalty Act had on Native American communities over the four decades it remained in place?

Document Text

. . . In all cases where any tribe or band of Indians has been, or shall hereafter be, located upon any reservation created for their use . . . the President of the United States . . . [can] allot the lands in said reservation in severalty to any Indian located thereon in quantities as follows:

To each head of a family, one-quarter of a section;

To each single person over eighteen years of age, one-eighth of a section;

To each orphan child under eighteen years of age, one-eighth of a section; and . . .

. . . Sec. 5. . . . And provided further . . . it shall be lawful for the Secretary of the Interior to negotiate with such Indian tribe for the purchase and release by said tribe . . . such portions of its reservation not allotted as such tribe shall, from time to time, consent to sell. . . .

Sec. 6. That upon the completion of said allotments . . . each and every member of the respective bands or tribes of Indians to whom allotments have been made shall have the benefit of and be subject to the laws, both civil and criminal, of the State or Territory in which they may reside . . . and every Indian born within the territorial limits of the United States who has voluntarily taken up, within said limits, his residence separate and apart from any tribe of Indians therein, and has adopted the habits of civilized life, is hereby declared to be a citizen of the United States, and is entitled to all the rights, privileges, and immunities of such citizens. . . .

Approved, February, 8, 1887.

3.4: Wounded Knee Massacre: Statements and Eyewitness Accounts (1891)

Historical Context

As we learned in the Dawes Severalty Act, native peoples were increasingly forced onto smaller reservations, and the land not allotted to tribe members was sold off to white settlers. Fearful of Native Americans, President Benjamin Harrison sent more troops to the West to protect settlers. Unsurprisingly, tensions increased as soldiers and settlers encroached on land long held by Native Americans. Some Native Americans, fearful that their way of life would be destroyed if they remained on the reservation, attempted to leave.

The story below recounts the experience of the Big Foot Band. The incident described took place on the Pine Ridge Indian Reservation on December 29, 1890. Although the exact number of casualties is the subject of controversy, at least 150 men, women, and children of the Lakota Sioux tribe were killed by soldiers of the U.S. Seventh Cavalry (with some estimates as high as 300 dead); 25 soldiers died on the field, and 39 were wounded (6 of whom later died).

As with any primary source, this document is somewhat incomplete, as it reveals the events from one perspective. The testimony of Turning Hawk says that a "crazy man" fired his gun at the soldiers. According to witnesses in other reports, a young man (named Black Coyote or Black Fox) refused to give up his gun, and when soldiers attempted to wrestle it from him, it accidentally fired. For our purposes, the cause of the event is less relevant than the outcome, but it is helpful to keep in mind who is providing the information and what factors affect their perception of an event.

Guiding Questions

1. What happened to the Big Foot Band, and why is the event known as the Wounded Knee Massacre?

2. Why might the Native American witnesses make a point of noting to reservation agency authorities that the man who started the conflict (intentionally or not) was a lone actor?

3. What does this event reveal about Native Americans' experiences during this time and about how the U.S Government and many U.S. citizens during this time viewed them? Can you draw parallels to today? What do you think

really happened before and during this event to trigger such an extreme response by the U.S. military? Is there a rational explanation or even a justification?

Document Text

Indian Reports to the Commissioner of Indian Affairs

The Indian Story of Wounded Knee

[The name of the speaker is indicated in bold]

. . . **Turning Hawk**. These people [members of the Big Foot band] were coming toward Pine Ridge agency [reservation], and when they were almost on the agency they were met by the soldiers and surrounded and finally taken to the Wounded Knee creek, and there at a given time their guns were demanded. When they had delivered them up, the men were separated from their families, from their tipis, and taken to a certain spot. When the guns were thus taken and the men thus separated, there was a crazy man, a young man of very bad influence and in fact a nobody, among that bunch of Indians fired his gun, and of course the firing of a gun must have been the breaking of a military rule of some sort, because immediately the soldiers returned fire and indiscriminate killing followed.

Spotted Horse. This man shot an officer in the army. . . . As soon as this shot was fired the Indians immediately began drawing their knives, and they were exhorted from all sides to desist, but this was not obeyed. Consequently the firing began immediately on the part of the soldiers.

Turning Hawk. All the men who were in a bunch were killed right there, and those who escaped that first fire got into the ravine, and as they went along up the ravine for a long distance they were pursued on both sides by the soldiers and shot down, as the dead bodies showed afterwards. The women were standing off at a different place from where the men were stationed, and when the firing began . . . [the women] went entirely in a different direction through an open field, and the women fared the same fate as the men who went up the deep ravine.

American Horse. . . . Then came next the village of the Indians and that was entirely surrounded by the soldiers also. . . . the women who were in the lodges [community groups] standing there under a flag of truce, and of course as soon as they were fired upon they fled, the men fleeing in one direction and the women running in two different directions. . . .

There was a woman with an infant in her arms who was killed as she almost touched the flag of truce, and the women and children of course were strewn all along the circular village until they were dispatched. Right near the flag of truce a mother was shot down with her infant; the child not knowing that its mother was dead was still nursing, and that especially was a very sad sight. The women as they were fleeing with their babes were killed together, shot right through, and the women who were very heavy with child were also killed. All the Indians fled in these three directions, and after most all of them had been killed a cry was made that all those who were not killed or wounded should come forth and they would be safe. Little boys who were not wounded came out of their places of refuge, and as soon as they came in sight a number of soldiers surrounded them and butchered them there.

3.5: Frederick Jackson Turner: "The Significance of the Frontier in American History" (1893)

Historical Context

Frederick Jackson Turner was a leading historian at the turn of the century. He presented this essay outlining his Frontier Thesis at the World's Columbian Exposition in Chicago in 1893. As the title indicates, the piece focuses on Turner's assessment of the role the frontier had on American society. Building on this idea, then, the "closing" of the frontier raised important questions about the nation's future and its expansion not only in North America, but overseas as well.

Guiding Questions

1. How, according to Turner, does the frontier lead to "Americanization?" Make a list of examples from the reading.

2. The excerpt from Turner concludes with his assessment of the nation's "Middle region." Why does he think the frontier and the Middle region are important to the United States?

3. Based on what you read in this excerpt, why do you think some people were concerned when they heard there was no more American frontier? How might this affect America's involvement in foreign affairs?

Document Text

In a recent bulletin of the Superintendent of the Census for 1890 appear these significant words: "Up to and including 1880 the country had a frontier of settlement, but at present the unsettled area has been so broken into by isolated bodies of settlement that there can hardly be said to be a frontier line."... This brief official statement marks the closing of a great historic movement. Up to our own day American history has been in a large degree the history of the colonization of the Great West. The existence of an area of free land, its continuous recession, and the advance of American settlement westward, explain American development.

... The frontier is the line of most rapid and effective Americanization. The wilderness masters the colonist. It finds him a European in dress, industries, tools, modes of travel, and thought.... It strips off the garments of civilization and arrays him in the hunting shirt and the moccasin. . . . In short, at the frontier the environment is at first too strong for the man. He must accept the conditions which it furnishes, or perish. . . . Little by little he transforms the wilderness, but the outcome is not the old Europe. . . . The fact is that here is a new product that is American. At first, the frontier was the Atlantic coast. It was the frontier of Europe in a very real sense. Moving westward, the frontier became more and more American. . . . The advance of the frontier has meant a steady movement away from the influence of Europe, a steady growth of independence on American lines. . . .

. . . First, we note that the frontier promoted the formation of a composite nationality for the American people. The coast was preponderantly English, but the later tides of continental immigration flowed across to the free lands. . . . The Scotch-Irish and the Palatine Germans, or "Pennsylvania Dutch," furnished the dominant element in the stock of the colonial frontier. . . . In the crucible of the frontier the immigrants were Americanized, liberated, and fused into a mixed race, English in neither nationality nor characteristics. . . .

In another way the advance of the frontier decreased our dependence on England. . . . Before long the frontier created a demand for merchants. As it retreated from the coast it became less and less possible for England to bring her supplies directly to the consumer's wharfs, and carry away staple crops. . . .

. . . The pioneer needed the goods of the coast, and so the grand series of internal improvement and railroad legislation began, with potent nationalizing effects. . . .

. . . The economic and social characteristics of the frontier worked against sectionalism. The men of the frontier had closer resemblances to the Middle region than to either of the other sections. . . . In short, it was a region mediating between New England and the South, and the East and the West. It represented that composite nationality which the contemporary United States exhibits. . . . Thus it became the typically American region. . . .

3.6: *Plessy v. Ferguson* (1896)

Historical Context

Homer Plessy was a Louisiana resident of "mixed descent." He self-identified as African American. According to the court case, his lineage was "seven-eighths Caucasian and one-eighth African blood." He purchased a first class ticket for a train on June 7, 1892. When he entered the car and took his seat, he identified himself as African American. The conductor asked him to give up his seat and move to the "colored" section of the train, saying the first class car was for whites only. Plessy refused, knowing he would be arrested for refusing. He hoped his case would become a test case that would work its way up through the court system to the Supreme Court, and eventually result in a ruling that would end Jim Crow [racial] segregation in Louisiana and throughout the South. The case did make it to the Supreme Court, but the outcome was not what he hoped.

Plessy argued that Louisiana's practice of racially segregating people violated his Thirteenth and Fourteenth Amendment rights. The Supreme Court rejected his Thirteenth Amendment argument outright, noting that this amendment primarily dealt with slavery, which was not a factor in this case. Though they took his Fourteenth Amendment argument more seriously, they concluded that his rights were not violated. Remember, the Fourteenth Amendment grants citizenship to all formerly enslaved people (naturalized citizens) and to all people born in the United States. That citizenship grants holders access to all the rights, privileges, and immunities associate with U.S. citizenship.

Before you read, note there are two sections in this reading—the Majority Opinion and the Dissent. As the name indicates, the Majority Opinion articulates the final decision of the Court and explains the logic of its ruling. (There are nine Supreme Court justices, so any decision requires a minimum of five people to get a majority.) Dissenting opinions are written by a justice (or a few justices) in the minority who disagree with the interpretation of the majority. Although a dissent has no legal impact on the rendered verdict, it allows the minority justices to air their grievances and explain why they came to a different conclusion regarding the majority's interpretation of the Constitution.

Guiding Questions

1. Summarize the Majority Opinion in your own words. What is its main argument and conclusion?

2. In time, Jim Crow laws were abolished, albeit many decades later. What impact did the *Plessy* case have on American history?

3. John Harlan Marshall wrote a dissenting opinion. What flaws does he identify in the majority's opinion?

Document Text

Henry Billings Brown: Majority Opinion

. . . So far, then, as a conflict with the fourteenth amendment is concerned, the case reduces itself to the question whether the statute of Louisiana is a reasonable regulation, and with respect to this there must necessarily be a large discretion on the part of the legislature. In determining the question of reasonableness, it is at liberty to act with reference to the established usages, customs, and traditions of the people, and with a view to the promotion of their comfort, and the preservation of the public peace and good order. Gauged by this standard, we cannot say that a law which authorizes or even requires the separation of the two races in public conveyances is unreasonable. . . .

We consider the underlying fallacy of the plaintiff's argument to consist in the assumption that the enforced separation of the two races stamps the colored race with a badge of inferiority. If this be so, it is not by reason of anything found in the act, but solely because the colored race chooses to put that construction upon it. . . . The argument also assumes that social prejudices may be overcome by legislation, and that equal rights cannot be secured to the negro except by an enforced commingling of the two races. We cannot accept this proposition. If the two races are to meet upon terms of social equality, it must be the result of natural affinities, a mutual appreciation of each other's merits, and a voluntary consent of individuals. . . . Legislation is powerless to eradicate racial instincts, or to abolish distinctions based upon physical differences, and the attempt to do so can only result in accentuating the difficulties of the present situation. If the civil and political rights of both races be equal, one cannot be inferior to the other civilly or politically. If one race be inferior to the other socially, the constitution of the United States cannot put them upon the same plane.

. . . The judgment of the court below [that segregation laws are legal] is therefore affirmed.

John Marshall Harlan: Dissent

. . . However apparent the injustice of such legislation [laws segregating railway carriages] may be, we have only to consider whether it is consistent with the constitution of the United States.

. . . The white race deems itself to be the dominant race in this country. And so it is, in prestige, in achievements, in education, in wealth, and in power. . . . But in view of the constitution, in the eye of the law, there is in this country no superior, dominant, ruling class of citizens. There is no caste here. Our constitution is color-blind, and neither knows nor tolerates classes among citizens. In respect of civil rights, all citizens are equal before the law. . . . It is therefore to be regretted that this high tribunal, the final expositor of the fundamental law of the land, has reached the conclusion that it is competent for a state to regulate the enjoyment by citizens of their civil rights solely upon the basis of race.

In my opinion, the judgment this day rendered will, in time, prove to be quite as pernicious as the decision made by this tribunal in the Dred Scott Case.

. . . If evils will result from the commingling of the two races upon public highways established for the benefit of all, they will be infinitely less than those that will surely come from state legislation regulating the enjoyment of civil rights upon the basis of race. We boast of the freedom enjoyed by our people above all other peoples. But it is difficult to reconcile that boast with a state of the law which, practically, puts the brand of servitude and degradation upon a large class of our fellow citizens, our equals before the law. The thin disguise of "equal" accommodations for passengers in railroad coaches will not mislead anyone, nor atone for the wrong this day done.

. . . I am of opinion that the state of Louisiana is inconsistent with the personal liberty of citizens, white and black, in that state, and hostile to both the spirit and letter of the constitution of the United States. . . .

. . . For the reason stated, I am constrained to withhold my assent from the opinion and judgment of the majority.

3.7: Unit 3 Review

At the beginning of this unit, we asked you to consider the following questions:

1. How would you characterize American identity **historically**? How would you describe American identity **today**? Draw a two-column comparison chart, listing historical American identity traits in one category and modern traits in another. How are the lists similar and different?

2. How did the nation's physical expansion intensify questions about American identity and citizenship? Before you answer this question, draw a simple map of today's United States. Then mark areas that you know were inhabited by many people that were not always considered "real" Americans in the past. Add notes to this map as you read these documents and learn more about these groups.

3. How can an individual or a nation's economic status affect their ability to access full rights or fair treatment by their own country or a neighboring country? Where do you see an example of this both historically and today?

This unit examined two related topics—American expansion and American identity.

Frederick Jackson Turner's Frontier Thesis is helpful for illustrating the overlapping nature of these two ideas. The excerpt from his piece explores the role the frontier had in shaping America and American identity, but it does not engage the challenges and conflicts that arose as white Americans engaged with larger numbers of non-white immigrants and Americans.

This unit demonstrated the physical expansion of the United States and the impact it had on Native Americans as settlers took more and more of their land. Settlers and the federal government believed these Americans of mostly North-Western European origins were culturally superior and therefore deserved the land. Conflicts over land and way of life could be devastating. In the Wounded Knee Massacre as many as 300 Native American men, women, and children lost their lives. Native Americans had not yet been granted citizenship—only those willing to leave their reservations and live amongst "civilized" white society could become citizens. (All Native Americans would become citizens in 1924.) Their exclusion from the American citizenry highlights the limited scope of American identity at this point in time.

Tensions continued to flare as white Americans began to turn a more hostile eye towards immigrants and people of color, including Asians and African Americans, who also appeared to exist outside the borders of American identity. As noted, Chinese immigrants were formally excluded from immigration and therefore could not legally access citizenship. While African Americans were obviously citizens, based on passage of the Fourteenth Amendment, white Americans found ways to diminish their citizenship rights until they essentially had only second-class status. This raises important questions about race and whiteness in America, and the answers are not as clear as they might seem.

Beginning in about the mid-1800s, Americans embraced staunch nativist and racist attitudes. Nativism is a philosophy in which individuals promote the rights of a nation's "native" people over the rights of others. Note that the term *native* is a highly subjective term and here means white, Anglo-Saxon, Protestants (WASPs). As we've seen, it obviously did not apply to Native Americans. Around the 1850s, immigrant Irish Catholics were the targets of early nativists. The Irish were seen as poor, dirty, anti-Protestant immigrants who stole American jobs and were not quite white.

For future reference, it's important to note that during this era, "whiteness" was not firmly linked to skin color, as it would be later. Someone's status as a "white" person was more often linked to the type of work they did, their socioeconomic status, native language, or religion. This attitude toward whiteness began to change around the turn of the century. Since then, it has resulted in a long history of discrimination for people of color in America. New immigrants, first the Germans and Irish and then later Southern and Eastern Europeans, quickly realized that in order to gain full access to American rights and privileges, it was better to be identified as "white" rather than as "non-white" or "colored." The latter terms were typically associated with African Americans, who were most obviously denied equal rights in the United States. As a result, immigrants around the turn of the twentieth century began to use the court system and immigration laws to link skin color to whiteness and the privileges associated with it. By the 1920s, this link was firmly established in Americans' minds. Many immigrants who were "not black" (e.g. not African American) became "white." This transition enabled millions of immigrants access to jobs and opportunities previously denied them, and they began the climb toward upward mobility associated with the American Dream. But it also meant they often increased their social status by adopting white supremacist attitudes and by seeking to limit African Americans' opportunities. In the next unit, "Industrialization and Social Reform," we'll learn more about America's immigrant working class and many people's ongoing quest for expanded civil rights.

4.1: Industrialization and Social Reform

Overview

The United States underwent a period of massive industrial growth at the end of the nineteenth and beginning of the twentieth century. Historians call this period the Second Industrial Revolution; the great American author Mark Twain coined the term *Gilded Age.* Several factors led to this economic development, including transportation improvements (more railroads, refrigerated cars, etc.), large scale immigration, and mechanization. Western settlement and an increased number of trains and canals linking the East and West allowed for a greater movement of people and raw materials between the two areas. Factories sprang up in eastern cities where large working class populations existed (many new immigrants hailed from southern and eastern Europe), thus leading to further urbanization, as workers moved from rural America to cities seeking jobs. Consumer demand at home and abroad underpinned this new economy. With fewer people living off the land, factories produced more of the material goods that people needed to live. At the same time, the era saw the growth of hugely powerful corporations and the business tycoons that owned them.

The turn of the century, then, was a period of great wealth but also one of significant struggle for working-class people. While men like Andrew Carnegie, Andrew W. Mellon, John D. Rockefeller, Henry Ford, and others accrued vast wealth, average people faced a host of challenges simply to survive.

Farmers in the Midwest and South began to look for ways to strengthen their precarious economic position. In the 1880s they first formed organizations like the Farmers' Alliance. By the 1890s the Populist, or People's, Party, emerged and essentially replaced the Farmers' Alliance. Populists wanted elected officials to embrace policies that would help farmers and strengthen America's democracy. They promoted ideas like "free silver," which would loosen the money supply by breaking with the gold standard and allowing currency to be linked to silver as well as gold. Economically, they also promoted left-leaning policies like a graduated income tax, which favored people in lower-income earning brackets, and nationalization of the railroads so that the government could help regulate prices. Politically, Populists called for the direct election of senators. Populists won some local elections but never won widespread national support. In the wake of the Populist Party collapse, some of their ideas would be adopted by Progressive Era reformers.

Social reformers called "Progressives" likewise emerged during this period. They hoped to improve the lives of average Americans and to clean up politics and American society. In the beginning, Progressivism was a social reform movement, not a political party. Progressive reformers came from different backgrounds and political parties, and they sought to address a range of problematic issues found throughout American life, ranging from education and women's rights to factory conditions and lynching.

The readings in this chapter illustrate two themes that defined the era—industrialization and social reform. As you read, keep in mind the following questions to help you understand the relationship between the two themes.

Unit Questions

1. Why did Mark Twain call this period the "Gilded Age"? How does that term stand in contrast to what many people's lives were like?

2. What do we learn about labor conditions during the Second Industrial Revolution? What were some of the ways in which Americans responded to these challenges?

3. What kinds of social reform issues are explicitly addressed in these readings?

4.2 Wendell Phillips: "The Foundation of the Labor Movement" (1871)

Historical Context

Wendell Phillips was a lifelong political agitator. He started out as an abolitionist, and once slavery was abolished in the United States, he began working for the labor movement. The term *labor movement* refers to efforts by working people to secure access to better wages and working conditions. Workers sought ways to fight a capitalist system under which wealthy people held the power and working-class people had few rights. In some cases, workers organized and formed unions. In others, they tried to form political coalitions.

An organization's "platform" is a declaration of the group's fundamental ideas and values. In this reading Phillips articulates the platform of the Labor Reform Convention, which was increasingly concerned about workers' rights as America rapidly industrialized. The group was a coalition of workers from different industries, so it structured its platform to reflect broad goals that would benefit most laboring people.

Guiding Questions

1. What does Phillips mean in the first sentence when he says that "labor, the creator of wealth, is entitled to all it creates"?

2. What kinds of demands does the labor movement make in this piece? Make a bulleted list as you read through the document.

3. How does the labor movement hope to bring about change in employment conditions?

Document Text

PLATFORM.

We affirm, as a fundamental principle, that labor, the creator of wealth, is entitled to all it creates.

Affirming this, we avow ourselves willing to accept the final results of the operation of a principle so radical,—such as the overthrow of the whole profit-making system, the extinction of all monopolies, the abolition of privileged classes, universal education and . . . the final obliteration of . . . the poverty of the masses. . . . we demand that some steps be taken in this direction: therefore,—

Resolved,—That we declare war with the wages system, which demoralizes alike the hirer and the hired, cheats both, and enslaves the working-man; war with the present system of finance, which robs labor, and gorges capital, makes the rich richer, and the poor poorer, . . . We demand a ten-hour day for factory-work, as a first step, and that eight hours be the working-day of all persons thus employed hereafter. We demand that, whenever women are employed at public expense to do the same kind and amount of work as men perform, they shall receive the same wages. We demand that all public debts be paid at once in accordance with the terms of the contract, and that no more debts be created. Viewing the contract importation of coolies as only another form of the slave-trade, we demand that all contracts made relative thereto be void in this country; and that no public ship, and no steamship which receives public subsidy, shall aid in such importation.

. . . [T]here is one great movement. It is for the people peaceably to take possession of their own. No more riots in the streets; no more disorder and revolution; no more arming of different bands; no cannon loaded to the lips. To-day the people have chosen a wiser method,—they have got the ballot in their right hands, and they say, "We come to take possession of the governments of the earth." In the interests of peace, I welcome this movement,—the peaceable marshalling of all voters toward remodelling the industrial and political civilization of the day. . . .

4.3 Samuel Gompers: Editorial on the Pullman Strike (1894)

Historical Context

Samuel Gompers was a longtime labor activist most notable for founding the American Federation of Labor (AFL) in 1886. The AFL would go on to become one of the largest, most influential labor unions in U.S. history.

In the late 1800s a series of labor strikes rattled America. The Great Railway Strike of 1877 kicked off a new era of workers rebelling against poor working conditions and low wages. Some of the more notable strikes of the era include the Homestead Strike in 1892 and the Pullman Strike in 1894. Gompers wrote the following editorial on behalf of the striking Pullman workers, who failed to secure labor and wage improvements through the strike. He specifically rails against the Pullman "company town." As the name implies, a company town is a town owned by the company. This meant that a single corporation owned the houses, stores, churches, schools, etc., in addition to serving as the primary source of employment. Thus, workers were generally forced to make all of their purchases from that corporation. Sometimes workers earned money for their labor, but in the most troublesome instances, they earned "company scrip" that could only be used to pay rent or purchase items at employer-owned stores.

Guiding Questions

1. What, according to the editorial, are some of the differences between what the public saw or heard about the Pullman company town and what the workers living there experienced? Make a list as you read.

2. What evidence does Gompers cite as a central cause of the strike? Write these out in your notes.

3. Why do you think going on strike was more difficult for workers living in company towns? What evidence can you use from the introduction and the reading to support your argument?

Reading Tip: "Arbitration" is when a neutral third party, with no vested interest in the issue, helps two disagreeing partners to come to a mutually agreed upon outcome.

It is a lamentable fact that success does not always attend the right of those who struggle to achieve it. If any doubt existed as to the truth of this statement, the strike at Pullman, and the strike of the American Railway Union in support of it, has dispelled that doubt.

It is indeed difficult to conceive a cause in which right was more on the side of those who were defeated as in the one under consideration.

. . . In the language of the picture drawn by Pullman, the philanthropist of Pullman, the town, he says: "That it is bordered with bright beds of flowers and green velvety stretches of land, that [it] is shaded with trees and dotted with parks and pretty water vistas and glimpses here and there of artistic sweeps and landscape gardening, a town where the homes even of the most modest are bright and wholesome and filled with pure air and light, a town, in a word, from which all that is ugly, discordant and demoralizing is eliminated and all that inspires to self-respect, to thrift and to cleanliness of person and of being is generally provided."

This description is unquestionably true so far as it refers to the view which the passer by sees upon the train; but back where the workers live and die, what a pitiful, horrible condition prevails. In whole blocks entire families have for years lived in one room in order that they might eke out an existence. In no community in the world, except possibly China, was there such a small proportion of families living in family privacy. . . .

. . . During the terrible suffering last winter the Company insisted that there was no destitution nor suffering in the place and with much nonchalance declared that "there could be none because it was not contemplated in the theory upon which the town was founded and controlled."

When a number of charitable ladies organized to relieve the destitution they were not permitted to carry on the work, for that would be an acknowledgment that there was need of relief.

. . . When the fact is borne in mind that Pullman has practically a monopoly in the building of his cars, is not the claim preposterous that he could not pay fair wages? Does anyone imagine that if Pullman's statement of his inability to pay the wage demanded was true that he would refuse to arbitrate? No arbitrator would make an award against him if he could prove his assertions; his refusal is the best evidence of his untruthfulness. In truth out of his own statements he convicts himself. . . .

4.4: Upton Sinclair: *The Jungle* (1906)

Historical Context

Chicago, Illinois, was perfectly situated as the gateway between the eastern and western regions of the United States at the turn of the century. In the years after the Civil War, entrepreneurs in Chicago began capitalizing on the expansion of railroads and new technologies like refrigeration. This new meat industry imported cattle and hogs from the West, slaughtered the animals, processed and packaged them into useable products, and finally shipped those goods to burgeoning urban populations in the East. Industrialized food processing decreased the cost of meat, which benefited consumers. Workers, however, paid dearly as meatpacking became a factory production. In his novel *The Jungle,* Upton Sinclair wrote about immigrant workers who toiled in the meatpacking industry in Chicago.

Guiding Questions

1. Upton Sinclair was a socialist focused on labor justice. After publishing *The Jungle,* Sinclair said "I aimed for the public's heart, and . . . hit it in the stomach." What did he mean?

2. As food processing shifted away from small farms to large-scale factory production, what happened to working conditions? Use the text to make a list of problems you see.

3. Make a prediction. What impact(s) do you think the *The Jungle* ends up having on America after its publication?

Document Text

Chapter 9

Of the butchers and floorsmen . . . you could scarcely find a person who had the use of his thumb; time and time again the base of it had been slashed, till it was a mere lump of flesh against which the man pressed the knife to hold it. . . . They would have no nails,—they had worn them off pulling hides; their knuckles were swollen so that their fingers spread out like a fan. . . . There were the wool-pluckers, whose hands went to pieces even sooner than the hands of the pickle men; for the pelts of the sheep had to be painted with acid to loosen the wool, and then the pluckers had to pull out this wool with their bare hands, till the acid had eaten their fingers off. . . . Some worked at the stamping machines, and it was very seldom that one could work long there at the pace that was set, and not give out and forget himself and have a part of his hand chopped off. . . . Worst of any, however, were the fertilizer men, and those who served in the cooking rooms. . . . the odor of a fertilizer man would scare any ordinary visitor at a hundred yards, and as for the other men, who worked in tank rooms full of steam, and in some of which there were open vats near the level of the floor, their peculiar trouble was that they fell into the vats; and when they were fished out, there was never enough of them left to be worth exhibiting. . . .

Chapter 14

With one member trimming beef in a cannery, and another working in a sausage factory, the family had a first-hand knowledge of the great majority of Packingtown swindles. . . . With what had been told them by Jonas, who had worked in the pickle rooms, they could now study the whole of the spoiled-meat industry on the inside, and read a new and grim meaning into that old Packingtown jest—that they use everything of the pig except the squeal.

Jonas had told them how the meat that was taken out of pickle would often be found sour, and how they would rub it up with soda to take away the smell, and sell it to be eaten on free-lunch counters; also of all the miracles of chemistry which they performed, giving to any sort of meat, fresh or salted, whole or chopped, any color and any flavor and any odor they chose. . . . And yet, in spite of this, there would be hams found spoiled, some of them with an odor so bad that a man could hardly bear to be in the room with them. To pump into these the packers had a second and much stronger pickle which destroyed the odor—a process known to the workers as "giving them thirty per cent." . . .

It was only when the whole ham was spoiled that it came into the department of Elzbieta. Cut up by the two-thousand-revolutions-a-minute flyers, and mixed with half a ton of other meat, no odor that ever was in a ham could make any difference. There was never the least attention paid to what was cut up for sausage; there would come all the way back from Europe old sausage that had been rejected, and that was moldy and white—it would be dosed with borax and glycerine, and dumped into the hoppers, and made over again for home consumption. There would be meat that had tumbled out on the floor, in the dirt and sawdust, where the workers had tramped and spit uncounted billions of consumption germs. There would be meat stored in great piles in rooms; and . . . a man could run his hand over these piles of meat and sweep off handfuls of the dried dung of rats. These rats were nuisances, and the packers would put poisoned bread out for them; they would die, and then rats, bread, and meat would go into the hoppers together. . . .

4.5: Ida B. Wells: "Lynching: Our National Crime" (1909)

Historical Context

This reading shifts the focus from industrialization to social reform. *Lynching* is a term used to describe mob violence against individuals. Hangings are most commonly associated with lynching, but the term includes a range of violence from severe beatings to other forms of torture or murder. In the United States after the Civil War, lynching became a common tactic deployed by white mobs against African Americans, particularly in the South.

Ida B. Wells was an African American journalist and activist. After three friends (Thomas Moss, Will Stewart, and Calvin McDowell) were lynched in Tennessee in 1892, she attacked the issue head on in a published editorial. The men were murdered for opening a grocery store in a mixed-race neighborhood, because local white grocery owners feared the men would siphon off some of their business. Wells was run out of town after publication of the piece, but this did not deter her. She continued to fight to end lynching in America for the rest of her life. Rather than simply highlighting the horror of lynchings, she used quantitative data to dispute the popular justifications of the day for why lynchings were necessary and acceptable.

Guiding Questions

1. What does Wells mean when she says that lynching is "color line murder"? What evidence does she use in the piece to support this assertion? Explain how she makes her case.

2. How did people historically justify lynching, according to Wells? And what evidence does she use to dispute those justifications?

3. What does Wells argue is the only way to end lynching in America?

Document Text

The lynching record for a quarter of a century merits the thoughtful study of the American people. It presents three salient facts:

First: Lynching is color line murder.

Second: Crimes against women is the excuse, not the cause.

Third: It is a national crime and requires a national remedy.

Proof that lynching follows the color line is to be found in the statistics which have been kept for the past twenty-five years. During the few years preceding this period and while frontier lynch law existed, the executions showed a majority of white victims. Later, however, as law courts and authorized judiciary extended into the far West, lynch law rapidly abated and its white victims became few and far between.

Just as the lynch law régime came to a close in the West, a new mob movement started in the South. This was wholly political, its purpose being to suppress the colored vote by intimidation and murder. Thousands of assassins banded together under the name of Ku Klux Klans, "Midnight Raiders," "Knights of the Golden Circle," etc., spread a reign of terror, by beating, shooting and killing colored people by the thousands. In a few years, the purpose was accomplished and the black vote was suppressed. But mob murder continued.

From 1882, in which year 52 were lynched, down to the present, lynching has been along the color line. Mob murder increased yearly until in 1892 more than 200 victims were lynched and statistics show that 3,284 men, women and children have been put to death in this quarter of a century. During the last ten years from 1899 to 1908 inclusive the number lynched was 959. Of this number 102 were white while the colored victims numbered 857. No other nation, civilized or savage, burns its criminals; only under the stars and stripes is the human holocaust possible. Twenty-eight human beings burned at the stake, one of them a woman and two of them children, is the awful indictment against American civilization—the gruesome tribute which the nation pays to the color line.

Why is mob murder permitted by a Christian nation? What is the cause of this awful slaughter? This question is answered almost daily—always the same shameless falsehood that "Negroes are lynched to protect womanhood."... John Temple Graves, at once champion of lynching and apologist for lynchers, said: "The mob stands to-day as the most potential bulwark between the women of the South and such a carnival of crime as would infuriate the world and precipitate the annihilation of the Negro race." This is the never varying answer of lynchers and their apologists. All know it is untrue. The cowardly lyncher revels in murder, then seeks to shield himself from public execration by claiming devotion to woman. But truth is mighty and the lynching record discloses the hypocrisy of the lyncher as well as his crime.

The Springfield, Illinois, mob rioted for two days, the militia of the entire state was called out, two men were lynched, hundreds of people driven from their homes, all because a white woman said a Negro had assaulted her. A mad mob went to the jail, tried to lynch the victim of her charge and, not being able to find him, proceeded to pillage and burn the town and to lynch two innocent men. Later, after the police had found that the woman's charge was false, she published a retraction, the indictment was dismissed and the intended victim discharged. But the lynched victims were dead. Hundreds were homeless and Illinois was disgraced....

...This nation must assert itself and defend its federal citizenship at home as well as abroad. The strong arm of the government must reach across state lines whenever unbridled lawlessness defies state laws....

Federal protection of American citizenship is the remedy for lynching....

4.6: Jane Addams: "Why Women Should Vote" (1910)

Historical Context

The following piece by Jane Addams, a progressive reformer who lived in Chicago at the turn of the twentieth century, illustrates the intersection of multiple issues requiring social reform. One such issue was women's rights. Women did not earn the right to vote nationally until 1920.

Guiding Questions

1. As the title indicates, Addams argued that women should have the right to vote. What evidence did she use to support this argument?

2. Make a chart illustrating the roles and responsibilities of men and women in the early 1900s. Use clues from the reading to help you make your chart.

3. How did Addams use the popular gendered ideas of the day about the roles of women in America to advocate for their right to vote?

Document Text

For many generations it has been believed that woman's place is within the walls of her home. . . .

. . . A woman's simplest duty, one would say, is to keep her house clean and wholesome and to feed her children properly. Yet if she lives in a tenement house . . . she cannot fulfill these simple obligations by her own efforts because she is utterly dependent upon the city administration for the conditions which render decent living possible. . . . In short, if woman would keep on with her old business of caring for her house and rearing her children she will have to have some conscience in regard to public affairs lying quite outside of her immediate household. . . .

In other words, if women would effectively continue their old avocations they must take part in the slow upbuilding of that code of legislation which is alone sufficient to protect the home from the dangers incident to modern life. . . .

. . . Ever since steam power has been applied to the processes of weaving and spinning woman's traditional work has been carried on largely outside of the home. . . . Because many thousands of those working in factories and shops are girls between the ages of fourteen and twenty-two there is a necessity that older women should be interested in the conditions of industry. The very fact that these girls are not going to remain in industry permanently makes it more important that someone should see to it that they shall not be incapacitated for their future family life because they work for exhausting hours and under insanitary conditions.

. . . To turn the administration of our civic affairs wholly over to men may mean that the American city will continue to push forward in its commercial and industrial development, and continue to lag behind in those things which make a city healthful and beautiful. . . .

. . . if woman would fulfill her traditional responsibility to her own children; if she would educate and protect from danger factory children who must find their recreation on the street; if she would bring the cultural forces to bear upon our materialistic civilization; and if she would do it all with the dignity and directness fitting one who carries on her immemorial duties, then she must bring herself to the use of the ballot—that latest implement for self government. May we not fairly say that American women need this implement in order to preserve the home?

4.7: Unit 4 Review

The readings in this unit illustrate the opportunities and challenges associated with the Second Industrial Revolution. Now that you've completed the readings, return to the guiding questions to see how you can add to your original responses.

> 1. Why did Mark Twain call this period the "Gilded Age"? How does that term stand in contrast to what many people's lives were like?
>
> 2. What do we learn about labor conditions during the Second Industrial Revolution? What were some of the ways in which Americans responded to these challenges?
>
> 3. What kinds of social reform issues are explicitly addressed in these readings?

As noted in Unit 3, America was grappling with issues of identity. This struggle continued well into the twentieth century. America saw massive immigration during this period, as poor people—including from southern and eastern Europe—flocked to America looking for new opportunities. These workers entered a difficult environment. Laissez-faire capitalism meant there were few, if any, restrictions in place to regulate wages and working conditions. As immigrants of non-western European stock, these newcomers also faced hostile racial attitudes. They were often seen as not-quite-white and therefore relegated to less desirable jobs and treated as second-class citizens. Many new immigrants quickly realized that in order to take advantage of America's full potential, they needed to gain access to "whiteness" and the privileges associated with it. Over time they used the courts, their lighter colored skin, and employment to become "white." This meant that the divide between African Americans and "white" Americans continued to grow.

African Americans, like Ida B. Wells and others, worked hard to eliminate this divide. As you'll see in the next unit, America faced great opportunities and challenges in the 1910s and 1920s, and African Americans used World War I and the economic prosperity of the "Roaring Twenties" to further their cause. Though they faced stiff opposition at times, they helped establish the foundation for the civil rights movement that arose in the 1950s and 1960s.

5.1: World War I and the Turbulent Twenties

Overview

The late 1890s to early 1900s was a period of major change for the United States. The U.S. government intervened in the Western Hemisphere in events like the Spanish American War (1898) and the building of the Panama Canal (1904-14), and it articulated its right to do so through interventionist policies like the Roosevelt Corollary (1904). At the same time, the nation also sought to exert its influence halfway around the globe in places like the Philippines, resulting in the Philippine-American War (1899-1902). It also expanded U.S. markets by promoting trade policies in China that would open up new markets for American goods. (These trading zones were called "spheres of influence.")

The Second Industrial Revolution helped propel the nation onto the world stage. Some individuals and companies amassed immense wealth, thanks to the government's laissez faire approach. Employers' gains, however, often came at the expense of workers. Wages and working conditions were deplorable. Workers had trouble creating and sustaining unions because of significant hostility towards organized labor. Employers feared unions would increase production costs and therefore drive down profits. Some Americans also feared labor unions would open the door to more radical political ideologies like socialism or communism.

As we learned in the last unit, reformers known as Progressives sought to help mitigate the worst conditions through legislation and community action. Not all Progressives had the same interests. For example, some Progressives promoted American activism and engagement abroad, and others believed the nation should focus on domestic affairs instead. By the mid-1910s the United States had a decision to make. Would it enter the "Great War" or not?

World War I, also known as the Great War, wracked Europe from 1914 to 1918. The United States avoided engagement during the early years of the war, pursuing an isolationist foreign policy and preferring to remain neutral. Following the sinking of the *Lusitania* in May 1915 and the deaths of many Americans, the United States moved closer to war. It eventually entered the war on the side of Britain and France in 1917.

For the United States, some of the most significant effects of the war happened not in Europe but on the home front. Millions of men signed up or were drafted to serve in the military. This left significant labor vacancies in northern factories. Women and African Americans joined the industrial workforce in record numbers. As for African Americans, roughly than one million left the South starting in the 1910s looking for better opportunities in the North. This movement of rural black Americans to urban centers would continue over the next few decades. It accelerated in the 1940s during World

War II, when once again a shortage of factory workers would enable African Americans to gain access to new jobs. Collectively, this decades-long movement of more than six million African Americans from rural to urban centers in the South, North, and West is called the Great Migration. (It is sometimes divided into two phases: the First Great Migration, which lasted roughly from 1916 to 1940; and the Second Great Migration, lasting roughly from 1940 to 1970.)

Like their counterparts on the home front, African Americans who served in World War I also underwent profound change. As the reading by W.E.B. Du Bois illustrates, fighting a war for "democracy" and "freedom" abroad provided returning soldiers with a stronger claim to those same rights at home. This experience, coupled with changing attitudes among urban black residents at home, ushered in a new movement in black communities. In Harlem, New York, this movement became known as the Harlem Renaissance. African Americans, though, were not the only Americans demanding change.

Women also used their increased role in American society during the war to push for political change. After centuries of demanding equal political rights, women finally secured the right to vote in 1920 with the passage and ratification of the Nineteenth Amendment. As you'll see in the readings, some women also sought greater social freedom, and this often caused a rift with older generations.

Guiding Questions

1. The early twentieth century was a period of significant change in America. Before you read the documents, brainstorm and make a basic list of social, political, and economic things that were happening in America between 1900 and 1920. Your list can include actual events as well as attitudes, issues challenging the nation, opportunities, and so on. (For example, the Second Industrial Revolution, America expanding its influence internationally, Jim Crow segregation, the draft, etc.) Make a prediction: How do you think these various elements might impact America in the 1920s?

2. The 1920s are often referred to as the "Roaring Twenties." Why do you think the era earned this nickname? As you read through the documents and learn more in class, make a list of evidence and support.

3. Make a prediction: How do you think the 1920s set the nation up for the Great Depression of the 1930s? What evidence do you have from the readings to support this prediction?

5.2: Navy Poster from World War I (1917)

Historical Context

European countries' borders were not as firmly established in 1917 as they are today. World War I highlights how different peoples and nations were attempting to assert their autonomy. The war began when Serbians assassinated the archduke and presumptive heir to the Austrian throne, Franz Ferdinand. Serbians hoped to unite Slavs throughout the region, even those living in territories controlled by other nation-states, like Austria-Hungary. As a result of various nations' alliances, much of the European continent was dragged into war.

The United States attempted to remain neutral at the start of the war. It was a small nation with limited military power at the time, and internally politicians and the public debated whether or not the country should pursue a more isolationist or interventionist foreign policy. By 1917 several key events compelled the United States to join the European conflict. Most notably were the sinking of the *Lusitania* and the Zimmermann Telegram. In 1915 a German U-boat sank the *Luisitania,* causing the deaths of 128 U.S. citizens. While tragic, this alone was not enough to compel America to intervene. In 1917, however, British intelligence intercepted a communication between Germany and Mexico that would become known as the Zimmermann Telegram. In that communication Germany offered to support Mexico in recovering its former lands (for example, Texas, New Mexico, and Arizona) that had been part of the United States for almost seventy years, in exchange for their alliance should the United States declare war on Germany. President Woodrow Wilson felt this telegram was an attack on American sovereignty that justified a response, so the United States declared war in 1917 and joined the conflict. (Mexico did not act upon Germany's offer.) The United States government sought to crush dissenting voices and undertook a significant propaganda campaign in order to prepare the nation for war. Laws like the Espionage Act, which included provisions often referred to as the Sedition Acts, seriously curtailed Americans' right to free speech during and after the war. The U.S. government also passed the Selective Service Act in 1917, which drafted approximately 4 million men into military service. Men of all ethnicities and races served in the military. As you'll see in the reading by W.E.B. Du Bois, many black men hoped their military service during World War I would translate into increased access to freedom and rights back home. In addition to drafting men into service, the government used propaganda posters like the one in this document to inspire patriotism and military support.

Guiding Questions

1. Why did the United States need to create posters like this one during World War I?

2. How does the poster use gender stereotypes to inspire men to join the military?

3. In what ways does this poster foreshadow changing attitudes, behaviors, and norms for women that followed in the wake of World War I?

Primary Source Image

5.3: W.E.B. Du Bois: "Returning Soldiers" (1919)

Historical Context

W.E.B. Du Bois was one of the greatest intellectuals of the early twentieth century and one of the most prominent African American activists. He was born to a free family in Massachusetts, and while he had experienced discrimination growing up, it was not until he moved to Tennessee to attend Fisk University that he was fully confronted with Jim Crow segregation. This experience caused him to deeply question black people's lives and opportunities in America. Grappling with these issues on an intellectual level, Du Bois went on to become the first African American to earn a Ph.D. from Harvard University and afterwards became a college professor.

Throughout his life Du Bois was a staunch civil rights activist. He cofounded the National Association for the Advancement of Colored People (NAACP) in 1909. Almost 100 years later it remains one of the most important civil rights organizations in America. Du Bois also served as the editor and a major contributor of the organization's monthly magazine, *The Crisis*. The following excerpt is from an article he wrote for *The Crisis* in 1919.

Guiding Questions

1. As you read through the document, compile a list of complaints Du Bois makes about the U.S. government.

2. Make an educated guess: Why would Du Bois encourage black men to serve in the military and support the United States during World War I, even though he obviously has significant complaints about the U.S. government?

3. What was this article's goal or purpose?

Document Text

We are returning from war! THE CRISIS and tens of thousands of black men were drafted into a great struggle. . . . we fought gladly and to the last drop of blood; for America and her highest ideals, we fought in far-off hope; for the dominant southern oligarchy entrenched in Washington, we fought in bitter resignation. For the America that represents and gloats in lynching, disfranchisement, caste, brutality and devilish insult—for this, in the hateful upturning and mixing of things, we were forced by vindictive fate to fight, also.

But today we return! We return from the slavery of uniform which the world's madness demanded us to don to the freedom of civil garb. We stand again to look America squarely in the face and call a spade a spade. We sing: This country of ours, despite all its better souls have done and dreamed, is yet a shameful land.

It lynches.

And lynching is barbarism of a degree of contemptible nastiness unparalleled in human history. Yet for fifty years we have lynched two Negroes a week, and we have kept this up right through the war.

It disfranchises its own citizens.

Disfranchisement is the deliberate theft and robbery of the only protection of poor against rich and black against white. The land that disfranchises its citizens and calls itself a democracy lies and knows it lies.

It encourages ignorance.

It has never really tried to educate the Negro. A dominant minority does not want Negroes educated. . . .

It steals from us.

It organized industry to cheat us. It cheats us out of our land; it cheats us out of our labor. It confiscates our savings. It reduces our wages. It raises our rent. It steals our profit. It taxes us without representation. It keeps us consistently and universally poor, and then feeds us on charity and derides our poverty.

It insults us.

It has organized a nation-wide and latterly a world-wide propaganda of deliberate and continuous insult and defamation of black blood wherever found. It decrees that it shall not be possible . . . for a black man to exist without tacit or open acknowledgment of his inferiority to the dirtiest white dog. . . .

This is the country to which we soldiers of Democracy return. This is the fatherland for which we fought! But it is our fatherland. It was right for us to fight. The faults of our country are our faults. Under similar circumstances, we would fight again. But by the God of Heaven, we are cowards and jackasses if now that that war is over, we do not marshal every ounce of our brain and brawn to fight a sterner, longer, more unbending battle against the forces of hell in our own land.

We return.

We return from fighting.

We return fighting.

Make way for Democracy! We saved it in France, and by the Great Jehovah, we will save it in the United States of America, or know the reason why.

5.4: Walter F. White: "The Eruption of Tulsa" (1921)

Historical Context

As noted in the Unit 2 review, the 1920s saw a resurgence of the Ku Klux Klan (KKK). Millions of immigrants, many of them from Eastern and Southern Europe, entered the United States during the Second Industrial Revolution hoping to earn money and improve their quality of life. "Native" Americans—white Americans who considered themselves native to the nation because their ancestors had immigrated earlier—feared these new immigrants were not sufficiently white, Protestant, or wealthy enough to become true "Americans." The KKK recruited these disillusioned Americans, resulting in a massive resurgence of the organization. Unsurprisingly, the KKK targeted African Americans as well in their terror campaigns. With the legalization of Jim Crow segregation, the KKK felt even more justified in proclaiming its avowed goal of white supremacy. Throughout the country, men and women who did not join the Klan itself also adopted their racist ideas. The era, then, saw an uptick in violence.

World War I ended in 1918, and by 1919 men were returning home from military service. Tensions increased, particularly in northern and midwestern cities, where large numbers of African Americans had moved during the First Great Migration to pursue better job opportunities. Returning white soldiers demanded their factory jobs back. They also resented the encroachment of black families in white neighborhoods. In twenty-five cities across the North and Midwest, tensions led to violent confrontations. The result was "Red Summer," a six month period of bloody, brutal, racial conflict in 1919. As you'll see in this article by Walter F. White, a civil rights activist who would eventually serve as NAACP president for almost twenty-five years, the violence did not end in 1919.

Tulsa, Oklahoma, had a thriving black community. The Greenwood neighborhood was so economically successful it was referred to as "Black Wall Street." Walter White estimated the damage done to the community at $1,500,000, following the race riot that convulsed the neighborhood in 1921.

Guiding Questions

1. What, according to White, were the causes of the Tulsa riot? Make a list as you read and explain why each was considered a cause.

2. How does the incident occurring between Sarah Page and Dick Rowland, and the subsequent events, relate to other articles you've read? Be specific in your analysis.

3. What happened to the black community of Tulsa during the riot? Provide evidence, both directly stated and implied.

Document Text

. . . What are the causes of the race riot that occurred in such a place?

First, the Negro in Oklahoma has shared in the sudden prosperity that has come to many of his white brothers, and there are some colored men there who are wealthy. This fact has caused a bitter resentment on the part of the lower order of whites, who feel that these colored men, members of an "inferior race," are exceedingly presumptuous in achieving greater economic prosperity than they who are members of a divinely ordered superior race. . . . Oklahoma is largely populated by pioneers from other [southern] States. . . . These have brought with them their anti-Negro prejudices. . . .

One of the charges made against the colored men in Tulsa is that they were "radical." Questioning the whites more closely regarding the nature of this radicalism, I found it means that Negroes were uncompromisingly denouncing "Jim-Crow" [railroad] cars, lynching, peonage; in short, were asking that the Federal constitutional guarantees of "life, liberty, and the pursuit of happiness" be given regardless of color. . . . Those of the whites who seek to maintain the old white group control naturally do not relish seeing Negroes emancipating themselves from the old system.

A third cause was the rotten political conditions in Tulsa. . . . Last July a white man by the name of Roy Belton, accused of murdering a taxicab driver, was taken from the county jail and lynched. According to the statements of many prominent Tulsans, local police officers directed traffic at the scene of the lynching, trying to afford every person present an equal chance to view the event. . . . The net result of these conditions was that practically none of the citizens of the town, white or colored, had very much respect for the law.

So much for the general causes. What was the spark that set off the blaze? On Monday, May 30, a white girl by the name of Sarah Page, operating an elevator in the Drexel Building, stated that Dick Rowland, a nineteen-year-old colored boy, had attempted criminally to assault her. . . . It was found afterwards that the boy had stepped by accident on her foot. It seems never to have occurred to the citizens of Tulsa that any sane person attempting criminally to assault a woman would have picked any place in the world rather than an open elevator in a public building with scores of people within calling distance. The story of the alleged assault was published Tuesday afternoon by the *Tulsa Tribune* . . . numerous other citizens all stated that there was talk Tuesday of lynching the boy.

. . . Remembering how a white man had been lynched after being taken from the same jail where the colored boy was now confined, they [the colored community] feared that Rowland was in danger. A group of colored men telephoned the sheriff and proffered their services in protecting the jail from attack. . . . A crowd of twenty-five armed Negroes set out immediately, but on reaching the jail found the report untrue. . . . They left, later returning, 75 strong. The sheriff persuaded them to leave. As they complied, a white man attempted to disarm one of the colored men. A shot was fired, and then—in the words of the sheriff—"all hell broke loose." . . . The fighting continued until midnight when the colored men, greatly outnumbered, were forced back to their section of the town.

Around five o'clock Wednesday morning the [white] mob, now numbering more than 10,000, made a mass attack on Little Africa [the black neighborhood in Tulsa]. Machine-guns were brought into use; eight aeroplanes were employed to spy on the movements of the Negroes and according to some were used in bombing the colored section. . . . Many are the stories of horror told to me—not by colored people—but by white residents. One was that of an aged colored couple, saying their evening prayers before retiring in their little home on Greenwood Avenue. A mob broke into the house, shot both of the old people in the backs of their heads, blowing their brains out and spattering them over the bed, pillaged the home, and then set fire to it. . . .

. . . It is highly doubtful if the exact number of casualties will ever be known. . . . For obvious reasons these officials wish to keep the number published as low as possible, but the figures obtained in Tulsa are far higher. Fifty whites and between 150 and 200 Negroes is much nearer the actual number of deaths.

5.5: Marcus Garvey: "The Principles of the Universal Negro Improvement Association" (1922)

Historical Context

Marcus Garvey was a Jamaican civil rights activist. He promoted an idea called Pan-Africanism. This means he wanted all people of African descent from around the world (called the African diaspora) to celebrate their African heritage and to create a thriving black world community. He founded the Universal Negro Improvement Association (UNIA) in Jamaica, and the organization quickly spread throughout the Caribbean and Central America, with chapters in countries like Cuba, Panama, Costa Rica, Nicaragua, and Honduras, to note a few. Around 1917 Garvey moved to New York City in an effort to grow the organization in the United States, particularly in large urban centers were witnessing an influx of African Americans migrating to them during the early years of the Great Migration. By the early 1920s there were more than 700 branches of the UNIA in 38 states. The UNIA was popular because it was a grassroots movement aimed at celebrating black people's African heritage and working to uplift individuals and communities by improving their daily lives.

After spending time in the United States, Garvey became convinced that full integration was impossible in America. He began to articulate an idea of black nationalism that built on the earlier ideas of unity and pride in one's African cultural heritage, but he added to this belief the concept of autonomy, or the right of black people to control their own lives. In the face of racism and violence in America, Garvey began advocating for a "back-to-Africa" movement in which he encouraged black people around the world to move back to Africa, where they could establish a thriving black nation. In the following document Garvey lays out the major principles of the UNIA. Remember that this document was written after Garvey witnessed the treatment returning soldiers faced after World War I and the bloodshed of Red Summer, as well as subsequent race riots.

Remember the article you read earlier this unit by W.E.B. Du Bois entitled "Returning Soldiers." Du Bois called upon African Americans to fight for their rights at home and explained why they were entitled to those rights. Compare that with Garvey's message in this document. Although they are quite different, they both articulate a new movement and a new identity among African Americans. This movement came to be called the New Negro Movement. New Negroes were typically men living in northern urban areas who had little patience for racism and discrimination. They were often the returning soldiers Du Bois wrote about. They had served in Europe during World War I and found that not all (white) societies discriminated against people of color the way white American society often did. They returned feeling empowered as men, to demand rights associated with manhood. The New Negro Movement, like Garveyism and the UNIA, embraced blackness as something beautiful and meant to be celebrated. The cultural manifestation of this attitude was the Harlem Renaissance.

Guiding Questions

1. Why did Garvey argue that black people should move "back to Africa"? List specific examples from the text.

2. What is nation-building and what, according to the UNIA, is the purpose in doing it?

3. What is the general tone in this piece? What feeling might it inspire in black people? If we compare this with Du Bois's quest for equal rights in the United States, what does this show us about different attitudes and beliefs about what was best "for the race" in the 1920s?

Document Text

Over five years ago the Universal Negro Improvement Association placed itself before the world as the movement through which the new and rising Negro would give expression of his feelings. This Association adopts an attitude not of hostility to other races and peoples of the world, but an attitude of self respect, of manhood rights on behalf of 400,000,000 Negroes of the world. . . .

We represent a new line of thought among Negroes. Whether you call it advanced thought or reactionary thought, I do not care. If it is reactionary for people to seek independence in government, then we are reactionary. If it is advanced thought for people to seek liberty and freedom, then we represent the advanced school of thought among the Negroes of this country. We of the U.N.I.A. believe that . . . if government is something that is appreciable and helpful and protective to others, then we also want to experiment in government. . . .

. . . We are not engaged in domestic politics, in church building or in social uplift work, but we are engaged in nation building. . . .

. . . We of the Universal Negro Improvement Association are determined to unite the 400,000,000 Negroes of the world . . . for the purpose of building a civilization of their own. And in that effort we desire to bring together the 15,000,000 of the United States, the 180,000,000 in Asia, the West Indies and Central and South America, and the 200,000,000 in Africa. We are looking toward political freedom on the continent of Africa, the land of our fathers. . . .

The difference between the Universal Negro Improvement Association and the other movements of this country, and probably the world, is that the Universal Negro Improvement Association seeks independence of government, while the other organizations seek to make the Negro a secondary part of existing governments. . . . the U.N.I.A. refuses to recognize any political or social system in Africa except that which we are about to establish for ourselves. . . .

. . . We should say to the millions who are in Africa to hold the fort, for we are coming 400,000,000 strong.

5.6: Ellen Welles Page: "A Flapper's Appeal to Parents" (1922)

Historical Context

Many American women had long demanded equal treatment, especially focusing on political equality. Some, like Jane Addams in the last unit, promoted women's voting rights while still outwardly supporting traditional gender roles. Although some women had always challenged stereotyped gender roles, the overt flaunting of traditional Victorian behaviors and values became more visible with the "flappers" of the 1920s.

As you read this piece, bear in mind that while all flappers were women, most women were not flappers. Some women preferred more traditional gendered roles, so they were not interested in becoming flappers. Other women wanted more liberalized gender roles, but they were not comfortable pushing social boundaries the way flappers did, since it could result in significant judgment and penalty from one's parents, peers, and community. Those who did embrace the new flapper identity came from all stations in life, from affluent to working-class.

Reading Tip: "Petting" was a term for intimate contact (not sexual intercourse) at the time. Victorian rules prohibited such interactions between courting couples (in other words, those "seeing" each other). Some men and women in the 1920s, however, wanted greater sexual freedom. At one point in the reading, Page says "And, most unpardonable infringement of all the rules and regulations of Flapperdom, I haven't a line!" She seems to be implying that she does not "have a line" of male suitors. Although she's a flapper, she is not as sexually liberal as some would expect. As you read, consider what evidence she provides to support this claim.

Guiding Questions

1. What does Page's letter reveal about differences among women, even those who considered themselves to be flappers?

2. As you read, create a two-column chart listing behaviors and values associated with the Victorian era (the preceding generation) and those associated with the new flappers. Why do you think the older generation of the Victorian Era disapproved of the younger generation? Who, in your opinion, are the modern equivalents of flappers?

3. How were young people's life expectations different from those of their parents? Consider documents you read in Unit 4 about working people's lives and compare that to what you see in Page's letter about their future goals.

December 6, 1922

If one judges by appearances, I suppose I am a flapper. I am within the age limit. I wear bobbed hair, the badge of flapperhood. . . . I powder my nose. I wear fringed skirts and bright-colored sweaters, and scarfs, and waists with Peter Pan collars, and and low-heeled "finale hopper" shoes. I *adore* to dance. I spend a large amount of time in automobiles. I attend hops, and proms, and ball-games, and crew races, and other affairs at men's colleges. But none the less [*sic*] some of the most thoroughbred superflappers might blush to claim sistership or even remote relationship with such as I. I don't use rouge, or lipstick, or pluck my eyebrows. I don't smoke (I've tried it, and don't like it), or drink, or tell "peppy stories." I don't pet. And, most unpardonable infringement of all the rules and regulations of Flapperdom, I haven't a line! But then— there are many degrees of flapper. There is the semi-flapper; the flapper; the superflapper. Each of these three main general divisions has its degrees of variation. I might possibly be placed somewhere in the middle of the first class.

I think everyone one [*sic*] realizes by this time that there has been a marked change in our much-discussed tactics. Jazz has been modified, and probably will continue to be until it has become obsolete. Petting is gradually growing out of fashion by being overworked. Yes, undoubtedly our hopeless condition is improving. But it was not for discussing these aspects of the case that I began this article.

I want to beg all you parents, and grandparents, and friends, and teachers, and preachers—you who constitute the "older generation"—to overlook our shortcoming, at least for the present, and to appreciate our virtues. I wonder if it ever occurred to any of you that it required *brains* to become and remain a successful flapper? Indeed it does! It requires an enormous amount of cleverness and energy to keep going at the proper pace. It requires self-knowledge and self-analysis. We must know our capabilities and limitations. We must be constantly on the alert. . . .

"Brains?" you repeat, skeptically. "Then why aren't they used to better advantage?" That is exactly it! And do you know who is largely responsible for all this energy's [*sic*] spent in the wrong directions! You! . . . .. . We have learned to take for granted conveniences, and many luxuries which not so many years ago were as yet undreamed of. . . . We have a tremendous problem on our hands. You must help us. . . . Be patient and understanding when we make mistakes. . . .

. . . In every person there is a desire, an innate longing, toward some special goal of achievement. Each of us has his place to fill. Each of us has his talent— be it ever so humble. And our hidden longing is usually for that which nature equipped us. Any one will do best and be happiest doing that which he really likes and for which he is fitted.

5.7: Unit 5 Review

The unit questions for this unit asked you to consider the following:

> 1. The early twentieth century was a period of significant change in America. Before you read the documents, brainstorm and make a basic list of social, political, and economic things that were happening in America between 1900 and 1920. Your list can include actual events as well as attitudes, issues challenging the nation, opportunities, and so on. (For example, the Second Industrial Revolution, America expanding its influence internationally, Jim Crow segregation, the draft, etc.) Make a prediction: How do you think these various elements might impact America in the 1920s?

> 2. The 1920s are often referred to as the "Roaring Twenties." Why do you think the era earned this nickname? As you read through the documents and learn more in class, make a list of evidence and support.

> 3. Make a prediction: How do you think the 1920s set the nation up for the Great Depression of the 1930s? What evidence do you have from the readings to support this prediction?

Upon reviewing these questions, you should assess whether your original predictions were on target or not. If they were incorrect, use the readings to help reshape your analysis. A review of the late 1910s and 1920s reveals several major themes.

At the start of World War I, the United States was grappling with whether to pursue an interventionist or isolationist foreign policy. Germany's actions led President Woodrow Wilson and Congress to declare war and enter the conflict, but once the war ended the isolationist/interventionist debate resumed. Many Americans were concerned about the cost of war on society, and so they embraced a more isolationist attitude. They rejected Wilson's proposal for a League of Nations, fearing that international entanglements would jeopardize American sovereignty and pull the nation into future conflicts. Many Americans also remained skeptical of political dissenters, especially following the Russian Revolution in 1917, which replaced the tsarist government with a new communist regime. Post-World War I America, then, saw a spike in anti-communism and anti-political radicalism in general. Historians refer to this period as the First Red Scare. (A Second Red Scare occurred following World War II.) Labor organizers and civil rights activists were often targeted in the late 1910s and 1920s because their messages of equal access to opportunity and capital sounded similar to communism or socialism according to their critics. These attacks illustrate one turbulent facet of the 1920s.

"New Negroes" of all nationalities, and African Americans primarily living in the urban

North, challenged the status quo by more vocally demanding civil rights and celebrating black culture. While they made some gains, they also met with violent resistance as demonstrated by the Tulsa riot. African Americans, particularly in the South, faced continued overt oppression, since Jim Crow segregation remained firmly intact. Even in northern cities, *de facto* segregation persisted and racial tensions escalated as more African Americans migrated from the South to the North and began competing with white residents for decent housing stock and job opportunities.

At the same time these racial tensions were playing out, so too were the forces of "tradition" and "modernity," or religion and science. The Scopes Monkey Trial in 1925 became known as the "trial of the century." Substitute teacher John T. Scopes was accused of violating Tennessee's Butler Act, which banned the teaching of human evolution in state-funded public schools. Activists, including Scopes, intentionally sought to trigger a court case over the teaching of evolution. The goal was to debunk the traditional, fundamentalist, creationist story of humankind's history in favor of modern science. The trial was basically a sham, with few long-term consequences, but it did highlight the intensely conflicting views of some religious fundamentalists and those of modernists who embraced scientific fact, inquiry, and change. The case is noteworthy because it adds yet another dimension to the complex feelings and thoughts circulating in America in the 1920s. Many Americans saw the trial as an extension of social changes already underway in the nation. Some Americans embraced these changes, while others believed they were tearing apart the fabric of American society.

As the World War I propaganda poster illustrates—intentional or not—American women and their place in society were on the brink of profound change. The poster tries to shame men into joining the military by showing that a good woman would be willing to serve in wartime, and therefore a man needs to do his manly duty and step up. The image of the woman in the poster, however, also breaks with the traditional Victorian woman of the late nineteenth and early twentieth century. The woman on the poster is sporting a bold attitude, short hair, and a man's uniform—imagery associated more with the flappers of the 1920s than their predecessors in the 1910s. The image, then, reminds us how society was changing during the period.

The Roaring Twenties, as the years of the 1920s are sometimes called, refer to the period's economic boom. The economy flourished as the government rolled back business regulations and Americans began consuming increasing numbers of finished goods. Mass consumption became the standard of the day. Henry Ford made significant headway in democratizing the automobile in the 1910s, and by the 1920s many American families could afford a basic car. Flapper Ellen Welles Page noted that young people took advantage of this fact and used cars to escape the oversight of their parents. Embracing more liberal attitudes, young men and women pushed moral boundaries and expectations. Some Americans were excited about these changes, but others feared they were undermining American society, values, and morals. Although most people did not realize it at the time, but the nation was also sitting on the brink of significant economic change.

As Americans re-embraced laissez faire economics and consumerism in the 1920s, they often failed to consider the possible consequences. Few Americans had any money in savings accounts. Those who did put their money in the banks had no guarantees it would be protected. Limited regulations meant that many banks and businesses engaged in risky practices. Partly as a result of speculators gaming the system, the stock market crashed in 1929. Although very few Americans invested in the stock market, its crash severely impacted the economy as a whole. The crash, combined with numerous bank closures, plunged the economy into depression. Farmers in rural America were already suffering an economic depression by the time the market collapsed. Many had taken out loans to pay for new technologies and land, to expand food production during World War I. So when the war ended and world demand for American food declined, they could not sell their crops at a decent price to pay off their loans. Many went bankrupt; others barely scraped by. For farmers, then, the 1920s were not a period of prosperity. Rather, their experiences foreshadowed the economic crisis that would sweep the nation in the 1930s.

6.1: The Great Depression

Overview

As Unit 5 concluded, we saw that while some Americans in the 1920s were reaping the benefits of a booming, largely unregulated economy, others were already suffering economic woes. Farmers entered a depression in the 1920s, and by the 1930s many were in the throes of economic ruin. Not only did they face problems from collapsing food prices and high loan repayments, but also in the 1930s the environment was also working against them.

In the Southern Plains region of the American West (covering portions of New Mexico, Colorado, Texas, Oklahoma, and Kansas), a severe drought and decades of poor policy decisions and terrible farming practices resulted in a farming and environmental crisis known as the Dust Bowl. Since the Civil War, the government had granted settlers moving west large swaths of prairie land if they worked to make the land "productive." Settlers and land speculators—individuals purchasing land hoping to get rich quickly—soon began clearing the land. Farming required tearing up native prairie grasses to make room for agricultural crops. The semi-arid region could not sustain this type of agricultural development. Prairie grass had long played a key role in the ecosystem, holding the sandy soil down and preventing it from drying out and blowing away. After years of farming, the ground no longer had enough natural habitat to hold the soil in place. When a severe drought began in 1931, farmers had no idea of the monster they had created. Winds whipped through the regions, sucking dust into the air and creating "black blizzards"—deadly dust storms that destroyed farms and suffocated people and livestock. So-called dust pneumonia killed many. People's and animals' lungs filled with fine particles of sand, making it impossible to breathe. Eventually their lungs gave out and they died. The drought lasted eight years.

In the face of such adversity, some farmers refused to give up and attempted to remain on the land, eking out a living. Others surrendered and migrated away from the Southern Plains, to places like California and the East Coast. (John Steinbeck, the great American author, memorialized the experience of farmers from Oklahoma and surrounding areas, known as "Okies," moving to California in search of a new life in his classic novel *The Grapes of Wrath*.) Millions of Americans joined the migrant labor stream, looking for work. As the Great Depression deepened, plunging rural and urban areas alike into dire economic straits, these impoverished workers faced incredible challenges. They often faced hostility because people did not want them settling in their communities, fearing that the increased job competition would drive down wages or push local residents out of work altogether.

If the Depression began for farmers in the 1920s, by October 29, 1929, the rest of the nation knew it had arrived as well. As with the agricultural crisis in the West, speculators played a role in the new crisis. Coupled with insufficient banking regulations, the stock market was a bubble waiting to burst by the end of the 1920s. The stock market crash did not cause the Great Depression, but it did contribute to the nation's economic decline.

The stock market was experiencing a bubble—stock prices skyrocketed, but the value listed on the New York Stock Exchange was not a real reflection of a company's value. Speculators, hoping to make money quickly, used weak banking laws to borrow money to purchase stocks. The goal was to purchase stocks and then quickly sell them at a profit when their price rose. The stock market crash revealed significant problems in the American economy.

A return to laissez faire economics in the 1920s meant there were few laws in place to regulate the economy. More and more of the nation's wealth resided in the pockets of a few wealthy individuals and corporations. This meant that the rest of the public was much more susceptible to economic swings. Failure to adequately regulate banks resulted in average customer's savings being loaned to speculators to purchase stocks. When the market tanked, individuals and banks alike lost their capital. Many banks were forced to close their doors, with investors unable to recover their lost money. Speculators were often to blame. As noted, agricultural overproduction kicked off the national crisis in rural America. However, the nation's factories also had a hand in the larger economic collapse, in part via overproduction of consumer goods. These factors taken together set the stage for the Great Depression, the severe economic downturn that lasted through most of the 1930s. The Depression was not limited to the United States but in fact affected much of the rest of the world economy as well.

Throughout history, the American economy has had periods of growth followed by periods of recession and depression. That is part of a normal economic cycle. What made the depression of the 1930s so "great," however, was the scope and scale of the disaster. Roughly a quarter of the nation was unemployed during the 1930s. (In a healthy economy, unemployment rates are typically about 4 to 5 percent.) Millions of Americans became migrants—people with no permanent home—because they had lost their land or jobs working in agriculture. No one knew how to end the Depression, because to date, the nation had never suffered such a severe one. Franklin Delano Roosevelt, elected president in 1932, promised to lead the country in a new direction.

Note: When you're referring explicitly to the Great Depression, "Depression" is capitalized. When speaking generally about an economic depression, it is lowercase.

Unit Questions

1. Why is the Great Depression seen as a watershed moment in American history? To answer this question, think about the many ways that it affected all sorts of people across the country.

2. How did different groups of people experience the Depression differently? Create a matrix or diagram with a list of different types of people (on the left) and the ways in which these people experienced the Depression (on the right).

3. How and why did the role of the U.S. government change in society from the 1920s through the 1930s? Here it would be helpful to make two lists of government policies: one for policies that contributed to the Depression and another one for policies that were designed to lift the country out of the Depression.

6.2: Herbert Hoover: "Rugged Individualism" Campaign Speech (1928)

Historical Context

Following World War I, the United States pulled back from international affairs and focused on domestic growth. The Republican Party led efforts to roll back Progressive-era legislation to stimulate business growth. Although Republicans did not call it *laissez faire,* since that term had fallen out of favor given its negative association with the poor working conditions during the Second Industrial Revolution, it basically was the same policy. Embracing free markets, several Republican presidents pursued economic policies aimed at maintaining economic growth. The excerpt below is from Herbert Hoover's 1928 presidential campaign. He won the election and took office in 1929.

Guiding Questions

1. What is the tone of Hoover's speech? Another way of asking this is, what message is he trying to send to the American public? To help you with this, make a list of key terms that apparently are important to Hoover.

2. Why do you think Hoover's idea of "rugged individualism" was popular with Americans in 1928? In your own words, explain what rugged individualism entails. Identify specific ideas or phrases in the reading that helped you develop your definition.

3. Make a prediction. The Great Depression begins in 1929, one year into Hoover's presidency. How do you think Americans' attitudes will change towards Hoover, and the ideas he promoted in this 1928 speech, by the time the 1932 election occurs?

Document Text

After the war [World War I], when the Republican Party assumed administration of the country, we were faced with the problem of determination of the very nature of our national life. During one hundred and fifty years we have [built] up a form of self-government and a social system which is peculiarly our own. It differs essentially from all others in the world. It is the American system.... It is founded upon a particular conception of self-government in which decentralized local responsibility is the very base. Further than this, it is founded upon the conception that only through ordered liberty, freedom, and equal opportunity to the individual will his initiative and enterprise spur on the march of progress. . . .

During the war we necessarily turned to the government to solve every difficult economic problem. . . . For the preservation of the state the Federal Government became a centralized despotism which undertook unprecedented responsibilities, assumed autocratic powers, and took over the business of citizens. To a large degree we regimented our whole people temporarily into a socialistic state. . . .

When the war closed, the most vital of all issues both in our own country and throughout the world was whether governments should continue their wartime ownership and operation of many instrumentalities of production and distribution. We were challenged with a peace-time choice between the American system of rugged individualism and a European philosophy of diametrically opposed doctrines—doctrines of paternalism and state socialism. The acceptance of these ideas would have meant the destruction of self-government through centralization of government. It would have meant the undermining of the individual initiative and enterprise through which our people have grown to unparalleled greatness. . . .

. . . There has been revived in this campaign . . . a series of proposals which, if adopted, would be a long step toward the abandonment of our American system . . . Because the country is faced with difficulty and doubt over certain national problems—that is prohibition, farm relief, and electrical power—our opponents propose that we must thrust government a long way into the businesses which give rise to these problems. . . .

I should like to state to you the effect that this projection of government in business. . . . It would impair the very basis of liberty and freedom. . . .

. . . I do not wish to be misunderstood in this statement. . . . I have already stated that where the government is engaged in public works for purposes of flood control, of navigation, of irrigation, of scientific research or national defense, or in pioneering a new art. . . . But they must be a by-product of the major purpose, not the major purpose itself.

Nor do I wish to be misinterpreted as believing that the United States is freeforall and devil-take-the-hindmost. . . . It is no system of laissez faire. . . .

. . . By adherence to the principles of decentralized self-government, ordered liberty, equal opportunity, and freedom to the individual, our American experiment in human welfare has yielded a degree of well-being unparalleled in all the world. It has come nearer to the abolition of poverty, to the abolition of fear of want, than humanity has ever reached before. Progress of the past seven years is the proof of it. . . .

6.3: Franklin D. Roosevelt: First Inaugural Address (1933)

Historical Context

Franklin Delano Roosevelt came from a wealthy, politically connected New York family. His distant cousin, Theodore, had been the president just after the turn of the century. Theodore was a Republican descended from the party of Abraham Lincoln. By the early 1900s, however, the Republican Party in general had moved towards becoming a more socially conservative party that embraced laissez faire economics. (Theodore would eventually break with the party and run for the president a second time, in 1912, as a progressive, in a party he called the Bull Moose Party.)

Franklin Roosevelt, however, was raised in a Democratic household in New York. He remained a Democrat and would eventually play a monumental role in reshaping the Democratic Party's constituency (voting base) and core philosophies. He was elected to the presidency in 1932 and took office in 1933. The excerpt below is from his First Inaugural Address to the nation.

Guiding Questions

1. Why do you think Franklin Roosevelt won the presidential election over Herbert Hoover in 1932? Based on the text below, what was the tone he wanted to set when he took office? Look for specific phrases or ideas you think would resonate with voters.

2. What are some of the immediate actions that Roosevelt planned to take (with or without the help of Congress) to help the nation?

3. How does this text reveal a very different attitude towards the role of government as compared to what you read in Hoover's campaign speech? Provide at least two specific examples from each man's speech.

Document Text

. . . first of all, let me assert my firm belief that the only thing we have to fear is fear itself. . .

In such a spirit on my part and on yours we face our common difficulties. They concern, thank God, only material things. Values have shrunken to fantastic levels; taxes have risen; our ability to pay has fallen; government of all kinds is faced by serious curtailment of income; the means of exchange are frozen in the currents of trade; the withered leaves of industrial enterprise lie on every side; farmers find no markets for their produce; the savings of many years in thousands of families are gone.

More important, a host of unemployed citizens face the grim problem of existence, and an equally great number toil with little return.

Yet our distress comes from no failure of substance. . . . Nature still offers her bounty and human efforts have multiplied it. . . .

. . . Restoration calls, however, not for changes in ethics alone. This Nation asks for action, and action now.

Our greatest primary task is to put people to work. . . . It can be accomplished in part by direct recruiting by the Government itself, treating the task as we would treat the emergency of a war. . . .

. . . The task can be helped by definite efforts to raise the values of agricultural products and with this the power to purchase the output of our cities. It can be helped by preventing realistically the tragedy of the growing loss through foreclosure of our small homes and our farms. . . .

. . . [I]n our progress toward a resumption of work we require two safeguards against a return of the evils of the old order; there must be a strict supervision of all banking and credits and investments; there must be an end to speculation with other people's money, and there must be provision for an adequate but sound currency. . . .

. . . [I]n the event that the Congress shall fail to take one of these two courses, and in the event that the national emergency is still critical . . . I shall ask the Congress for the one remaining instrument to meet the crisis—broad Executive power to wage a war against the emergency, as great as the power that would be given to me if we were in fact invaded by a foreign foe. . . .

We do not distrust the future of essential democracy. The people of the United States have not failed. In their need they have registered a mandate that they want direct, vigorous action. They have asked for discipline and direction under leadership. They have made me the present instrument of their wishes. In the spirit of the gift I take it.

6.4: Wayne W. Parrish: Letter to Harry Hopkins (1934)

Historical Context

The Roosevelt Administration started countless programs and agencies during the Great Depression aimed at putting people back to work or providing material support to help them survive the severe economic collapse. Facing an unprecedented economic downturn, Roosevelt and his advisors embraced Keynesian economic theory. Named for British economist John Maynard Keynes, this theory holds that government intervention can stabilize the economy during a period of economic downturn. Keynes essentially argued that when free markets fail to promote full employment, the government can help the process by increasing its spending and therefore stimulate economic growth. Facing few viable alternatives, Roosevelt decided to put the theory into practice.

Federal Emergency Relief Administration (FERA) and the Civilian Conservation Corps (CCC) were the first two major "relief" programs set up by the Roosevelt Administration. Applying Keynesian theory, Roosevelt believed the government could help stabilize the economy and put people back to work by hiring them to do a variety of jobs. FERA allocated federal funds to states to help set up work programs so that people could earn money through jobs, rather than collecting direct payments. (At the time, such direct payments were referred to as "the dole"; today, they would be called "welfare" or "food stamps"). This idea was popular because people generally wanted to work and provide for themselves and their families, rather than having to take a handout from the government. In this document, Wayne W. Parrish is writing to Harry Hopkins, the director of FERA. Parrish was a field investigator, which meant he visited the communities in his assigned territory to report on conditions.

Historical Note: FERA was replaced in 1935 by the more widely known and highly successful Works Progress Administration.

Guiding Questions

1. Read through the entire document, then return to the first full paragraph. What does Parrish mean when he says "the psychology of relief has gone through the whole population within the past year"? What does his document reveal about people's attitudes towards "relief" (also known as "welfare" in modern times)?

2. Draw conclusions from the context about the overall social, economic, and political circumstances in which this letter was written. How do you think Americans' attitudes towards welfare had changed since the start of the Great Depression? Why do you think their attitudes changed?

3. What does this document reveal about people's evolving attitudes towards the role of government in the United States? How is this different from what we saw in the 1920s?

Document Text

November 11, 1934

My dear Mr. Hopkins:

This is my first report to you on the survey of New York and metropolitan New Jersey....

Relief rolls are still increasing. No private jobs are in sight....

... [T]he psychology of relief has gone through the whole population within the past year. Relief is regarded as permanent by both clients and relief workers. Clients are assuming that the government has a responsibility to provide. The stigma of relief has almost disappeared except among white collar groups....

Jobs is the cry everywhere, and I can't over-emphasize this point. All agree that this is the one solution, and with no jobs in private business, they must be created by the government. There is no stigma attached to work relief jobs, but there is a growing hatred of home relief. Neither clients nor relief workers understand why jobs can't be created.

All report that mental deterioration has increased in the past year. An evolutionary process, except for the lowest classes, and they are better off than ever before. Clothes present the most serious need at present, with 25 percent of clients in critical need and 75 percent in need. Household equipment is worse because of lack of money for maintenance.

There is a surprisingly uniform belief—at least to me—among supervisors and case workers that they feel the government has a definite responsibility and obligation to provide a minimum subsistence level for every person, regardless of jobs. If private jobs bring in income below this level, then the government should supplement. This feeling has also gained amazing tenacity among clients, who are definitely more dependent on the government....

As for health, the lowest classes are better off. I am referring to the minority of clients who were always in the poverty classification and who never had permanent homes or jobs. Now they have medical care and go to clinics, and some take advantage of educational facilities which they never had before. . . . Most investigators consider the health problem "serious", but not one of them is able to compare health with pre-depression days because they have never been connected with medical institutions. It is probably a safe conclusion, however, that health conditions are worse among the better class of relief clients because of their inability to use private facilities they formerly enjoyed. . . .

. . . In reference to criticism often made that people are getting relief that don't need it, I can say that as far as I have gone the percentage of frauds is very low. Only a very small percentage are getting away with anything. Most of the chiseling is on a small scale and the people who do it use the money for essential maintenance. . . . The investigators I talked with are not only consci-entious but are active in tracing down frauds, and I say this knowing that they would make a good appearance to an investigator from above. . . .

Yours very sincerely,

Wayne W. Parrish

6.5: New Deal Legislation (selected excerpts from 1935 and 1938)

Historical Context

The "New Deal" is the name given to President Franklin D. Roosevelt's legislation and programs aimed at stopping the nation's downward spiral, and encouraging improvement, during the Great Depression. The New Deal is considered the start of the modern "welfare state" in America. The term *welfare* means different things to different people around the world. For all intents and purposes, "welfare" simply describes governmental efforts to provide basic necessities to its population.

The three documents listed below provide selections from New Deal legislation designed to create basic protections for workers and the American public. While this legislation provided protections for some people, however, it also excluded some categories of workers.

Roosevelt put together a unique political coalition in order to win the 1932 election. He worked with long-time Democrats in northern urban centers, as well as minorities including newly naturalized immigrants and African Americans in those areas. He also tapped into labor unions, recognizing their ability to marshal members' support during election times. As a Democrat, Roosevelt also looked to southern white voters, who had long belonged to the Democratic Party.

Guiding Questions

1. What are some of the welfare policies implemented by the three laws listed below? How were they designed to help people? You might find it useful to create a table or a matrix to organize your notes.

2. As you read, write down what groups of people were excluded from certain benefits. Why do you think Roosevelt allowed some groups of workers to be excluded? (Hint: Consider his political coalition in answer to this question. The answer is not explicit in the reading, but with some deductive reasoning you can figure out the answer.)

3. How did New Deal legislation reshape the American workplace? Identify specific provisions or practices that are still in place today (even if somewhat modified to accommodate economic inflation).

Social Security Act (1935)

An act to provide for the general welfare by establishing a system of Federal old-age benefits, and by enabling the several States to make more adequate provision for aged persons, blind persons, dependent and crippled children, maternal and child welfare, public health, and the administration of their unemployment compensation laws. . .

DEFINITIONS

SEC. 811. . .

(b) The term employment means any service, of whatever nature, performed within the United States by an employee for his employer, except—

(1) Agricultural labor;

(2) Domestic service in a private home;

National Labor Relations Act (1935)

An act to diminish the causes of labor disputes burdening or obstructing interstate and foreign commerce, to create a National Labor Relations Board. . . .

. . . Experience has proved that protection by law of the right of employees to organize and bargain collectively safeguards commerce . . . and promotes the flow of commerce by removing certain recognized sources of industrial strife and unrest. . . .

It is hereby declared to be the policy of the United States to eliminate the causes of certain substantial obstructions to the free flow of commerce and to mitigate and eliminate these obstructions when they have occurred by encouraging the practice and procedure of collective bargaining and by protecting the exercise by workers of full freedom of association, self-organization, and designation of representatives of their own choosing, for the purpose of negotiating the terms and conditions of their employment or their mutual aid or protection. . . .

Definitions . . .

(3) The term "employee" shall not . . . include any individual employed as an agricultural laborer, or in the domestic service of any family or person at his home. . . .

Prevention of Unfair Labor Practices. . . .

Sec. 10. (a) The Board is empowered, as hereinafter provided, to prevent any person from engaging in any unfair labor practice (listed in Section 8) affecting commerce. . . .

Fair Labor Standards Act (1938)

AN ACT

To provide for the establishment of fair labor standards in employment in and affecting interstate commerce, and for other purposes. . . .

DEFINITIONS

SEC. 3. As used in this Act—. . . .

(l) "Oppressive child-labor" means a condition of employment under which (1) any employee under the age of sixteen years is employed by an employer (other than a parent or a person standing in place of a parent employing his own child or a child in his custody under the age of sixteen years in an occupation other than manufacturing or mining) in any occupation. . . .

MINIMUM WAGES. . . .

SEC. 6. (a) Every employer shall pay to each of his employees who is engaged in commerce or in the production of goods for commerce wages at the following rates—

(1) during the first year from the effective date of this section, not less than 25 cents an hour,

(2) during the next six years from such date, not less than 30 cents an hour. . . .

MAXIMUM HOURS. . . .

SEC. 7. (a) No employer shall, except as otherwise provided in this section, employ any of his employees who is engaged in commerce or in the production of goods for commerce—....

(3) for a workweek longer than forty hours....

EXEMPTIONS....

(5) any employee employed in the catching, taking, harvesting, cultivating or farming of any ... aquatic forms of animal and vegetable life ... or (6) any employee employed in agriculture ... (c) The provisions of section 12 relating to child labor shall not apply with respect to any employee employed in agriculture while not legally required to attend school or to any child employed as an actor in motion pictures or theatrical productions.

6.6: John P. Davis: "A Black Inventory of the New Deal" (1935)

Historical Context

The Great Depression affected different populations in different parts of the country in different ways. As we have seen, historically, African American communities economically lagged behind white communities because of laws and policies explicitly designed to undermine their economic growth and freedom.

John P. Davis, a journalist and activist, traveled throughout the South interviewing black Americans to learn more about the impact that New Deal programs had on people's lives. Below is an excerpt from his findings.

Guiding Questions

1. From what you can glean in the reading, what did the Agricultural Adjustment Act do? What impact did the AAA have on black farmers and farmworkers? To help you organize your notes, make lists.

2. Why did many New Deal programs fail to sufficiently support black populations, the way they did with white populations? Provide specific examples from the text to support your argument.

3. Why and how did the exclusion of agricultural workers and domestic workers from unemployment insurance severely affect black communities?

Document Text

It is highly important for the Negro citizen of America to take inventory of the gains and losses which have come to him under the "New Deal." . . .

. . . As a matter of fact federal relief officials themselves admit that grave abuses exist in the administration of rural relief to Negroes. And this is reliably borne out by the disproportionate increase in the number of urban Negro families on relief to the number of rural Negro families on relief. Thus the increase in the number of Negroes in relief families is an accurate indication of the deepening of the economic crisis for black America. . . .

. . . The Agricultural Adjustment Administration has used cruder methods in enforcing poverty on the Negro farm population. . . . The reduction of the acreage under cultivation through the government rental agreement rendered unnecessary large numbers of tenants and farm laborers. Although the contract with the government provided that the land owner should not reduce the number of his tenants, he did so. . . . Farm laborers are now jobless by the hundreds of thousands, the conservative government estimate of the decline in agricultural employment for the year 1934 alone being a quarter of a million. The larger portion of these are unskilled Negro agricultural workers—now without income and unable to secure work or relief. . . .

. . . The past year has seen an extension of poverty even to the small percentage (a little more than 20 per cent) of Negro farmers who own their own land. For them compulsory reduction of acreage . . . has meant drastic reduction of their already low income. . . .

Nor has the vast public works program, designed to give increased employment to workers in the building trades, been free from prejudice. State officials in the South are in many cases in open rebellion against the ruling of PWA [Public Works Administration] that the same wage scales must be paid to Negro and white labor. Compliance with this paper ruling is enforced in only rare cases. . . .

. . . Recovery legislation of the present session of Congress reveals the same fatal flaws which have been noted in the operation of previous recovery ventures. Thus, for example, instead of genuine unemployment insurance we have the leaders of the administration proposing to exclude from their plans domestic and agricultural workers, in which classes are to be found 15 out of every 23 Negro workers. . . .

6.7: Unit 6 Review

The unit began with an overview of the Great Depression's causes and effects in the 1920s and 1930s. We asked you to think about the following questions before you began the unit. Now that you've completed the unit, look at what you originally wrote down. What would you add to your notes?

1. Why is the Great Depression seen as a watershed moment in American history?

2. How did different groups of people experience the Depression differently? Add the new information you've learned to your matrix.

3. How and why did the role of the U.S. government change in society from the 1920s through the 1930s? What new evidence do you have from the readings to support your conclusions?

The three questions are deeply interrelated. The Great Depression is a watershed moment in U.S. history because it redefined the role of government in America. As the readings demonstrate, many people shifted from supporting former President Hoover's vision of a hands-off government (laissez faire) where people succeeded by "pulling themselves up by their bootstraps" ("rugged individualism") to embracing Roosevelt's vision that government can play a key role in helping people survive and thrive. You should be asking yourself, why did people change their attitude so dramatically? The answer to this question is alluded to in Wayne Parrish's letter to Harry Hopkins.

Prior to the Great Depression, many Americans believed that they had succeeded through hard work. When the Depression hit and millions of people lost their money and jobs through no fault of their own, they started to believe that there was a flaw in the system. African Americans and many of the working poor who had never been able to move into a higher economic standing had long known that larger structural problems existed that often prevented them from reaping the economic benefits promoted in the 1920s. But when these inequalities became apparent to a broader swath of the American public, that public began to demand changes.

President Roosevelt recognized the shift in American attitudes early on and built his career around creating programs and policies to slow the economic freefall and rebuild the national economy. He sought to put people back to work and pass legislation to prevent something like this from happening again. After the private sector collapsed, Roosevelt initially tried to support Americans simply by providing them opportunities to earn a paycheck through government sponsored jobs. Eventually, however, the economy got so bad that he called on government to begin providing direct aid to the nation's neediest communities.

Programs like Social Security emerged during the Great Depression, and they started to form the basis of the modern American welfare state. (The U.S. welfare state would never develop as fully as its western European counterparts, but it did take steps to try and create a minimal safety net.) As we see, however, politics affected Roosevelt's decision-making. In order to maintain his political coalition, he excluded some working people from important labor provisions or welfare policies like Social Security. Unsurprisingly, in order to keep southern Democrats in the party, Roosevelt limited government support to African Americans by excluding workers in agriculture and domestic service. While this impacted some white workers in those fields, it effectively excluded roughly 65 percent of America's black population. (Keep Roosevelt's New Deal political coalition in mind as we progress through the 20th Century. By bringing together northern urban democrats, minorities, and unions and working-class people, Roosevelt played a major role in helping shape the modern Democratic Party.)

Many people embraced Roosevelt's new policies, while many others disagreed with this new approach to government. (Note, Franklin Roosevelt was the only president in history to be elected four times! He died early on in his fourth term. In 1947 Congress passed the Twenty-second Amendment, setting a two-term limit on presidents. The amendment was ratified by the states in 1951.) Over the course of the Great Depression, the Supreme Court ruled some New Deal programs unconstitutional, while others flourished. In the end, scholars still debate the overall efficacy of New Deal programs in ending the Depression. Most historians agree that various policies prevented the Depression from getting worse but argue that World War II is what finally pulled the nation (and the rest of the world) out of the massive economic slump.

7.1: World War II and the Home Front

Overview

World War II was a major turning point in U.S. history and the world. It caused global turmoil and disrupted the lives of millions of people. This unit specifically examines the war and the home front in order to focus attention on how it directly affected the United States.

The last unit explored the Great Depression, including its impact on Americans and government efforts to help people suffering as a result of it. President Franklin D. Roosevelt tried countless policies and programs aimed at ending the Depression. Many helped to mitigate the worst effects of the Depression, but most scholars agree World War II was responsible for bringing it to a close. The reasons for this are similar to what you read about during World War I. Large numbers of men (and increasingly women) left the workforce to join the military. At the same time, the United States increased its industrial production and food supply. Initially, it did this in a limited quantity to support its allies. Following the Japanese attack on Pearl Harbor in December 1941 and the United States' declaration of war, however, the nation dramatically increased production. This required more workers in virtually all sectors of the economy.

American workers began shifting jobs looking for better opportunities. For example, agricultural workers often left farm work looking for better paying industrial jobs. In extreme cases this left labor shortages resulting in U.S. farmers demanding access to foreign workers to tend their crops. The United States government brought in workers from Mexico, under the Bracero Program, as well as people from the Bahamas and the Caribbean under the British West Indian Emergency Farm Labor Program. In both instances workers were imported to work temporarily, and then they returned to their native countries at the close of the harvest season. This program provided migrant workers with the opportunity to earn higher wages than they often could at home, but it came at a cost. Working conditions were often poor and laborers had little recourse, since they could easily be deported for complaining about wages or conditions. Additionally, by importing workers, farm owners made it more difficult for domestic workers to push for better wages and conditions because they could be replaced by the foreign workers.

In the American South, African Americans had dominated the agricultural labor pool prior to World War II. As you'll read in this unit, much like in World War I, they leveraged the war to gain access to better paying jobs. This time, however, conditions were in their favor and they began to get more permanent access to those jobs. Franklin Roosevelt had retained significant political power through his "New Deal Coalition," which was composed of working people, union members, urban minorities in the North, and southern whites. (Most black voters in the South were disenfranchised—in other words, unable to vote—at this time due to discriminatory voting laws, like poll taxes, literacy tests, and violent voter suppression through murder, abuse, and fear tactics.) Northern black voters, however, were ready to put pressure on Roosevelt to deliver on his political promises of better wages and job opportunities for those willing to work.

As much as the war benefited many Americans by pulling them out of economic dire straits, others suffered during the war. World War II increased people's fear and hostility especially towards those whose ancestry traced back to the countries the nation was fighting. Among these, Japanese Americans were targeted most fiercely following the attack on Pearl Harbor.

Unit Questions

1. Why did the United States originally try to stay out of World War II? What eventually led to its involvement? Create an annotated timeline that begins in the late 1930s and ends in 1945 to help you get a better overview.

2. How did the war affect the U.S. home front during and after the war? A cause-and-effect concept map may be helpful here.

3. Make a prediction. Why is World War II considered a turning point in the nation's history? (Hint: Try to explain how and why the United States became a world superpower after the war. Consider here which countries were left weakened the most after the end of World War II.)

7.2: Franklin D. Roosevelt: Four Freedoms Message to Congress (1941)

Historical Context

U.S. presidents typically deliver the State of the Union address in January. In January 1941, when President Franklin D. Roosevelt (known as FDR) delivered his State of the Union speech, he gave it during a period of intense international anxiety. (Domestic tensions were also quite high, since the Great Depression was still well underway.) In the mid-to-late 1930s, Italy, Germany, and Japan had begun hostile expansions into neighboring countries, taking them over directly or setting up puppet regimes under their control. Collectively, Germany, Italy, and Japan came to be known as the Axis Powers during World War II.

By 1941 the Axis Powers controlled large swaths of land in Europe, Asia, and north Africa. The United States had long been protected from European affairs based on its geography, but President Roosevelt began to argue that America could not stay safe if it remained unprepared for war. The country had a fairly small military in the late 1930s, but in 1940 it instituted a draft to build up its armed forces. As you'll see in Roosevelt's speech, he also acknowledges the need for America to build up its material resources as well. The United States had passed a series of Neutrality Acts in the 1930s, because it did not want to be pulled into a violent, bloody conflict that appeared to have little to do with its interests. However, by the late 1930s and early 1940s, it was becoming clear that these acts limited the U.S.'s ability to fight tyranny in the world, so the government repealed most of them by 1941.

As time progressed, the United States supported the Allied Powers, composed primarily of Great Britain and the Soviet Union. France had been part of the Allied Powers until it fell under German control in 1940 (a control that lasted into 1944). China and many other smaller nations also supported the Allies during World War II. Starting in March 1941 the United States supported the Allies through programs like the Lend-Lease policy. Under this law, the United States supplied needed wartime materials to the Allied Powers at no cost (the "lend" portion of the policy). In exchange for these materials, the United States "leased," at no cost, army and naval bases in Allied territories during the war.

American involvement in World War II changed dramatically after the Japanese attack on Pearl Harbor on December 7, 1941. The United States immediately declared war on Japan. Four days later Germany declared war on the United States, and shortly after that the U.S. in turn declared war on Germany. The United States, then, was fully engaged in World War II and would be fighting a war on two fronts—a war against the Japanese in the Pacific Theater and one against Germany and Italy in Europe and North Africa.

At the time of Roosevelt's speech in January 1941, however, he knew none of the events that would transpire. He knew the world was a hostile place where dictators were taking over and destroying democracy. He used his State of the Union speech as a proverbial call to arms. He was asking the United States to stand up for its core belief in democracy and freedom and to support those fighting for it around the world.

Guiding Questions

1. Early in the speech Roosevelt lays out three main pillars of American "national policy." What are they? What are the United States' goals based on those three policies, and how does it plan to achieve them?

2. What principles and policies, according to FDR, make a democracy strong? How does his interpretation of those ideas align with those of the modern Democratic Party he helped to create?

3. How does FDR define freedom in this speech? After it was delivered, it became known as the "Four Freedoms" speech. What are those four freedoms? What is the fifth freedom he explicitly mentions but does not list along with the other four?

Document Text

. . . I find it, unhappily, necessary to report that the future and the safety of our country and of our democracy are overwhelmingly involved in events far beyond our borders. . . .

. . . Our national policy is this:

First . . . we are committed to all-inclusive national defense.

Second . . . we are committed to full support of all those resolute peoples, everywhere, who are resisting aggression and are thereby keeping war away from our Hemisphere. . . .

Third . . . we are committed to the proposition that principles of morality and considerations for our own security will never permit us to acquiesce in a peace dictated by aggressors and sponsored by appeasers. We know that enduring peace cannot be bought at the cost of other people's freedom. . . .

. . . Therefore, the immediate need is a swift and driving increase in our armament production.

. . . Our most useful and immediate role is to act as an arsenal for them [our allies] as well as for ourselves. They do not need man power, but they do need billions of dollars worth of the weapons of defense. . . .

. . . [T]here is nothing mysterious about the foundations of a healthy and strong democracy. The basic things expected by our people of their political and economic systems are simple. They are:

Equality of opportunity for youth and for others.

Jobs for those who can work.

Security for those who need it.

The ending of special privilege for the few.

The preservation of civil liberties for all.

The enjoyment of the fruits of scientific progress in a wider and constantly rising standard of living.

. . . The inner and abiding strength of our economic and political systems is dependent upon the degree to which they fulfill these expectations.

Many subjects connected with our social economy call for immediate improvement. As examples:

We should bring more citizens under the coverage of old-age pensions and unemployment insurance.

We should widen the opportunities for adequate medical care.

We should plan a better system by which persons deserving or needing gainful employment may obtain it.

I have called for personal sacrifice. I am assured of the willingness of almost all Americans to respond to that call.

A part of the sacrifice means the payment of more money in taxes. . . . I shall recommend that a greater portion of this great defense program be paid for from taxation . . . No person should try, or be allowed, to get rich out of this program....

...In the future days, which we seek to make secure, we look forward to a world founded upon four essential human freedoms.

The first is freedom of speech and expression—everywhere in the world.

The second is freedom of every person to worship God in his own way—everywhere in the world.

The third is freedom from want—which, translated into world terms, means economic understandings which will secure to every nation a healthy peace-time life for its inhabitants—everywhere in the world.

The fourth is freedom from fear—which, translated into world terms, means a world-wide reduction of armaments to such a point and in such a thorough fashion that no nation will be in a position to commit an act of physical aggression against any neighbor—anywhere in the world.

...Freedom means the supremacy of human rights everywhere. Our support goes to those who struggle to gain those rights or keep them. Our strength is our unity of purpose. To that high concept there can be no end save victory.

7.3: Executive Order 8802: Banning Discrimination in Government and Defense Industries (1941)

Historical Context

The American home front during World War II looked very similar to that of World War I. Large numbers of men left their jobs voluntarily or through the draft to serve in the U.S. military. Their absence provided new employment opportunities for women, African Americans, and other minority groups. As we saw in earlier readings, many African Americans had hoped that their service during World War I would improve their position in America, but this largely did not happen. African Americans still faced extreme discrimination throughout the country in all facets of life. They were excluded from many professions and denied access to better paying jobs. A. Philip Randolph, a long-time labor organizer and founder and president of the most successful black union, the Brotherhood of the Sleeping Car Porters, saw World War II as an opportunity to again highlight black people's contributions to the nation and to demand equal rights.

Randolph met with President Roosevelt in 1941 and offered him an ultimatum. Roosevelt could either open up good paying jobs to African Americans, or Randolph would call upon thousands of African Americans throughout the country to march on Washington, D.C., to voice their discontent with the government and the nation. Roosevelt, knowing this would reflect poorly on the nation and undermine the war effort, signed Executive Order 8802. An executive order allows the president to enact a law without congressional approval. In 1941 it would have been difficult for the president to get members of Congress to support a law banning discrimination, so he bypassed them by using an executive order.

Guiding Questions

1. Based on the document, in what ways was it now illegal to discriminate? To what specific types of employment did this law apply? As you read, make a list in your notes.

2. What enforcement mechanism did the law create to help people seek recourse if they suffered discrimination? In what ways do you think this new enforcement mechanism might be successful and why might it prove to be insufficient?

3. Draw connections. During World War II, Nazi Germany was taking over its neighbors and killing millions of people based largely on their religious and racial/ethnic identities and origins. Nazi ideology was based on the belief that certain people (i.e. Aryans) were superior to others. Why would this context make it less acceptable for the United States to discriminate against African Americans?

Reaffirming Policy of Full Participation in The Defense Program by All Persons, Regardless of Race, Creed, Color, or National Origin, and Directing Certain Action in Furtherance of Said Policy

June 25, 1941

WHEREAS it is the policy of the United States to encourage full participation in the national defense program by all citizens of the United States, regardless of race, creed, color, or national origin, in the firm belief that the democratic way of life within the Nation can be defended successfully only with the help and support of all groups within its borders; and:

WHEREAS there is evidence that available and needed workers have been barred from employment in industries engaged in defense production solely because of considerations of race, creed, color, or national origin, to the detriment of workers' morale and of national unity:

NOW, THEREFORE, by virtue of the authority vested in me by the Constitution and the statutes, and as a prerequisite to the successful conduct of our national defense production effort, I do hereby reaffirm the policy of the United States that there shall be no discrimination in the employment of workers in defense industries or government because of race, creed, color, or national origin, and I do hereby declare that it is the duty of employers and of labor organizations, in furtherance of said policy and of this order, to provide for the full and equitable participation of all workers in defense industries, without discrimination because of race, creed, color, or national origin;

And it is hereby ordered as follows:

1. All departments and agencies of the Government of the United States concerned with vocational and training programs for defense production shall take special measures appropriate to assure that such programs are administered without discrimination because of race, creed, color, or national origin;

2. All contracting agencies of the Government of the United States shall include in all defense contracts hereafter negotiated by them a provision obligating the contractor not to discriminate against any worker because of race, creed, color, or national origin;

3. There is established in the Office of Production Management a Committee

on Fair Employment Practice, which shall consist of a chairman and four other members to be appointed by the President. The Chairman and members of the Committee shall serve as such without compensation but shall be entitled to actual and necessary transportation, subsistence and other expenses incidental to performance of their duties. The Committee shall receive and investigate complaints of discrimination in violation of the provisions of this order and shall take appropriate steps to redress grievances which it finds to be valid. The Committee shall also recommend to the several departments and agencies of the Government of the United States and to the President all measures which may be deemed by it necessary or proper to effectuate the provisions of this order.

Franklin D. Roosevelt

7.4: Order for Internment of Japanese Americans in San Francisco (1942)

Historical Context

Following the Japanese attack on Pearl Harbor, many Americans let their fears take over. As a result, they embraced some policies, like internment, that were misguided and racist. Some people in the United States believed that Americans of Japanese descent could not be loyal Americans because of ties to their ancestral homeland. They also feared that Japanese Americans and immigrant spies had helped facilitate the 1941 attack on Pearl Harbor. There was never any evidence to corroborate this theory. Nonetheless, President Roosevelt signed Executive Order 9066 outlining the internment of people of Japanese descent. As the following document notes, it is from the Western Defense Command and Fourth Army Wartime Civil Control Administration in the state of California, and it outlines important logistical information for those affected by the order.

Several decades after the war, in 1988, the U.S. government—recognizing its mistakes—passed the Civil Liberties Act, which provided a formal apology and monetary compensation to the more than 100,000 people who had been incarcerated in internment camps during World War II.

Guiding Questions

1. What was internment? How and why did it violate Japanese Americans' civil liberties?

2. The document provides logistical information for individuals and families of Japanese descent. What does this information reveal about possible impacts internment may have on their lives?

3. How did the U.S. government attempt to walk the fine line between violating people's rights and attempting to make the forced move to an internment camp less damaging or difficult for families?

Western Defense Command and Fourth Army Wartime Civil Control Administration

Presidio of San Francisco, California

April 1, 1942

INSTRUCTIONS TO ALL PERSONS OF JAPANESE ANCESTRY

Living in the Following Area:

. . . All Japanese persons, both alien and non-alien, will be evacuated from the above designated area by 12:00 o'clock noon Tuesday, April 7, 1942.

No Japanese person will be permitted to enter or leave the above described area after 8:00 a.m., Thursday, April 2, 1942, without obtaining special permission from the Provost Marshal. . . .

. . . The Civil Control Station is equipped to assist the Japanese population affected by this evacuation in the following ways:

1. Give advice and instructions on the evacuation.

2. Provide services with respect to the management, leasing, sale, storage or other disposition of most kinds of property including real estate, business and professional equipment, household goods, boats, automobiles, livestock, etc.

3. Provide temporary residence elsewhere for all Japanese in family groups.

4. Transport persons and a limited amount of clothing and equipment to their new residence as specified below.

The Following Instructions Must Be Observed:

1. A responsible member of each family, preferably the head of the family, or the person in whose name most of the property is held, and each individual living alone must report to the Civil Control Station to receive further instructions. . . .

2. Evacuees must carry with them on departure for the Reception Center, the following property:

a. Bedding and linens (no mattress) for each member of the family.

b. Toilet articles for each member of the family.

c. Extra clothing for each member of the family.

d. Sufficient knives, forks, spoons, plates, bowls and cups for each member of the family.

e. Essential personal effects for each member of the family.

All items carried will be securely packaged, tied and plainly marked with the name of the owner and numbered in accordance with instructions received at the Civil Control Station.

The size and number of packages is limited to that which can be carried by the individual or family group. . . .

. . . 3. The United States Government through its agencies will provide for the storage at the sole risk of the owner of the more substantial household items, such as iceboxes, washing machines, pianos and other heavy furniture. Cooking utensils and other small items will be accepted if crated, packed and plainly marked with the name and address of the owner. Only one name and address will be used by a given family.

4. Each family, and individual living alone, will be furnished transportation to the Reception Center. Private means of transportation will not be utilized. All instructions pertaining to the movement will be obtained at the Civil Control Station. . . .

J. L. DeWITT

Lieutenant General, U. S. Army

Commanding

7.5: GI Bill (Servicemen's Readjustment Act of 1944)

Historical Context

The Servicemen's Readjustment Act of 1944 became known as the GI Bill. Americans began to use the term "GI" (the abbreviation for "government issue") as a shorthand for soldiers in World War II as well as other material items.

The GI Bill is credited with helping establish the American middle class after World War II. An estimated 16 million Americans served in World War II. If an individual met the criteria established in the law, then he or she could take advantage of the many benefits provided in the bill.

Reading note: The GI Bill's authors repeatedly had to identify which servicemen qualified for the programs and benefits it outlined. In general, the bill covered "Any person who shall have served in the active military or naval service of the United States at any time after September 16, 1940, and prior to the termination of the present war, and who shall have been discharged or released from active service under conditions other than dishonorable, after active service of ninety days or more, or by reason of an injury or disability incurred in service in line of duty." Therefore, beneficiaries would have had to meet the above criteria (and any other listed in the original document) to qualify for any of the programs outlined in the following reading. To simplify the reading, however, we have deleted many of the specific requirements. Our goal is to focus attention on the *types of benefits* available to veterans.

Guiding Questions

1. What are some of the major benefits provided to qualifying veterans in the GI Bill? Read through the document and make a list of the basic categories (e.g. healthcare).

2. Draw conclusions: How would access to benefits like those listed in this selection help an individual or family join the American middle class? Explain your answer.

3. Make a prediction. Where do you think many new homes, paid for through the GI Bill, were built? What impact might this have on America? To help you with this task, look around to see where most single-family homes were built after the war and in the decades to come.

. . .

Title I

Chapter I—Hospitalization, Claims and Procedures

Sec. 100. The Veterans' Administration is hereby declared to be an essential war agency and entitled . . . to priorities in personnel, equipment, supplies, and material under any laws, Executive orders, and regulations. . . .

Title II

Chapter IV—Education of Veterans

. . ."1. Any [qualified] person . . . whose education or training was impeded, delayed, interrupted, or interfered with by reason of his entrance into the service, or who desires a refresher or retraining course, and who either shall have served ninety days or more. . . .

. . ."5. The Administrator shall pay to the educational or training institution, for each person enrolled in full time or part time course of education or training, the customary cost of tuition, and such laboratory, library, health, infirmary, and other similar fees as are customarily charged, and may pay for books, supplies, equipment, and other necessary expenses, exclusive of board, lodging, other living expenses, and travel, as are generally required for the successful pursuit and completion of the course by other students in the institution." . . .

Title III—Loans for the Purchase or Construction of Homes Farms, and Business Property

. . .

Purchase or Construction of Homes

Sec 501. (a) Any application made by a veteran under this title for the guaranty of a loan to be used in purchasing residential property or in constructing a dwelling on unimproved property owned by him to be occupied as his home may be approved the Administrator of Veterans' Affairs. . . .

Purchase of Farms and Farm Equipment

Sec. 502. Any application made under this title for the guaranty of a loan to be used in purchasing any land, buildings, livestock, equipment, machinery, or implements, or in repairing, altering, or improving any buildings or equipment, to be used in forming operations conducted by the applicant, may be approved by the Administrator of Veterans' Affairs. . . .

Purchase of Business Property

Sec. 503. Any application made under this title for the guaranty of a loan to be used in purchasing any business, land, buildings, supplies, equipment, machinery, or tools, to be used by the applicant in pursuing a gainful occupation (other than farming) may be approved by the Administrator of Veterans' Affairs. . . .

Title IV

Chapter VI—Employment of Veterans

Sec. 600. (a) In the enactment of the provisions of this title Congress declares as its intent and purpose that there shall be an effective job counseling and employment placement service for veterans, and that, to this end, policies shall be promulgated and administered, so as to provide for them the maximum of job opportunity in the field of gainful employment. . . .

Title V

Chapter VII—Readjustment Allowances for Former Members of the Armed Forces Who Are Unemployed

Sec. 700. (a) Any [qualified] person . . . shall be entitled . . . to receive a readjustment allowance as provided herein for each week of unemployment, not to exceed a total of fifty-two weeks. . . .

7.6: Harry S. Truman: Statement Announcing the Use of the Atomic Bomb on Hiroshima (1945)

Historical Context

The U.S. government used the code name *Manhattan Project* to describe its efforts to create an atomic bomb during World War II. The project began in 1942 under President Franklin D. Roosevelt. The leading theoretical physicist on the project was J. Robert Oppenheimer, who was stationed in Los Alamos, New Mexico. Many other scientists, researchers, and factory workers also worked on the project throughout the United States. As the following speech by President Harry Truman reveals, sometimes they knew they were working on the project and sometimes they did not. The project required incredible government spending and employed thousands of American workers.

In August 1945 the United States dropped atomic bombs on two major Japanese cities, Hiroshima and Nagasaki. The United States had celebrated VE Day—or Victory in Europe—in May 1945 when the Germans surrendered, thus marking the end of World War II in Europe. The war in the Pacific, though, raged on. In June 1945 Allied forces captured the Japanese Island of Okinawa, but it was with heavy casualties on both sides. Many officials feared that without decisive action, the war would continue and the death toll would rise. President Truman took the controversial step of deciding to use the U.S.'s new atomic weapons. The first bomb was dropped on Hiroshima on August 6, 1945, and three days later, the United States dropped a second bomb on Nagasaki. Shortly thereafter, the Japanese Emperor Hirohito announced Japan's unconditional surrender.

Some military experts and scholars have argued that the bombs were essential to bringing about Japan's immediate surrender. Others have argued that the Japanese were already on their way to losing the war and surrendering, and they have questioned the necessity of dropping the bombs. Specifically, many have questioned if it was necessary to drop the two bombs within such a short period of time, or if one would have been sufficient to force a Japanese surrender. A third group has argued that America never should have used the bombs because the consequences were too severe. We cannot definitively know the answer to this debate, but considering all sides helps us to understand the event's importance in history.

The bombs devastated Japan in countless ways. The bombs physically destroyed vast swaths of the two cities and killed more than 100,000 civilians on impact. Upwards of another 100,000 died in subsequent months as a result of radiation exposure from the nuclear fallout. In addition to the devastating effect these bombs had on Japan and its citizens, creating and using nuclear weapons during World War II led to unforeseen consequences that you'll learn more about during the next unit on the Cold War.

Science note: There are two types of nuclear bombs: atomic and hydrogen. An atomic bomb is a type of nuclear bomb that explodes as a result of splitting atoms (fission). A hydrogen bomb (or thermonuclear bomb) is an even more powerful weapon that gets its explosive power by fusing atoms together (fusion). Fusion requires very high temperatures, so often an atomic bomb is used to trigger the hydrogen bomb. (If a hydrogen bombs uses this process, it can also be called an atomic bomb.)

Guiding Questions

1. Why, according to the reading, was the atomic bomb developed in the United States with the help of scientists from Allied countries?

2. President Truman uses the speech to explain, or justify, to the American people why it was necessary to drop such a devastating bomb on Hiroshima. What reasons does he give? Make a list.

3. Truman was aware that nuclear power could be abused. What is his plan to prevent this in the United States?

Document Text

Sixteen hours ago an American airplane dropped one bomb on Hiroshima, an important Japanese Army base. That bomb had more power than 20,000 tons of TNT. It had more than 2,000 times the blast power of the British "Grand Slam," which is the largest bomb ever yet used in the history of warfare.

The Japanese began the war from the air at Pearl Harbor. They have been repaid manyfold. And the end is not yet. With this bomb we have now added a new and revolutionary increase in destruction to supplement the growing power of our armed forces. . . .

It is an atomic bomb. . . .

The battle of the laboratories held fateful risks for us as well as the battles of the air, land, and sea, and we have now won the battle of the laboratories as we have won the other battles. . . .

. . . The United States had available the large number of scientists of distinction in the many needed areas of knowledge. It had the tremendous industrial and financial resources necessary for the project . . . the laboratory work and the production plants, on which a substantial start had already been made, would be out of reach of enemy bombing, while at that time Britain was exposed to constant air attack and was still threatened with the possibility of invasion. For these reasons Prime Minister Churchill and President Roosevelt agreed that it was wise to carry on the project here.

We now have two great plants and many lesser works devoted to the production of atomic power. Employment during peak construction numbered 125,000 and over 65,000 individuals are even now engaged in operating the plants. Many have worked there for two and a half years. Few know what they have been producing. . . . We have spent $2 billion on the greatest scientific gamble in history—and won. . . .

. . . We are now prepared to obliterate more rapidly and completely every productive enterprise the Japanese have above ground in any city. We shall destroy their docks, their factories, and their communications. Let there be no mistake; we shall completely destroy Japan's power to make war.

It was to spare the Japanese people from utter destruction that the ultimatum of July 26 was issued at Potsdam. Their leaders promptly rejected that ultimatum. If they do not now accept our terms they may expect a rain of ruin from the air, the like of which has never been seen on this earth. . . .

I shall recommend that the Congress of the United States consider promptly the establishment of an appropriate commission to control the production and use of atomic power within the United States. I shall give further consideration and make further recommendations to the Congress as to how atomic power can become a powerful and forceful influence towards the maintenance of world peace.

7.7: Unit 7 Review

The unit introduction asked you to answer the following questions:

1. Why did the United States originally try to stay out of World War II? What eventually led to its involvement? Create an annotated timeline that begins in the late 1930s and ends in 1945 to help you get a better overview.

2. How did the war affect the U.S. home front during and after the war? A cause-and-effect concept map may be helpful here.

3. Make a prediction. Why is World War II considered a turning point in the nation's history? (Hint: Try to explain how and why the United States became a world superpower after the war. Consider here which countries were left weakened the most after the end of World War II.)

These questions grow progressively more complex. The first is fairly straightforward and mainly focuses on careful reading and minimal analysis. The second question, however, asks you to identify specific information clearly presented in the readings, but it also requires you to apply knowledge across the readings. As noted in the introduction, World War II pulled the U.S. economy out of the Great Depression. Its impacts reached beyond general economic improvement, however. Franklin Roosevelt's executive order banning discrimination clearly articulates a major shift in American society and work. It specifically banned racial discrimination in government jobs or defense contracting positions. This was a major breakthrough for the nation. It provided African Americans access to better jobs, and it set the nation on course towards ending segregation. On the flip side, while African Americans were securing their civil rights, Japanese Americans were suffering a denial of their basic civil liberties. Internment resulted in American citizens and legal residents of Japanese descent being rounded up in large numbers and incarcerated based on their ethnic identity alone. They had not committed any crimes; yet they were locked up and detained by the U.S. government.

The GI Bill, introduced at the end of the war, also changed the U.S. home front. It granted more men the opportunity to attend college, buy homes, and start businesses. Not all veterans benefited equally, however. African Americans and other minority veterans were often excluded from access to benefits like the GI Bill. Sometimes, local officials would intentionally discriminate against African Americans, denying them home loans or access to education, even though they were entitled under the GI Bill. Similarly, new suburban communities often used covenants to prevent African Americans, Jews, and other minorities from purchasing homes in those areas for years to come. Access to equal housing opportunities would become a key issue during the civil rights movement of the 1960s.

The third unit question requires the most critical thinking. It asks you to synthesize the main points of each reading and draw conclusions about how that information can be applied. In making a prediction, you need to think about the possible impacts that may result, even though you do not yet have all the information.

World War II was a turning point in American history because it began the modern era for the nation. Following the war, the United States emerged as one of the world's two superpowers. The Soviet Union was the other. During the war, the United States invested significant money in developing a strong military and superior military weaponry. Additionally, much of Western Europe was destroyed during the war, so the United States, under the Marshall Plan, offered to help nations rebuild. It pushed nations to improve production, increase trade, and support capitalism. The United States provided much of the money and materials to rebuild, which helped keep the domestic economy strong even after the war ended. Furthermore, although the United States had joined forces with the Soviet Union during the war, it was an uneasy alliance since the Soviet Union was a communist nation. The Truman Doctrine (1947), also implemented in the postwar period, sought to contain communist threats in Greece and Turkey. The doctrine implied that the United States would support other nations facing a communist threat. Shortly thereafter, in 1949, the United States formed the North American Treaty Organization (NATO) to shore up its military alliances. Taken together, each of these actions deepened the political and ideological divide between the Soviet Union and the United States. As you will learn in the next unit, the two countries began a nearly 50-year conflict known as the Cold War.

8.1: The Cold War

Overview

Unit 7, World War II and the Home Front, concluded by introducing post-war tensions that set the United States and the Union of Soviet Socialist Republics (USSR or the "Soviet Union") on a path that changed the course of history. The ideological divide between the two nations—the United States promoting capitalism and democracy and the Soviet Union supporting communism—defined one of the most tense periods in world history.

The readings in this unit illustrate how the conflict developed and played out over time. The Cold War began almost immediately after World War II and lasted until 1991, when the Soviet Union collapsed. For nearly 45 years the United States and the Soviet Union were locked in a largely ideological struggle. Proxy battles occurred in places like Korea and Vietnam, and the two nations nearly engaged in a direct conflict during the 1962 Cuban Missile Crisis; but overall, the two world superpowers successfully avoided direct military confrontation, thus earning the period the name the "Cold War." To understand this period, you have to understand the key vocabulary, concepts, and major players.

Capitalism is based on free markets (with no or limited government regulation) and private ownership of the means of production. The government generally embraces a hands-off approach to the economy. The government may provide some basic regulations, but it does not generally own the companies that produce goods or provide utilities. Likewise, workers own their own labor and can negotiate for wages with their employer. Under a communist system, the government owns the means of production and establishes the wage rates for workers based on their abilities and needs. Communism rejects private property ownership because it creates inequality among the population (social, political, and economic). Communists strive to create a society where all people are treated equally. Karl Marx is considered the father of modern communism.

Americans typically pair capitalism (an economic system) with democracy (a political system). Under American democracy, each citizen is granted the right to vote, and government leaders are elected representatives of the population. Under a communist political system, leaders are selected from the broader community, with all members of that community occupying the same socio-political class. In reality, though, most communist countries in the twentieth century saw small groups of leaders emerge and retain power through intimidation and violence. Often countries ended up with single-party rule where political dissent was not tolerated. Communist leaders sought to control the press to limit people's access to information, and in some extreme cases they imprisoned or killed wealthy, elite, or highly educated members of society in order to eliminate class distinctions and threats to the Communist Party leadership.

Americans deeply valued the idea of freedom, and they associated communism with dictatorships that restricted people's rights. The rapid expansion of communism around the world in the mid-twentieth century, then, concerned Americans who feared that if left unchecked, communism could eventually threaten American freedom and that of its allies. As a result of this perceived attack on a fundamental value, many Americans developed a strong fear of communism and the Soviet Union in the 1950s. As noted, some fears stemmed from economic concerns, but others were rooted in the territorial spread of communism as nations fell under authoritarian rule.

Russia became a communist nation in 1917 following the Bolshevik Revolution, and throughout the 1920s it united with neighboring socialist republics to form the USSR. During and after World War II, the USSR continued to expand and shore up its alliances. Many Eastern Europe nations had Soviet-supported communist governments. They essentially acted as puppet states carrying out Soviet policies. At the same time, communists in China under Mao Zedong won the Chinese Civil War in 1949. With this victory, a huge portion of the Asian landmass was under communist control. This stoked American fears that a showdown between the Soviet Union (and its communist allies) and the United States was practically inevitable. Reflecting on their experience fighting Adolf Hitler's Germany during World War II, Americans also believed that unless they remained hypervigilant, it would be possible for Josef Stalin (the Soviet Premier until his death in 1953) or his successor to become the next dictator bent on conquering the world.

By the early 1950s Americans were increasingly concerned about communism spreading internationally and at home. In 1950 the United States sent troops to support South Korea and prevent North Korea, backed by the Soviet Union, from taking over the southern portion of the peninsula. The Korean War lasted from 1950 to 1953. The conflict ended in a stalemate, and the two countries returned to pre-war conditions, which are still in effect today. Although South Korea and the United States failed to overtake North Korea and impose democracy, the war succeeded in preventing the North from overtaking the South and imposing communism.

In some ways, then, the United States could argue this was a victory of sorts thanks to the containment theory, which stopped the domino effect of neighboring countries "falling communist." This reference comes from President Dwight Eisenhower, who in 1954 coined a term that would come to dominate America's Cold War foreign policy—"domino theory." The idea was that if you looked at neighboring countries like dominoes stacked closely together on their ends, if one fell over and hit the next, they would all fall. Politically this meant that if one country "fell" communist it could easily influence neighboring states to embrace communism as well. As you will see in the first document by George Kennan, "containment" became a central pillar of U.S. Cold War foreign policy.

The most controversial application of containment and domino theories also began in 1954, when the United States began aiding the French conflict in Southeast Asia. The French were attempting to maintain control of their colony, French Indochina, which included present day Cambodia, Laos, and Vietnam. As you'll learn about in Unit 11, this conflict would set the United States on the path to war in Vietnam in the 1960s and 1970s.

In conclusion, then, communism after World War II appeared anathema to many Americans who firmly believed in the American Dream. Americans embraced the notion that an individual could rise above his/her original station in life through hard work. Many believed that communism diminished an individual's ability and interest in hard work and personal achievement. Furthermore, the United States was founded on the principle of democracy, which espoused the idea that every person had a vote and the right to determine the nation's future. From the beginning the United States valued ideals like free speech and religion—these ideas are written into the nation's Constitution. In practice, communism deprived people of the right to freely choose their leaders, express their views openly and engage in public debates, and practice whatever religion they wanted. In essence, then, communism appeared to be an attack on America's most basic values. This ideological divide—between capitalism/democracy and communism—defined the Cold War period and set the stage for a showdown between the two superpowers. Each side sought to exert its influence on the world, build up its military power and weapons capabilities, and control politics at home.

Unit Questions

1. What was the Cold War and why did the United States get involved in it?

2. How did the United States fight the Cold War internationally?

3. How did the Cold War play out domestically?

8.2: George F. Kennan: "Long Telegram" (1946)

Historical Context

George F. Kennan (1904-2005) was a diplomat with the U.S. Foreign Service. Kennan quickly realized that U.S.-Soviet relations would likely decline when World War II ended. He wrote the following telegram in 1946, expressing concerns over the difference in attitude and policies between the two countries. Kennan's telegram included recommendations for dealing with these differences, and attempting to mitigate potential Soviet impact on the world, while avoiding direct confrontation. Eventually, the ideas he promoted became known as "containment policy."

In the next document you will read about the Truman Doctrine, which also sought to prevent the spread of communism in the world. That was not the United States' only approach, however. The country also implemented the Marshall Plan in 1948. Essentially, this plan represented Kennan's intended vision of containment policy in action. As part of the Marshall Plan, the United States provided billions of dollars of aid to Western Europe to rebuild countries and their economies after World War II. As noted in the last unit, the goal of the Marshall Plan was to strengthen trading relationships and prevent the spread of communism. As historian Anthony Santoro has argued in *Milestone Documents of American Leaders,* "Although Kennan's influence on foreign policy was strong, he was unable to prevent containment from being implemented almost exclusively as a military policy rather than the economic and political strategy that he had envisioned. In devising the policy of containment, Kennan envisaged that policy makers would choose their conflicts in such a way as to maximize potential gains while minimizing potential losses, in terms of life, political capital, and economic resources." Unit 11 on the Vietnam War will demonstrate how the containment policy became militarized.

Guiding Questions

1. Why does George Kennan think that the Soviet Union (also referred to as Russia or the Kremlin, its seat of government) does not get along with the United States? Look for specific evidence from the text to support your response. Write it in your own words.

2. What evidence do you see in the reading that supports the "containment policy" attributed to Kennan?

3. What steps does Kennan recommend the United States take to stay strong and mitigate Soviet influence in the world? Create a numbered list.

Part 2: Background of Outlook

... At bottom of Kremlin's neurotic view of world affairs is traditional and instinctive Russian sense of insecurity. ... as Russia came into contact with economically advanced West ... Russian rulers have invariably sensed that their rule was ... unable to stand comparison or contact with political systems of Western countries. For this reason they have always feared foreign penetration, feared direct contact between Western world and their own. ... [T]hey have learned to seek security only in patient but deadly struggle for total destruction of rival power, never in compacts and compromises with it. ...

Part 5: [Practical Deductions from Standpoint of US Policy]

... [W]e have here a political force committed fanatically to the belief that with US there can be no permanent modus vivendi [peaceful coexistence][;] that it is desirable and necessary that the internal harmony of our society be disrupted, our traditional way of life be destroyed, the international authority of our state be broken, if Soviet power is to be secure. ...

(1) Soviet power ... does not take unnecessary risks. Impervious to logic of reason, and it is highly sensitive to logic of force. For this reason it can easily withdraw—and usually does when strong resistance is encountered at any point. Thus, if the adversary has sufficient force and makes clear his readiness to use it, he rarely has to do so. If situations are properly handled there need be no prestige-engaging showdowns. ...

(4) All Soviet propaganda beyond Soviet security sphere is basically negative and destructive. It should therefore be relatively easy to combat it by any intelligent and really constructive program.

For those reasons I think we may approach calmly and with good heart [the] problem of how to deal with Russia. As to how this approach should be made, I only wish to advance, by way of conclusion, following comments:

... (2) We must see that our public is educated to realities of Russian situation. I cannot over-emphasize importance of this. ... I am convinced that there would be far less hysterical anti-Sovietism in our country today if realities of this situation were better understood by our people. There is nothing as dangerous or as terrifying as the unknown. It may also be argued that to reveal more information on our difficulties with Russia would reflect unfavorably on Russian-American relations. ...

(4) We must formulate and put forward for other nations a much more positive and constructive picture of sort of world we would like to see than we have put forward in past. It is not enough to urge people to develop political processes similar to our own. . . .

(5) Finally we must have courage and self-confidence to cling to our own methods and conceptions of human society. After all, the greatest danger that can befall us in coping with this problem of Soviet communism is that we shall allow ourselves to become like those with whom we are coping.

8.3: Harry S. Truman: Truman Doctrine (1947)

Historical Context

President Franklin Roosevelt died during his fourth term in office as President of the United States in 1945. (Congress passed the Twenty-second Amendment setting presidential term limits in 1947. Prior to that point, it was precedent for presidents to serve a maximum of two terms, but it was not mandated by law.) Roosevelt's vice president, Harry S. Truman, assumed the presidency and guided the United States through the end of World War II and the post-war period. Shortly after the war ended, the United States' wartime alliance with the Soviet Union began to deteriorate. By 1947 tensions had escalated. The Soviet Union had installed puppet regimes loyal to Josef Stalin throughout Eastern Europe, and in 1946 the Soviets refused to withdraw from northern Iran. The following speech is from 1947, one year after George Kennan submitted his "Long Telegram."

Guiding Questions

1. President Truman delivered this speech to Congress. Why do you think he was giving them this speech? What does he hope the outcome will be following his speech? Keep in mind what Congress' role is in the U.S. government.

2. What, according to Truman, were the threats facing Greece and Turkey? Why did the United States care about the two countries? Look for specific examples from the text to explain why he focused on these two countries in particular. If necessary, look at a map of the region that contains Greece, Turkey, and Russia to give you a better idea of the geographic context.

3. How does the Truman Doctrine reflect George Kennan's containment policy in practice? Read the text carefully and list examples of the U.S.'s proposed plans to further its interests in the world. Explain each in your own words.

Document Text

. . . The gravity of the situation which confronts the world today necessitates my appearance before a joint session of the Congress. The foreign policy and the national security of this country are involved.

One aspect of the present situation, which I wish to present to you at this time for your consideration and decision, concerns Greece and Turkey.

The United States has received from the Greek Government an urgent appeal for financial and economic assistance. . . .

. . . The very existence of the Greek state is today threatened by the terrorist activities of several thousand armed men, led by Communists, who defy the government's authority at a number of points, particularly along the northern boundaries. . . .

Meanwhile, the Greek Government is unable to cope with the situation. The Greek army is small and poorly equipped. It needs supplies and equipment if it is to restore the authority of the government throughout Greek territory. Greece must have assistance if it is to become a self-supporting and self-respecting democracy.

The United States must supply that assistance. . . .

. . . I am fully aware of the broad implications involved if the United States extends assistance to Greece and Turkey, and I shall discuss these implications with you at this time.

. . . At the present moment in world history nearly every nation must choose between alternative ways of life. The choice is too often not a free one.

One way of life is based upon the will of the majority, and is distinguished by free institutions, representative government, free elections, guarantees of individual liberty, freedom of speech and religion, and freedom from political oppression.

The second way of life is based upon the will of a minority forcibly imposed upon the majority. It relies upon terror and oppression, a controlled press and radio; fixed elections, and the suppression of personal freedoms.

. . . It is necessary only to glance at a map to realize that the survival and integrity of the Greek nation are of grave importance in a much wider situation. If Greece should fall under the control of an armed minority, the effect upon its neighbor, Turkey, would be immediate and serious. Confusion and disorder might well spread throughout the entire Middle East.

. . . I therefore ask the Congress to provide authority for assistance to Greece and Turkey. . . .

In addition to funds, I ask the Congress to authorize the detail of American civilian and military personnel to Greece and Turkey, at the request of those countries, to assist in the tasks of reconstruction, and for the purpose of supervising the use of such financial and material assistance as may be furnished....

The seeds of totalitarian regimes are nurtured by misery and want. They spread and grow in the evil soil of poverty and strife. They reach their full growth when the hope of a people for a better life has died. We must keep that hope alive.

The free peoples of the world look to us for support in maintaining their freedoms....

8.4: Joseph McCarthy: "Enemies from Within" Speech (1950)

Historical Context

The United States developed the atomic bomb during World War II secretly with aid of Great Britain, but it did not extend participation to its Russian allies during the war. The Soviets assumed that the Americans were developing a "superweapon" and began to develop one themselves. Initially, the project moved slowly, but when the United States dropped atomic bombs on Hiroshima and Nagasaki in 1945, the Soviet Union accelerated its program. It produced and successfully tested its first bomb in 1949. The quick production of the weapon raised questions about how they got the technological know-how. This development, coupled with the trial of American citizens Julius and Ethel Rosenberg—who were charged and found guilty of being spies for the Soviet Union—escalated American fears about communism both at home and abroad.

Beginning in the late 1930s the U.S. House of Representatives had created a special committee, the House Un-American Activities Committee (HUAC), to investigate allegations of communist activity in the United States. In their quest to identify and punish communists, HUAC trampled on people's civil liberties and ruined the careers, reputations, and lives of many Americans. One of the most famous examples was when the committee targeted Hollywood in 1947. At that time ten writers, directors, and producers were called to testify. They refused to cooperate and were blacklisted from working in Hollywood. HUAC's activities helped set the stage for Joseph McCarthy's political career.

McCarthy was a staunch anticommunist who capitalized on people's fears. He contributed to hysteria at home as he accused government workers of being suspected communists and communist sympathizers. Eventually, in 1954, McCarthy would be censured by his colleagues in the Senate because of his behavior during this era. By that time, though, he had already caused significant damage. This period is often referred to as the Second Red Scare. (The First Red Scare occurred after World War I, when politicians similarly targeted political radicals.)

Guiding Questions

1. How does McCarthy frame the Cold War as a moral conflict as well as a political one?

2. How does McCarthy stoke listeners' fears about the spread of communism?

3. Who, according to McCarthy, poses the greatest threat to the United States? What is his proposed solution for solving this problem?

. . . Five years after a world war has been won, men's hearts should anticipate a long peace. . . . But . . . this is not a period of peace. This is a time of "the cold war." This is a time when all the world is split into two vast, increasingly hostile armed camps—a time of a great armament race. . . .

. . . The great difference between our western Christian world and the atheistic Communist world is not political, gentlemen, it is moral. . . .

. . . Karl Marx dismissed God as a hoax, and Lenin and Stalin have added in clear-cut, unmistakable language their resolve that no nation, no people who believe in a god, can exist side by side with their communist state. . . .

. . . Today we are engaged in a final, all-out battle between communistic atheism and Christianity. . . .

. . . Six years ago, . . . there was within the Soviet orbit, 180,000,000 people. . . . Today, only six years later, there are 800,000,000 people under the absolute domination of Soviet Russia—an increase of over 400 percent. . . .

This indicates the swiftness of the tempo of Communist victories and American defeats in the cold war. As one of our outstanding historical figures once said, "When a great democracy is destroyed, it will not be from enemies from without, but rather because of enemies from within." . . .

The reason why we find ourselves in a position of impotency is not because our only powerful potential enemy has sent men to invade our shores . . . but rather because of the traitorous actions of those who have been treated so well by this Nation. It has not been the less fortunate, or members of minority groups who have been traitorous to this Nation, but rather those who have had all the benefits that the wealthiest Nation on earth has had to offer . . . the finest homes, the finest college education and the finest jobs in government we can give.

This is glaringly true in the State Department. There the bright young men who are born with silver spoons in their mouths are the ones who have been most traitorous. . . .

I have here in my hand a list of 205 . . . a list of names that were made known to the Secretary of State as being members of the Communist Party and who nevertheless are still working and shaping policy in the State Department. . . .

As you know, very recently the Secretary of State proclaimed his loyalty to a man guilty of what has always been considered as the most abominable of all crimes—being a traitor to the people who gave him a position of great trust. . . .

He has lighted the spark which is resulting in a moral uprising and will end only when the whole sorry mess of twisted, warped thinkers are swept from the national scene so that we may have a new birth of honesty and decency in government.

8.5: Richard M. Nixon: "Kitchen" Debate with Nikita Khrushchev (1959)

Historical Context

Vice President Richard Nixon flew to Moscow in 1959 to engage in a cultural exchange with the Soviet Union. (Nixon served as Dwight D. Eisenhower's vice president from 1953 to 1961, and he served as president from 1969 to 1974.) Nixon attended an event in Russia sponsored by the American government called the American National Exhibition. (A similar USSR-sponsored event was held in New York.) The goal was to improve American-Soviet understanding of one another and showcase their achievements to the world. Both sides could potentially benefit from the propaganda the event generated.

Nixon met the Soviet Premier Nikita Khrushchev for the first time as the two men walked through the exhibit space. They talked about a variety of issues including both sides' desire to live in peace, perceptions of one another, and ongoing areas of tension, like weapons development and limitations on free speech. The excerpt below illustrates how the Cold War played out on a diplomatic and cultural level.

Guiding Questions

1. What ideological points did Nixon and Khrushchev make as they talked about the kitchen exhibit? Make a two-column chart listing each man's position. Align their points and counterpoints when possible.

2. How did the two men use the "kitchen debate" to address broader Cold War issues?

3. What is the tone of this exchange? What does it tell us about Cold War diplomacy strategies? How does it compare to the McCarthy document?

Nixon [halting Khrushchev at model kitchen in model house]: "You had a very nice house in your exhibition in New York. My wife and I saw and enjoyed it very much. I want to show you this kitchen. It is like those of our houses in California."

Khrushchev: [after Nixon called attention to a built-in panel-controlled washing machine]: "We have such things."

Nixon: "This is the newest model. . . . Let me give you an example you can appreciate. Our steelworkers, as you know, are on strike. But any steelworker could buy this house. They earn $3 an hour. This house costs about $100 a month to buy on a contract running 25 to 30 years."

Khrushchev: "We have steel workers and we have peasants who also can afford to spend $14,000 for a house. . . .

"Many things you've shown us are interesting but they are not needed in life. . . . They are merely gadgets. . . .

"The Americans have created their own image of the Soviet man and think he is as you want him to be. But he is not as you think. You think the Russian people will be dumbfounded to see these things, but the fact is that newly built Russian houses have all this equipment right now. Moreover, all you have to do to get a house is to be born in the Soviet Union. You are entitled to housing. I was born in the Soviet Union. So I have a right to a house. In America, if you don't have a dollar—you have the right to choose between sleeping in a house or on the pavement. Yet you say that we are slaves of communism." . . .

Nixon: "You can learn from us and we can learn from you. There must be a free exchange. Let the people choose the kind of house, the kind of soup, the kind of ideas they want. . . .

"We do not claim to astonish the Russian people. We hope to show our diversity and our right to choose. We do not wish to have decisions made at the top by government officials who say that all homes should be built in the same way. Would it not be better to compete in the relative merits of washing machines than in the strength of rockets? Is this the kind of competition you want?"

Khrushchev: "Yes that's the kind of competition we want. But your generals say: "Let's compete in rockets. We are strong and we can beat you.' But in this respect we can also show you something."

Nixon: "To me you are strong and we are strong. . . . Neither should use that strength to put the other in a position where he in effect has an ultimatum. In this day and age that misses the point. With modern weapons it does not make any difference if war comes. We both have had it."

"We want peace too and I believe that you do also."

8.6: John F. Kennedy: Report to the American People on the Soviet Arms Buildup in Cuba (1962)

Historical Context

John F. Kennedy won the 1960 presidential election. Shortly after taking office, he learned that former President Eisenhower had planned a CIA-supported invasion of Cuba by Cubans who opposed the communist leader of that country, Fidel Castro. Kennedy authorized the invasion, known as the Bay of Pigs, and it turned out to be an enormous failure. In response to the attack on Castro, Soviet Premier Nikita Khrushchev decided to help install nuclear missiles in Cuba. American reconnaissance planes provided evidence of the plan. This led to an international incident known as the Cuban Missile Crisis in October 1962, when the United State and the Soviet Union came perilously close to a nuclear war. During the crisis, on October 22, Kennedy went on national television to inform the American public and demand the Soviets withdraw their missiles.

Guiding Questions

1. How did Kennedy use history to support his demands for Soviet withdrawal of the missiles?

2. What steps did Kennedy want taken to peacefully end the conflict? Make a numbered list and summarize Kennedy's points in your own words.

3. How did Kennedy try to frame the issue as one that jeopardized not only Americans but Cubans as well?

Document Text

Good evening, my fellow citizens:

This Government, as promised, has maintained the closest surveillance of the Soviet military buildup on the island of Cuba. Within the past week, unmistakable evidence has established the fact that a series of offensive missile sites is now in preparation on that imprisoned island. The purpose of these bases can be none other than to provide a nuclear strike capability against the Western Hemisphere. . . .

In addition, jet bombers, capable of carrying nuclear weapons, are now being uncrated and assembled in Cuba, while the necessary air bases are being prepared.

This urgent transformation of Cuba into an important strategic base ... constitutes an explicit threat to the peace and security of all the Americas. ...

... We no longer live in a world where only the actual firing of weapons represents a sufficient challenge to a nation's security to constitute maximum peril. Nuclear weapons are so destructive and ballistic missiles are so swift, that any substantially increased possibility of their use or any sudden change in their deployment may well be regarded as a definite threat to peace. ...

... This secret, swift, and extraordinary buildup of Communist missiles ... is a deliberately provocative and unjustified change in the status quo which cannot be accepted by this country. ...

The 1930's taught us a clear lesson: aggressive conduct, if allowed to go unchecked and unchallenged, ultimately leads to war. This nation is opposed to war. ... Our unswerving objective, therefore, must be to prevent the use of these missiles against this or any other country, and to secure their withdrawal or elimination from the Western Hemisphere. ...

... In the defense of our own security and of the entire Western Hemisphere ... I have directed that the following initial steps be taken immediately:

First: To halt this offensive buildup, a strict quarantine on all offensive military equipment under shipment to Cuba is being initiated. All ships ... if found to contain cargoes of offensive weapons, be turned back. ...

Second: I have directed the continued and increased close surveillance of Cuba and its military buildup. ...

Third: It shall be the policy of this Nation to regard any nuclear missile launched from Cuba against any nation in the Western Hemisphere as an attack by the Soviet Union on the United States, requiring a full retaliatory response upon the Soviet Union. ...

Sixth: Our resolution will call for the prompt dismantling and withdrawal of all offensive weapons in Cuba, under the supervision of U.N. observers, before the quarantine can be lifted. ...

Finally, I want to say a few words to the captive people of Cuba ... your leaders . . . are puppets and agents of an international conspiracy which has turned Cuba against your friends and neighbors in the Americas. . . .

These new weapons are not in your interest. They contribute nothing to your peace and well-being. They can only undermine it. . . .

. . . Our goal is . . . peace and freedom, here in this hemisphere, and, we hope, around the world.

8.7: Unit 8 Review

The Unit Questions asked you to consider the following:

> 1. What was the Cold War and why did the United States get involved in it?

> 2. How did the United States fight the Cold War internationally?

> 3. How did the Cold War play out domestically?

Most of the documents in this unit illustrated the international aspects of the Cold War. The speech by Senator Joseph McCarthy about "enemies within" highlighted how the conflict played out at home as well. To fully answer question three, however, you need to know more about the Cold War's impacts at home.

The Second Red Scare, or "McCarthyism" as it is sometimes referred to, targeted communists and political radicals and aimed to silence their voices and influence in American society. Some people targeted by HUAC were famous figures, like the Hollywood 10 or musicians like Pete Seeger, but many were average individuals like teachers, labor organizers, government workers, and journalists going about their daily lives. Many Americans began to fear that they would be targeted if they spoke out against the movement even though it clearly violated people's civil liberties. As a result, the 1950s are often described as a period of conformity.

The era reinforced traditional gender roles. After World War II, men returned from military service and re-entered the workforce or went to college. Women were expected to give up their wartime jobs and return to the home. Even women attending college were generally expected to find a husband. Technological advancements like the television also promoted and reinforced numerous gender, racial, and ethnic stereotypes. Some people embraced the conformity and traditional ideas promoted in the 1950s; and, as you'll see in the next unit, others chafed under the pressure to conform and the often-offensive ideas promoted during the period.

As you work through the next few units remember that the Cold War lasted from roughly 1945 to 1991, when the Soviet Union collapsed. This undercurrent of tension and conflict is woven into nearly five decades of U.S. history. Keep this in mind as you read, and think about how the Cold War affected American attitudes and actions.

9.1: Affluence, Unrest, and Civil Rights

Overview

Historians often refer to the 1950s as a period of both affluence and unrest. The period is defined by post-war prosperity and a return to traditional gender roles, as well as significant unrest resulting from people who did not want to return to the status quo.

Consumerism flourished in the 1950s. The American economy shifted from wartime production to mass production of consumer goods. Advertising expanded exponentially, and it began to craft narratives about American society and people's roles within that society. As the advertisements of the 1950s reveal, though, there were some deeply disturbing attitudes towards women and their perceived place in society. The majority of advertisements also focused on white patrons, making little effort to create or market products to other racial or ethnic demographics. Most advertisements also avoided addressing any of the controversial issues of the day, like race relations. The messaging of the 1950s, then, was often overly optimistic and rarely confronted the reality that many people faced in their daily lives.

The GI Bill (1944) provided many soldiers returning from World War II with the opportunity to secure home, business, and school loans. This wide-reaching federal assistance program helped create the American middle class. As the 1950s progressed, more Americans—especially white Americans—shored-up their position within the new middle class. They bought homes in suburbs, many of which developed in the post-war period. Suburban communities often used covenants to prevent certain racial or ethnic groups from purchasing homes in that community. The rise of suburban America deepened the divide between America's white middle class and working-class communities of color left behind in urban centers.

Political and social unrest had long simmered under the surface of American society, but by the mid-1950s it became more visible. Cold war political tensions emerged immediately after World War II ended. The United States' uneasy alliance with the Soviet Union collapsed, and tensions escalated. The ideological clash between the communist USSR and the democratic United States highlighted one of America's greatest failures—the country's incredibly undemocratic and unequal treatment of African Americans. Aside from the political advertisements, the four remaining documents in this unit deal explicitly with social unrest and the rise of the modern black civil rights movement. In that movement, African Americans confronted the nation's long history of white supremacy, racism, and discrimination head-on. Read together, these documents reveal the various approaches activists took in an effort to secure equal rights.

1. Why are the 1950s described as a period of both affluence and unrest? Identify evidence from the documents that illustrate these two themes.

2. How do the documents authored by Martin Luther King Jr. and Stokely Carmichael, respectively, illustrate the evolution of the black civil rights movement? Compare and contrast these two documents. In what ways are they similar and in what ways are they different?

3. Make a prediction. How do you think the civil rights movement will expand in the 1960s and 1970s to other groups of people frustrated by the status quo? Who may those groups be?

9.2: Advertisements from the 1950s and 1960s

Historical Context

Similar to the 1920s, the 1950s were characterized by mass consumption. Advertising, which increased significantly during this period, provides valuable insights into the social norms, values, and stereotypes of the day.

Guiding Questions

1. Scroll through the following advertisements and identify three that you want to focus on. What is each ad trying to sell? What kind of messaging is the ad using to sell that product?

2. What similarities do you notice about your three selected advertisements? What does this reveal about people's attitudes or stereotypes about certain groups of people? How is humor (or an attempt at humor) used to push a product in ways that most people would find disturbing or unacceptable today?

3. Using your three ads, explain why certain groups of Americans end up actively pushing for civil rights in the 1950s, 1960s, and 1970s.

A 1935 advertisement for Elliott's Paint and Varnish (© Pictures from History/ Bridgeman Images)

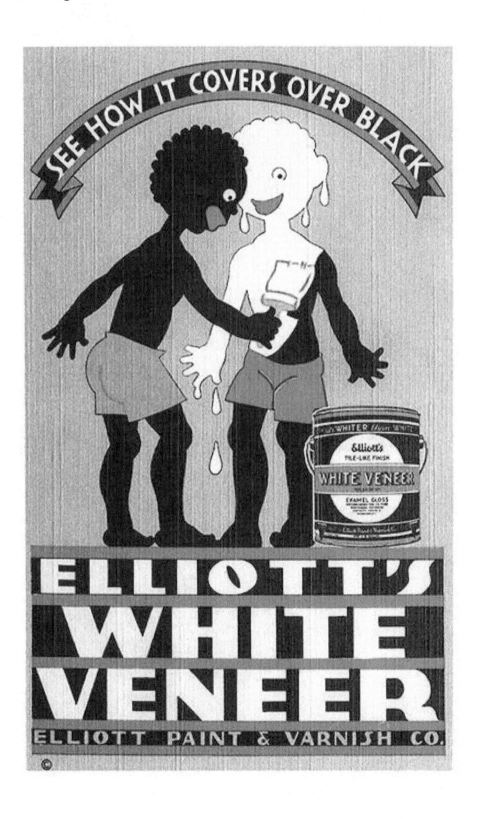

A magazine advertisement for Hoover Vacuums from the 1950s (© The Advertising Archives/Bridgeman Images)

A magazine advertisement for Alcoa Aluminum from the 1950s (© The Advertising Archives/Bridgeman Images)

You mean a <u>woman</u> can open it?

Easily—without a knife blade, a bottle opener, or even a husband! All it takes is a dainty grasp, an easy, two-finger twist—and the catsup is ready to pour.

We call this safe-sealing bottle cap the Alcoa HyTop. It is made of pure, food-loving Alcoa Aluminum. It spins off—and back on again—without muscle power because an exclusive Alcoa process tailors it to each bottle's threads

after it is on the bottle. By vacuum sealing both top and sides, the HyTop gives purity a double guard.

You'll recognize the attractive, tractable HyTop when you see it on your grocer's shelf. It's long, it's white, it's grooved—and it's on the most famous and flavorful brands. Put the bottle that wears it in your basket . . . save fumbling, fuming and fingers at opening time with the most cooperative cap in the world—the Alcoa HyTop Closure.

A 1972 magazine advertisement for Weyenberg Shoes (© The Advertising Archives/Bridgeman Images)

9.3: *Brown v. Board of Education* (1954)

Historical Context

Brown v. Board of Education is a landmark civil rights test case in U.S. history. It directly challenged segregation. School segregation was one of the most pervasive, persistent, and damaging forms of discrimination present throughout the United States in the mid-twentieth century (and it remains a significant problem today). Schools, especially in the South, were explicitly designed to be unequal facilities. White communities routinely provided inadequate educational opportunities to African Americans while seeking to keep white and black children from being educated in the same schools. Black communities throughout the South worked hard to close the gap and provide quality education from elementary school to university. These communities made important gains, such as creating Historically Black College and Universities, or HBCUs. For many African Americans, though, the ultimate goal was to gain equal access to existing, mostly white, educational institutions. *Brown v. Board of Education* was a critical ruling that furthered that goal.

Guiding Questions

1. What did the Supreme Court rule in this case? What evidence did it use to justify its ruling? Provide specific evidence from the text that explains the Court's logic.   .

2. *Brown v. Board* directly makes reference to the case of *Plessy v. Ferguson*, which you read in Unit 3. First, compare the results of each of these two rulings in their respective times. Think about the message that each of these two rulings sent. Think about how members of the racial minority would feel about the way they are being discussed. Second, what does the chief justice's opinion express about the case of *Plessy v. Ferguson*? What impact does this newer ruling have on the older ruling?

3. Make an educated guess: Why do you think it was important to Chief Justice Earl Warren that the Supreme Court issue a unanimous decision in the *Brown v. Board* case?

Opinion

Mr. Chief Justice Warren Delivered the Opinion of the Court

. . . In each of the cases, minors of the Negro race, through their legal repre-sentatives, seek the aid of the courts in obtaining admission to the public schools of their community on a nonsegregated basis. In each instance, they had been denied admission to schools attended by white children under laws requiring or permitting segregation according to race. This segregation was alleged to deprive the plaintiffs of the equal protection of the laws under the Fourteenth Amendment. In each of the cases other than the Delaware case, a three-judge federal district court denied relief to the plaintiffs on the so-called "separate but equal" doctrine announced by this Court in *Plessy v. Ferguson*, 163 U.S. 537. Under that doctrine, equality of treatment is accorded when the races are provided substantially equal facilities, even though these facilities be separate. . . .

The plaintiffs contend that segregated public schools are not "equal" and can-not be made "equal," and that hence they are deprived of the equal protection of the laws. . . .

. . . In approaching this problem, we cannot turn the clock back to 1868, when the Amendment was adopted, or even to 1896, when *Plessy v. Ferguson* was written. We must consider public education in the light of its full development and its present place in American life throughout the Nation. Only in this way can it be determined if segregation in public schools deprives these plaintiffs of the equal protection of the laws.

Today, education is perhaps the most important function of state and local governments. . . . It is the very foundation of good citizenship. Today it is a principal instrument in awakening the child to cultural values, in preparing him for later professional training, and in helping him to adjust normally to his environment. In these days, it is doubtful that any child may reasonably be expected to succeed in life if he is denied the opportunity of an education. Such an opportunity, where the state has undertaken to provide it, is a right which must be made available to all on equal terms.

We come then to the question presented: Does segregation of children in public schools solely on the basis of race, even though the physical facilities and other "tangible" factors may be equal, deprive the children of the minority group of equal educational opportunities? We believe that it does.

... The effect of this separation on their educational opportunities was well stated by a finding in the Kansas case by a court which nevertheless felt compelled to rule against the Negro plaintiffs.

Segregation of white and colored children in public schools has a detrimental effect upon the colored children. The impact is greater when it has the sanction of the law, for the policy of separating the races is usually interpreted as denoting the inferiority of the negro group. A sense of inferiority affects the motivation of a child to learn. Segregation with the sanction of law, therefore, has a tendency to [retard] the educational and mental development of negro children and to deprive them of some of the benefits they would receive in a racial[ly] integrated school system.

... We conclude that, in the field of public education, the doctrine of "separate but equal" has no place. Separate educational facilities are inherently unequal. Therefore, we hold that the plaintiffs and others similarly situated for whom the actions have been brought are, by reason of the segregation complained of, deprived of the equal protection of the laws guaranteed by the Fourteenth Amendment....

9.4: Southern Manifesto (1956)

Historical Context

Following *Brown v. Board of Education*, white southern Democratic senators began a legal and political campaign to fight the Court's desegregation order. This resulted in the Southern Manifesto, published in 1956. It essentially argued that the *Brown* ruling violated southern states' rights to conduct their societies as they saw fit. The document helped establish the ideological foundation for fighting desegregation. It moved away from traditional arguments of "black inferiority" or southern fears of "miscegenation" and instead made more historical and constitutional arguments against desegregation. The document promoted the idea that southern states had a right and responsibility to shield their populations from "damaging" policies (e.g. desegregation) promoted by the federal government.

Guiding Questions

1. On what grounds did southern Democrats reject the Supreme Court's ruling in *Brown v. Board*? Make a list of the main reasons they identify.

2. Based on the document text, what evidence do you see that might reveal very different attitudes about segregation when comparing white and black southerners? Remember that this manifesto was authored by white southerners. Which of their characterizations of race relations in the South might black southerners feel differently about?

3. Based on the reading, make a prediction. What do you think white southerners might do to resist desegregation efforts?

Document Text

The unwarranted decision of the Supreme Court in the public school cases is now bearing the fruit always produced when men substitute naked power for established law.

. . . We regard the decisions of the Supreme Court in the school cases as a clear abuse of judicial power. It climaxes a trend in the Federal Judiciary undertaking to legislate, in derogation of the authority of Congress, and to encroach upon the reserved rights of the States and the people.

The original Constitution does not mention education. Neither does the Fourteenth Amendment nor any other amendment. The debates preceding the submission of the Fourteenth Amendment clearly show that there was no intent that it should affect the system of education maintained by the States.

. . . Every one of the 26 States that had any substantial racial differences among its people, either approved the operation of segregated schools already in existence or subsequently established such schools by action of the same law-making body which considered the Fourteenth Amendment.

. . . In the case of *Plessy v. Ferguson* in 1896 the Supreme Court expressly declared that under the Fourteenth Amendment no person was denied any of his rights if the States provided separate but equal facilities. . . .

. . . This interpretation, restated time and again, became a part of the life of the people of many of the States and confirmed their habits, traditions, and way of life. It is founded on elemental humanity and commonsense, for parents should not be deprived by Government of the right to direct the lives and education of their own children.

. . . This unwarranted exercise of power by the Court, contrary to the Constitution, is creating chaos and confusion in the States principally affected. It is destroying the amicable relations between the white and Negro races that have been created through 90 years of patient effort by the good people of both races. It has planted hatred and suspicion where there has been heretofore friendship and understanding.

. . . We commend the motives of those States which have declared the intention to resist forced integration by any lawful means.

. . . We pledge ourselves to use all lawful means to bring about a reversal of this decision which is contrary to the Constitution and to prevent the use of force in its implementation.

9.5: Martin Luther King Jr.: "Letter from Birmingham Jail" (1963)

Historical Context

Martin Luther King Jr. is the most famous civil rights activist in American history. He was a Baptist minister with a PhD in theology and was one of the greatest orators in American history. He essentially became the face of the civil rights movement after he went to Montgomery, Alabama, to assist in the Montgomery Bus Boycott in 1955. King was important to the movement, since he provided a charismatic leader for the media to follow. His presence, and the male-dominated Southern Christian Leadership Conference (SCLC) that he cofounded, often overshadowed the major role that average men and women played behind the scenes in carrying out the work of civil rights activism. (Most notably, women were central to the success of the movement, working tirelessly to organize the campaigns and marches that King helped lead.) Starting in the mid-1950s, black men, women, and children pushed the civil rights movement forward by putting their bodies on the line in the quest for civil rights.

By 1963 the press typically followed wherever King went in the South, since his presence and the nonviolent protests he helped organize and carry out often resulted in significant confrontation and reactionary violence. King used the press to further the cause, drawing attention to the violent resistance that African Americans faced when trying to exercise their basic civil rights. Birmingham, Alabama, was one of the most hostile cities toward African Americans in the United States. King was invited there by local leaders in 1963 to help draw national attention to the plight of residents who were routinely denied access to public facilities and to the right to vote. A peaceful protest turned violent as police attacked marchers. King, like many others, was arrested for protesting, since an Alabama court had previously ruled that King could not hold a protest march in the state. From his jail cell, King penned one of his most famous works, "Letter from a Birmingham Jail." The following text is an excerpt from that letter.

Today, King is widely admired and celebrated by white and black Americans alike. The reality was very different during his lifetime, however. Many white Americans, in both the North and the South, thought King was a radical and a threat to the nation. His ideas of respect, equal treatment, desegregation, and access to full political rights fundamentally challenged white supremacy throughout the nation, and this scared many Americans. Keep this in mind as you read the following selection.

Guiding Questions

1. King wrote this open letter, published in newspapers across the country, to the religious leaders (clergy) in Birmingham. As you read through the letter, make a two-column chart. In the left column, identify the argument the cler-

gy made as to why King should not lead a protest in Birmingham. In the right column, identify and explain why King rejects each of those arguments.

2. Many white Americans thought King and his strategies were "extremist." How does King refute this claim? Look specifically at the text where he directly addresses this claim. He saw himself and his movement in the middle. What, according to him, are the "two opposing forces in the Negro community" on either side of him? Why does he see his strategy as the best option?

3. How, according to King, does nonviolent direct action work? Why does he think it is the right tool for change?

Document Text

My Dear Fellow Clergymen:

While confined here in the Birmingham city jail, I came across your recent statement calling my present activities "unwise and untimely." . . . I want to try to answer your statements in what I hope will be patient and reasonable terms.

. . . I cannot sit idly by in Atlanta and not be concerned about what happens in Birmingham. Injustice anywhere is a threat to justice everywhere. . . .

. . . Birmingham is probably the most thoroughly segregated city in the United States. . . . There have been more unsolved bombings of Negro homes and churches in Birmingham than in any other city in the nation. .. . .

. . . You may well ask: "Why direct action? Why sit-ins, marches and so forth? Isn't negotiation a better path?" You are quite right in calling for negotiation. Indeed, this is the very purpose of direct action. Nonviolent direct action seeks to . . . create a situation so crisis-packed that it will inevitably open the door to negotiation. . . .

One of the basic points in your statement is that the action that I and my associates have taken in Birmingham is untimely. . . .

. . . We know through painful experience that freedom is never voluntarily given by the oppressor; it must be demanded by the oppressed. . . . For years now I have heard the word "Wait!" It rings in the ear of every Negro with piercing familiarity. This "Wait" has almost always meant "Never." We must come to see, with one of our distinguished jurists, that "justice too long delayed is justice denied."

. . . You express a great deal of anxiety over our willingness to break laws. This is certainly a legitimate concern. Since we so diligently urge people to obey the Supreme Court's decision of 1954 outlawing segregation in the public schools, at first glance it may seem rather paradoxical for us consciously to break laws. One may well ask: "How can you advocate breaking some laws and obeying others?" The answer lies in the fact that there are two types of laws: just and unjust. I would be the first to advocate obeying just laws. One has not only a legal but a moral responsibility to obey just laws. Conversely, one has a moral responsibility to disobey unjust laws. I would agree with St. Augustine that "an unjust law is no law at all."

. . . I must make two honest confessions to you . . . over the past few years I have been gravely disappointed with the white moderate. . . . [T]he Negro's great stumbling block in his stride toward freedom is not the White Citizens Counciler or the Ku Klux Klanner, but the white moderate, who is more devoted to "order" than to justice; . . . who constantly says: "I agree with you in the goal you seek, but I cannot agree with your methods of direct action"; who paternalistically believes he can set the timetable for another man's freedom . . . who constantly advises the Negro to wait for a "more convenient season." . . .

. . . You speak of our activity in Birmingham as extreme. . . . I stand in the middle of two opposing forces in the Negro community. One is a force of complacency, made up in part of Negroes who, as a result of long years of oppression, are . . . adjusted to segregation; and in part of a few middle-class Negroes who, because of a degree of academic and economic security and because in some ways they profit by segregation, have become insensitive to the problems of the masses. The other force is one of bitterness and hatred, and it comes perilously close to advocating violence. It is expressed in the various black nationalist groups that are springing up across the nation, the largest and best-known being Elijah Muhammad's Muslim movement. Nourished by the Negro's frustration over the continued existence of racial discrimination, this movement is made up of people who have lost faith in America, who have absolutely repudiated Christianity, and who have concluded that the white man is an incorrigible "devil."

. . . Let me take note of my other major disappointment. I have been so greatly disappointed with the white church and its leadership.

. . . I felt that the white ministers, priests and rabbis of the South would be among our strongest allies. Instead, some have been outright opponents, refusing to understand the freedom movement and misrepresenting its leaders; all too many others have been more cautious than courageous and have remained silent . . .

. . . Before closing I feel impelled to mention one other point in your statement that has troubled me profoundly. You warmly commended the Birmingham police force for keeping "order" and "preventing violence." I doubt that you would have so warmly commended the police force if you had seen its dogs sinking their teeth into unarmed, nonviolent Negroes . . . if you were to watch them push and curse old Negro women and young Negro girls; if you were to see them slap and kick old Negro men and young boys. . . .

9.6: Stokely Carmichael: "Black Power" (1966)

Historical Context

Stokely Carmichael (also known as Kwame Ture) was a Trinidadian-American black civil rights activist who became a key leader among the movement's younger generation. Carmichael joined the Student Nonviolent Coordinating Committee (SNCC, pronounced "snick"), a group founded by long-time activist Ella Baker. For a while, SNCC worked with Martin Luther King Jr. and his organization, the SCLC, to organize nonviolent protests and marches. As time progressed, however, Carmichael and other young people grew frustrated with the slow pace of change.

Carmichael took over leadership of SNCC in 1966 and made his frustrations known. He moved to shift the historically biracial SNCC to an all-black organization. And after activist James Meredith was shot and injured during a solo protest march through Mississippi, Carmichael publicly rejected the nonviolent strategy promoted by King. When asked by the press if he would continue supporting nonviolent direct confrontation, he responded, "We been saying 'freedom' for six years. . . . What we are going to start saying now is 'Black Power.'"

Guiding Questions

1. What are the major issues and/or conflicts that Carmichael addresses in this excerpt from his "Black Power" speech? Make a list of the topics and annotate that list with his views on those issues.

2. What is "Black Power" according to Carmichael, and what is it not? What does this document reveal about people's attitudes towards black power?

3. How would you characterize the tone of Carmichael's speech compared to King's letter? Explain how and why you think the two sound similar or different, and explain how comparing the two helps illustrate the evolution of as well as the different voices within the civil rights movement in the 1960s.

Reading tip: The following text is from a speech. Read the text out loud to better hear the cadence and rhythm.

... I knew that I could vote and that that wasn't a privilege; it was my right. Every time I tried I was shot, killed or jailed, beaten or economically deprived. So somebody had to write a bill for white people to tell them, "When a black man comes to vote, don't bother him."...

So that the failures to pass a civil rights bill isn't because of Black Power, isn't because of the Student Nonviolent Coordinating Committee; it's not because of the rebellions that are occurring in the major cities. It is incapability of whites to deal with their own problems inside their own communities....

... How can we move to begin to change what's going on in this country. I maintain, as we have in SNCC, that the war in Vietnam is an illegal and immoral war. And the question is, What can we do to stop that war? What can we do to stop the people who, in the name of our country, are killing babies, women, and children? What can we do to stop that? And I maintain that we do not have the power in our hands to change that institution, to begin to recreate it, so that they learn to leave the Vietnamese people alone, and that the only power we have is the power to say, "Hell no!" to the draft.

... Now, then, we want to touch on nonviolence because we see that again as the failure of white society to make nonviolence work. I was always surprised at Quakers who came to Alabama and counseled me to be nonviolent, but didn't have the guts to start talking to James Clark to be nonviolent. That is where nonviolence needs to be preached—to Jim Clark, not to black people. They have already been nonviolent too many years. The question is, Can white people conduct their nonviolent schools in Cicero where they belong to be conducted, not among black people in Mississippi....

... [W]e're never going to get caught up in questions about power. This country knows what power is. It knows it very well. And it knows what Black Power is 'cause it deprived black people of it for 400 years. So it knows what Black Power is. That the question of, Why do black people—Why do white people in this country associate Black Power with violence? And the question is because of their own inability to deal with "blackness." If we had said "Negro power" nobody would get scared. Everybody would support it. Or if we said power for colored people, everybody'd be for that, but it is the word "black"—it is the word "black" that bothers people in this country, and that's their problem, not mine—their problem, their problem.

... In Lowndes County, we developed something called the Lowndes County Freedom Organization. It is a political party. The Alabama law says that if you have a Party you must have an emblem. We chose for the emblem a black panther, a beautiful black animal which symbolizes the strength and dignity of black people, an animal that never strikes back until he's back so far into the wall, he's got nothing to do but spring out. Yeah. And when he springs he does not stop. . . .

9.7: Unit 9 Review

The Unit Questions in the Overview asked you the following:

1. Why are the 1950s described as a period of both affluence and unrest? Identify evidence from the documents that illustrate these two themes.

2. How do documents authored by Martin Luther King Jr. and Stokely Carmichael, respectively, illustrate the evolution of the black civil rights movement? Compare and contrast these two documents. In what ways are they similar and in what ways are they different?

3. Make a prediction. How do you think the civil rights movement will expand in the 1960s and 1970s to other groups of people frustrated by the status quo? Who may those groups be?

The 1950s and 1960s were a turning point in U.S. history. Internationally, the nation was fully enmeshed in the Cold War, and at home it faced a host of challenges. Economically, the nation flourished in the post-war years as consumerism increased thanks to advertising and the emergence of a middle class. Not everyone benefited equally during this time, though. As the advertising reflects, women were seen and treated as objects or commodities to be enjoyed, rather than as people deserving equal treatment as members of society. African Americans, too, were largely excluded from the new national bounty and access to civil rights.

Schools were prime locations for testing the boundaries of civil rights. *Brown v. Board* made educational segregation illegal, but southern states were loath to give it up. Incidents like the one involving the Little Rock Nine, where in 1957 the governor of Arkansas called out the National Guard to try and prevent students from integrating public schools in Little Rock, highlighted the long road ahead. While the Supreme Court declared that schools must desegregate with "all deliberate speed," it provided no mechanism for forcing states and local governments to comply. Thus, many states dragged their feet and were slow to integrate. Facing such staunch opposition, African Americans grappled with determining the best way to move forward.

The black civil rights movement had many significant events and leaders. The readings in this unit by King and Carmichael were selected to illustrate differences in opinion within the black community and how the movement changed over time. King authored his piece before the two landmark civil rights achievements of the era, the Civil Rights Act of 1964 and the Voting Rights Act of 1965, while Carmichael spoke after those achievements, in 1966. In King's case, nonviolent direct action campaigns worked well in the South, where white supremacists violently reacted to protesters. Images of police officers and white mobs verbally and physically attacking peaceful protestors shocked the nation and the world. The conflicts led President Lyndon Johnson to promote civil rights through legislation. The Civil Rights Act of 1964 banned segregation in public places and made it illegal to discriminate based on a person's "race, color, religion, sex or national origin." Throughout the South, however, African Americans still faced significant obstacles to voting, so Congress passed the Voting Rights Act of 1965 in order to eliminate barriers to voting. While these were incredibly important pieces of legislation, they had their limitations.

In general these laws did little to address or alleviate the needs of northern, urban black communities. They also lacked significant mechanisms to force communities to immediately change their practices and behaviors. Frustrated by the slow pace of change, Carmichael expressed a new belief and attitude that would take root in the later years of the 1960s and into the 1970s. He was not the first person to use the term *Black Power,* but his public, unapologetic use of it moved it into the mainstream. As you can see in the text of his speech, his language and political organizing would influence subsequent developments, like the emergence of the Black Panther Party in Oakland, California, in 1966.

Many white Americans were afraid of the new Black Power movement. Black Power, and the militancy associated with the Black Panther Party, intimidated lots of white people who were not comfortable with African Americans demanding full and immediate access to civil rights. Additionally, there appeared to be no room for white liberals in the movement. The evolution of the black civil rights movement to the left, coupled with the 1968 assassination of King, left many whites concerned about the future of the movement and the nation. Some continued to support civil rights activism, but as we'll see in Unit 12 (The Triumph of Conservatism), a significant number of white Americans began to withdraw their support, instead focusing on their own needs. Before examining that shift, however, we also need to see how other groups capitalized on the activism of the 1960s and 1970s to expand their quest for civil rights.

10.1: Expanding Civil Rights

Overview

The last unit focused on changes occurring throughout America, especially the black civil rights struggle. African Americans made significant gains, but they continued to face challenges, especially in northern and urban areas where segregation and discrimination were pervasive and not easily eradicated by new legislation. The Civil Rights Act of 1964, however, proved incredibly helpful to women of all backgrounds, since it banned discrimination on the basis of "sex" in addition to race, religion, color, and national origin. As a result, women and other minority groups that witnessed African Americans' successes sought to replicate them in their own lives.

Women, who had entered the workforce in larger numbers to support the war effort during World War II, felt mixed emotions about being pushed out of their jobs to make space for returning men. Some women were ready to return to the home and start their lives as mothers and homemakers. Other women wanted to remain in the workforce, fulfilling their professional desires, earning money, and living more independent lives. Women with professional aspirations faced stiff opposition from a society that increasingly emphasized marriage and motherhood, but eventually their frustrations spilled over into public action. It was the dawn of the women's movement. The beginning was fairly quiet, however. Women began to talk amongst themselves about their discontent with the status quo. By the end of the movement, though, there would be a tidal wave of change.

Women faced a range of issues that extended well beyond employment. They rejected advertising common in the 1950s that depicted women as objects to be enjoyed or that characterized them as juvenile or stupid. As the women's movement grew, more women demanded respect as well as the right to control their bodies. They began to seek greater legislative remedies for things like sexual harassment and physical assault. Birth control and abortion also became hot button issues. Cases such as *Roe v. Wade* emerged and still divide the nation to this day.

Like women, other minority groups sought access to full civil rights and legal protections. Latino workers in the West, under the leadership of activists such as César Chávez and Dolores Huerta, organized the most successful farm worker union the nation had ever seen. These organizers faced many struggles as employers sought to retain power. For many Latinos working in agriculture, the most basic civil rights were about access to fair wages and working conditions.

Native Americans too sought remedies for past wrongs. They wanted the U.S. government to support Native peoples and make up for many past wrongs. In some cases they protested using traditional marches and rallies, and other times they took more dramatic steps that would elicit national attention.

Gay Americans also came out of the shadows in the late 1960s and 1970s. Prior to the 1970s, most U.S. states had laws criminalizing homosexual encounters. Capitalizing on the civil rights movement sweeping the nation, gay men and women began to openly identify as homosexual and to challenge laws that criminalized their personal lives. Gay bars in places like New York City were regularly targeted by police, who would arrest (and sometimes beat) the bar's patrons. Following a police raid at the Stonewall Inn one night in 1969, however, patrons did not go quietly. The resulting riot is now frequently cited as the beginning of the gay liberation movement.

The quest for civil rights diversified and expanded in the 1960s and 1970s. As you will read in this unit, different people had different reasons for protesting and different goals they hoped to achieve. At their core, however, everyone wanted access to the full civil rights guaranteed under the Constitution.

Unit Questions

1. What kinds of rights were different groups of Americans trying to secure in the 1960s and 1970s? Make a list of the issues you identified in the introduction and as you read the documents. (Be specific about what may constitute a "civil right.")

2. Use deductive reasoning. (Deductive reasoning is looking at the available evidence and trying to draw likely conclusions.) Based on the readings, what kinds of opposition do you think people faced in their quest for civil rights? Why might some people oppose these civil rights goals?

3. Make a prediction. How do you think the expansive and ongoing civil rights movements of the 1950s, 1960s, and 1970s might cause fatigue and pushback among some Americans? How might this affect the country in the 1980s and onward?

10.2: Betty Friedan: *The Feminine Mystique* (1963)

Historical Context

During the 1950s, America was caught in an intense Cold War with the Soviet Union. Americans sought stability in a volatile Cold War-world. The conflict profoundly impacted people's lives and attitudes, even if Americans did not realize it at the time. As Betty Friedan notes in this excerpt, many women married at young ages and had lots of children. Children born in this period would come to be called "Baby Boomers" because of the rash of births from the late 1940s through the early 1960s. The GI Bill of 1944 provided many Americans with a new path to the emerging middle class. And the development of suburbs enabled people to move away from cities and extended families and focus on the nuclear family. In this case "nuclear" means one's immediate family members (e.g., parents and children). Consumerism also encouraged many people to look for new products that would improve their lives. Large numbers of women focused on their homes and personal lives, then, rather than on professional opportunities.

Not all women, however, were happy with this shift to focusing on family life alone. Friedan's 1963 book, *The Feminine Mystique,* was a scathing critique of the suburban woman's condition. Revealing deep and intense dissatisfaction among many of the nation's middle class housewives, her book helped articulate their frustrations and launch the modern women's movement.

Guiding Questions

1. What was "the problem that has no name"? Make a list of what caused this problem, according to Friedan.

2. Why might some women, especially contented homemakers, be offended by Friedan's assessment of the situation? Look for specific examples.

3. In what ways do you think Friedan's analysis was deeply impacted by her own biases as a well-educated, middle-class white woman? Asked another way, how might working-class women, especially women of color, have been frustrated with Friedan's analysis?

Chapter 1: "The Problem That Has No Name"

The problem lay buried, unspoken, for many years in the minds of American women. It was a strange stirring, a sense of dissatisfaction, a yearning that women suffered in the middle of the twentieth century in the United States. Each suburban wife struggled with it alone. As she made the beds, shopped for groceries, matched slipcover material, ate peanut butter sandwiches with her children, chauffeured Cub Scouts and Brownies, lay beside her husband at night—she was afraid to ask even of herself the silent question—"Is this all?"

For over fifteen years there was no word of this yearning in the millions of words written about women, for women, in all the columns, books and articles by experts telling women their role was to seek fulfillment as wives and mothers. . . . They learned that truly feminine women do not want careers, higher education, political rights. . . .

By the end of the nineteen-fifties, the average marriage age of women in America dropped to 20, and was still dropping, into the teens. Fourteen million girls were engaged by 17. The proportion of women attending college in comparison with men dropped from 47 per cent in 1920 to 35 per cent in 1958. A century earlier, women had fought for higher education; now girls went to college to get a husband. By the mid-fifties, 60 per cent dropped out of college to marry, or because they were afraid too much education would be a marriage bar. . . .

. . . By the end of the fifties, the United States birthrate was overtaking India's. . . . Statisticians were especially astounded at the fantastic increase in the number of babies among college women. Where once they had two children, now they had four, five, six. . . .

. . . In the late fifties . . . a third of American women now worked, but most were no longer young and very few were pursuing careers. They were married women who held part-time jobs, selling or secretarial, to put their husbands through school, their sons through college, or to help pay the mortgage. Or they were widows supporting families. Fewer and fewer women were entering professional work. . . .

. . . In the fifteen years after World War II, this mystique of feminine fulfillment became the cherished and self-perpetuating core of contemporary American culture. . . . They gloried in their role as women, and wrote proudly on the census blank: "Occupation: housewife."

. . . If a woman had a problem in the 1950's and 1960's, she knew that something must be wrong with her marriage, or with herself. Other women were satisfied with their lives, she thought. What kind of a woman was she if she did not feel this mysterious fulfillment waxing the kitchen floor? . . .

. . . I heard a mother of four, having coffee with four other mothers in a suburban development . . . say in a tone of quiet desperation, "the problem." And the others knew, without words . . . they all shared the same problem, the problem that has no name.

. . . If I am right, the problem that has no name stirring in the minds of so many American women today is not a matter of loss of femininity or too much education, or the demands of domesticity. . . . We can no longer ignore that voice within women that says: "I want something more than my husband and my children and my home."

10.3: Indians of All Tribes Occupation of Alcatraz: Proclamation (1969)

Historical Context

Historically, Native Americans have suffered extensive abuse at the hands of the American government. Recall how the government under the Dawes Severalty Act essentially required Native Americans to give up their indigenous culture if they wanted to become citizens. In other instances, like Wounded Knee, they were massacred by federal troops.

Roughly eighty years later, many Native Americans remained deeply frustrated with the U.S. government. Witnessing the many successes of the black civil rights movement, Native Americans too began to vocalize their discontent. Some opted to take more radical actions as well, as demonstrated by the following reading.

Guiding Questions

1. There are two distinct parts to this text. Where does one end and the other begin? What is each of these two parts about?

2. Why do the occupying Native Americans want to "reclaim" Alcatraz? Compare the literal meaning with the actual meaning of this passage.

3. How did they hope to use the island, if they were able to have it? Do you think that the author meant this literally?

Document Text

To the Great White Father and All His People:

We, the native Americans, re-claim the land known as Alcatraz Island in the name of all American Indians by right of discovery.

We wish to be fair and honorable in our dealings with the Caucasian inhabitants of this land, and hereby offer the following treaty:

We will purchase said Alcatraz Island for twenty-four dollars ($24) in glass beads and red cloth, a precedent set by the white man's purchase of a similar island about 300 years ago. We know that $24 in trade goods for these 16 acres is more than was paid when Manhattan Island was sold, but we know that land values have risen over the years. Our offer of $1.24 per acre is greater than the 47 cents per acre the white men are now paying the California Indians for their land.

. . . We feel that this so-called Alcatraz Island is more than suitable for an Indian Reservation, as determined by the white man's own standards. By this we mean that this place resembles most Indian reservations, in that:

1. It is isolated from modern facilities, and without adequate means of transportation.

2. It has no fresh running water.

3. It has inadequate sanitation facilities.

4. There are no oil or mineral rights.

5. There is no industry so unemployment is great.

6. There are no health care facilities.

7. The soil is rocky and non-productive; and the land does not support game.

8. There are no educational facilities.

9. The population has always exceeded the land base.

10. The population has always been held as prisoners and kept dependent upon others.

. . . USE TO BE MADE OF ALCATRAZ ISLAND

Since the San Francisco Indian Center burned down, there is no place for Indians to assemble and carry on our tribal life here in the white man's city. Therefore, we plan to develop on this island several Indian institutes:

1. A Center for Native American Studies will be developed which will train our

young people in the best of our native cultural arts and sciences, as well as . . . learn the traditional values . . .

2. An American Indian Spiritual center will be developed which will practice our ancient tribal religious ceremonies and medicine. . . .

3. An Indian Center of Ecology will be built which will train and support our young people in scientific research and practice in order to restore our lands and waters to their pure and natural state. . . .

4. A Great Indian Training School will be developed to teach our peoples how to make a living in the world, improve our standards of living, and end hunger and unemployment among all our peoples. . . .

5. Some of the present buildings will be taken over to develop an American Indian Museum, which will depict our native foods and other cultural contributions we have given to all the world. Another part of the Museum will present some of the things the white man has given to the Indians, in return for the land and the life he took: disease, alcohol, poverty, and cultural decimation (as symbolized by old tin cans, barbed wire, rubber tires, plastic containers, etc.). Part of the museum will remain a dungeon, to symbolize both Indian captives who were incarcerated for challenging white authority, and those who were imprisoned on reservations. The Museum will show the noble and the tragic events of Indian history, including the broken treaties, the documentary of the Trail of Tears, the Massacre of Wounded Knee, as well as the victory over Yellow-Hair Custer and his army. . . .

SIGNED, INDIANS OF ALL TRIBES

10.4: Statement of César E. Chávez before the U.S. Senate (1969)

Historical Context

César Chávez, with the assistance of Dolores Huerta, became the most famous Latino civil rights activist in America in the 1960s. He focused on organizing farm workers, mainly in western states, where the vast majority lived. He was the cofounder and director of the United Farm Workers Union, which was affiliated with the AFL-CIO (American Federation of Labor-Congress of Industrial Organizations). Historically it had been very difficult to organize farm workers, since they were excluded from New Deal-era labor laws such as the National Labor Relations Act (NLRA). The NLRA, also known as the Wagner Act, explicitly granted working people in other industries federal protection in organizing unions.

Chávez and Huerta, capitalizing on the 1960s civil rights movement in America, worked to unionize farm workers in order to secure better wages and working conditions for some of America's most impoverished people. In the past, most worker strikes had failed. Successfully organizing workers under the UFW, Chávez tried a new tactic, in addition to waging a prolonged strike.

Unions protected by the Wagner Act could not conduct secondary boycotts. However, farm workers were excluded from the Wagner Act, so they were not required to follow the rules around boycotts. The workers, then, organized something called a "secondary boycott." In a secondary boycott, the farm workers targeted not only the grape growers they were striking against, but they also picketed outside stores that sold table grapes or grape products, like wine. This tactic proved successful, since many consumers did not want to cross the picket lines to buy grape products. Although it took several years of boycotting, leading grape growers eventually agreed to sit down and negotiate with the UFW and its workers.

In the following excerpt, Chávez testifies before the U.S. Senate Subcommittee on Labor and Public Welfare. At the same time he was testifying in 1969, workers were still striking and conducting boycotts.

Guiding Questions

1. Chávez specifically mentions "illegals and green carders" in this excerpt. Why does he say their presence can be problematic for striking American workers?

2. How were farm workers affected by New Deal policies? How did this affect their general welfare?

3. What was the main goal Chávez hoped to achieve by testifying before Congress?

Document Text

. . . How can the nation, how can Congress help the farm worker close the yawning gap between his own social and economic condition and that of the other wage earners, even those of comparable skill in other industries such as manufacturing and construction?

Answer? Through strong, effective, well-run unions. . . .

. . . Unionization cannot make progress in the face of hostile employer attitudes unless it receives effective governmental support. . . .

. . . What we ask is some way to keep the illegals and green carders from breaking strikes; some civil remedy against growers who employ behind our picket lines those who have entered the United States illegally, and, likewise those green carders who have not permanently moved their residence and domicile to the United States.

An especially serious problem in agricultural employment is the concerted refusal of growers even to discuss their use of economic poisons or pesticides. . . .

. . . Thirty-four years ago a nation groping its uncharted course through the seas of the Great Depression faced the threatening storms of social and economic revolution.

The late President Franklin D. Roosevelt met the challenge with the Wagner Act and with other New Deal measures, then considered quite revolutionary, such as Social Security, unemployment insurance and the Fair Labor Standards Act.

While these measures modified the existing capitalistic system somewhat, they also saved the nation for free enterprise.

They did not save the farm worker. He was left out of every one of them. The social revolution of the New Deal passed him by. . . .

The relief we seek from Congress today, however, is neither very new nor very revolutionary. It had proved beneficial to the nation in the past when unions were weak and industry strong. We need and favor NLRA amendments along the lines of the original Wagner Act. . . .

10.5: Gay Liberation Front: Program Platform Statement (1970)

Historical Context

From the nation's founding, many American colonies (and later states) enacted laws targeting homosexual encounters. The result was that thousands of individuals lived secret lives, often in fear of being exposed by people seeking to harm their reputations or destroy their lives. Immigration laws, like the Immigration Act of 1917, one of the first intensely restrictive immigration policies in U.S. history, also reinforced homophobic attitudes by allowing agents at ports of entry to bar immigrants thought to be homosexual under the "mentally defective" provision. The idea that homosexuality was the result of some kind of mental deficiency persisted well into the twentieth century.

In 1952, when the American Psychiatric Association (APA) published its first *Diagnostic and Statistical Manual of Mental Disorders* (DSM), it identified homosexuality as "sociopathic personality disturbance." The 1950s saw explicitly anti-gay policies like President Dwight D. Eisenhower's executive order banning homosexuals from working in the federal government because they were a perceived security risk. Government officials assumed that knowledge of an individual's homosexuality could be used to blackmail them by enemies. The FBI itself frequently targeted individuals and used their sexual identity to harass and discredit them. In 1968 the APA again classified homosexuality as a mental disorder. Gay patients, voluntarily or by force from family, often underwent aversion therapy treatments aimed at "turning" them heterosexual. Also around this period, however, gay Americans—like other minority groups—tired of the mistreatment and discrimination, began to fight back. In New York City in 1969, for example, a group of gay bar patrons clashed with police after a raid at the Stonewall Inn. The resulting riots are seen as one of the most important events in the gay liberation movement.

The 1960s marked a period of intense debate about personal identity, and during this time the APA classification of homosexuality as a mental disorder fell out of favor. By 1973 a majority of APA members voted to change the classification. As a compromise, they created the label "sexual orientation disturbance" to classify people who felt conflicted about their homosexual identity. Throughout this period individual psychiatrists approached the issue differently. Some continued trying to "treat" homosexual patients and "cure" them of their gayness, while others abandoned the practice, fully believing it was unethical and/or impossible. A little over a decade later, in 1987, homosexuality was fully removed from the DSM. That did not mean, however, that gay Americans had gained access to full civil rights. Throughout the 1990s President Bill Clinton, a Democrat, signed two key pieces of legislation that limited gay Americans' rights. The first, in 1993, became popularly known as "Don't Ask, Don't Tell." Under this policy, openly gay men and women were banned from serving in the military, but the policy also prohibited the harassment of gay servicemen and women who were still "in the closet" (not publicly open about their sexual identity). In addition, in 1996 Clinton signed the Defense of Marriage Act (DOMA), which defined marriage as a union between a man and a woman.

This history illustrates the challenges the gay community faced in the mid-twentieth century. Embracing the activism and civil rights demands that other groups made in the 1960s and 1970s, organizations like the Gay Liberation Front (GLF) organized and began to push for gay people's civil rights.

Guiding Questions

1. What, according to the document, are the three types of oppression that activists sought to free gay people from in America? How did each of these types of oppression harm people?

2. What actions did the organization plan to take to combat homophobia? Put this into your own words.

3. Draw a conclusion based on the document evidence and by applying general knowledge. Gay Americans were a minority of the population, similar to other groups fighting for civil rights during this period (like African Americans, Native Americans, Latinos, etc.). In the statement, the GLF plans to unite with other oppressed people to fight for equal rights for everyone. Why might some people welcome their support, and why might other people not want to be linked to the gay community at this point in time? Provide at least one specific example for these two types of response.

Document Text

Adapted by Seattle Gay Liberation Front on . . . December 2, 1970

The basic purpose of GLF is the liberation of homosexual men and women in this society [who] suffer under three principal types of oppression:

1) Societal oppression: Much of society's oppression of homosexuals stems from ignorance which produces fear, and the consequent alienation of heterosexual society from the recognition of homosexuals as individual men and women. . . .

2) Psychological oppression: The psychological oppression of homosexuals takes two forms. One is an internalized oppression of the homosexual by himself. This reflects that programming perpetuated in the society that creates the feeling within many homosexuals that they are somehow "sick" or "perverted." The ramifications of such a feeling for the individual are extremely damaging, since he or she is unable to accept him/herself fully and feel free and healthy in his/her sexuality. The second form of psychological oppression is homosexual's oppression of other homosexuals. . . . entrenched societal programming which causes the homosexual to reflect the sexist views of heterosexual society onto other homosexuals. Hence, . . . we find homosexuals practicing sexism toward other homosexuals.

3) Legal/Quasi-political oppression: Reinforcing and embodying societal ignorance is the "legal" oppression of homosexuals. This facet of oppression encompasses a wide range of laws, discriminatory practices, and more insidious harassment. . . . Often even more oppressive than the letter of the law and more difficult to deal with is the misuse of legal avenues to harass homosexuals, particularly as they frequent gay establishments.

PROGRAM ACTIONS

. . . this group would like to see GLF undertake as part of the struggle against oppression:

Homosexuals as they relate to heterosexual society:

GLF should . . . educate straight society about homosexuality with the aim to alleviate fear by eliminating ignorance. . . .

. . . GLF should have a central Speakers Bureau which would arrange for gays to speak at institutions or organizations. . . .

Homosexuals as they relate to institutions:

GLF should undertake to draw up and disseminate all laws, local ordinances, or semi-legal practices oppressive to homosexuals.

GLF should selectively violate these laws openly, then obtain legal aid in fighting them in the courts. . . .

Homosexuals dealing with other homosexuals:

Consciousness raising sessions in which small groups of homosexual men, women or both relate on a personal basis to each other in order to collectively build for each other a healthy freedom and dignity in coming to terms with their sexuality. . . .

. . . A GLF library of gay writings should be started and centrally located so that it is available to anyone—gay or straight—who is interested. . . .

POLITICAL STATEMENT

The goals of GLF revolve around social change. In order to accomplish this social change, political action is necessary. The Gay Liberation Front is interested in homosexual freedom, but we must realize and support the cause of freedom for all people. . . . Our goal is to establish a society in which all people enjoy freedom of existence and freedom to relate to each other in whatever manner they see fit, without fear of oppression or condemnation.

10.6: *Roe v. Wade* (1973)

Historical Context

Roe v. Wade is one of the most divisive Supreme Court cases of modern times. It focuses on whether or not a woman has a constitutional right to privacy and if that privacy extends to reproductive health and the right to access legal abortion services.

The woman in the case used the pseudonym Jane Roe, because she was seeking an abortion in Texas, where it was illegal. According to the Supreme Court ruling, Roe "wished to terminate her pregnancy by an abortion "performed by a competent, licensed physician, under safe, clinical conditions." However, "she was unable to get a 'legal' abortion in Texas because her life did not appear to be threatened by the continuation of her pregnancy." Denied this opportunity, Roe sued the state of Texas, arguing that the law preventing her access to abortion services violated her privacy rights.

Guiding Questions

1. How did Harry Blackmun, writing for the majority, explain the Court's logic in supporting Roe's claim that her privacy rights had been violated? Make a list of the specific examples, or evidence, that Blackmun cited.

2. Read the second to last paragraph and explain what is meant by "viability." What is the logic behind this ruling?

3. What did the Texas state statute originally say about a woman's right to an abortion? How did this Supreme Court ruling affect that rule?

Document Text

Harry Blackmun: Majority Opinion

... the District Court held that the fundamental right of single women and married persons to choose whether to have children is protected by the Ninth Amendment, through the Fourteenth Amendment, and that the Texas criminal abortion statutes were void on their face because they were both unconstitutionally vague and constituted an overbroad infringement of the plaintiffs' Ninth Amendment rights. ...

. . . The principal thrust of appellant's attack on the Texas statutes is that they improperly invade a right, said to be possessed by the pregnant woman, to choose to terminate her pregnancy. . . .

. . . The Constitution does not explicitly mention any right of privacy. In a line of decisions, however . . . the Court has recognized that a right of personal privacy . . . does exist under the Constitution. . . .

This right of privacy, whether it be founded in the Fourteenth Amendment's concept of personal liberty and restrictions upon state action . . . or . . . in the Ninth Amendment's reservation of rights to the people, is broad enough to encompass a woman's decision whether or not to terminate her pregnancy. The detriment that the State would impose upon the pregnant woman by denying this choice altogether is apparent. Specific and direct harm medically diagnosable even in early pregnancy may be involved. Maternity, or additional offspring, may force upon the woman a distressful life and future. Psychological harm may be imminent. . . . All these are factors the woman and her responsible physician necessarily will consider in consultation.

. . . throughout the major portion of the 19th century, prevailing legal abortion practices were far freer than they are today, persuades us that the word "person," as used in the Fourteenth Amendment, does not include the unborn. . . .

. . . Texas urges that, apart from the Fourteenth Amendment, life begins at conception and is present throughout pregnancy, and that, therefore, the State has a compelling interest in protecting that life from and after conception.

. . . Viability is usually placed at about seven months (28 weeks) but may occur earlier, even at 24 weeks. . . .

. . . With respect to the State's important and legitimate interest in potential life, the "compelling" point is at viability. This is so because the fetus then presumably has the capability of meaningful life outside the mother's womb. . . . If the State is interested in protecting fetal life after viability, it may go so far as to proscribe abortion during that period, except when it is necessary to preserve the life or health of the mother. . . .

. . . Our conclusion that Art. 1196 is unconstitutional means, of course, that the Texas abortion statutes, as a unit, must fall.

10.7: Unit 10 Review

This unit began with an overview of various movements. We asked you to consider the following as you read:

1. What kinds of rights were different groups of Americans trying to secure in the 1960s and 1970s? Make a list of the issues you identified in the introduction and as you read the documents. (Be specific about what may constitute a "civil right.")

2. Use deductive reasoning. (Deductive reasoning is looking at the available evidence and trying to draw likely conclusions.) Based on the readings, what kinds of opposition do you think people faced in their quest for civil rights? Why might some people oppose their goals?

3. Make a prediction. How do you think the expansive and ongoing civil rights movements of the 1950s, 1960s, and 1970s might cause fatigue among some Americans? How might this affect the country in the 1980s and onward?

This unit looked at the women's movement as well as similar movements from other minority groups seeking access to full civil rights. For their part, women focused national attention on a host of issues. As Betty Friedan argued in *The Feminine Mystique*, although many women had healthy families and significant material goods, not all of them were satisfied with their role as the happy homemaker and having their lives defined by their roles as a wife and/or mother.

Feminists—who believed in the equal treatment of women—helped pave the way for women to enter the professional workforce in larger numbers and secure equal treatment more generally. (Note that men can also be feminists, since the term only means a person who believes in the equal treatment of women.) Women's rights activists rejected the objectification of women and fought for legislation that would protect women from sexual harassment and abuse. As noted, they also pushed for greater control over their bodies in all ways, including reproductive health. This issue proved to be particularly divisive in American society, with abortion rights emerging and remaining one of the most contentious issues of the modern era.

Like the black civil rights movement that preceded it, the women's movement increased in scope and scale as time progressed, and this led to some fracturing of the movement. Unsurprisingly, as with the black civil rights movement, different women (particularly younger women) wanted more immediate and drastic change. Taken together, all of these women's efforts helped fundamentally change a woman's status in America.

Native Americans, Latinos, gay Americans, and other groups also capitalized on the civil-rights focus of the 1960s and 1970s to push for change in their lives. Reading the documents should make it possible for you to brainstorm an extensive list of "civil rights" that people pushed for during this era. Native Americans sought respect and remediation for past wrongs committed against them by the federal government. They wanted access to better education, jobs, and programs aimed at cultural preservation. Likewise, Latinos throughout the nation wanted to end discrimination and, in some places, outright segregation. César Chávez and Dolores Huerta led farm workers in unionizing, seeking to improve labor conditions and wages. Gay Americans, like women, were on the forefront of social change. They sought legal protections for gay people, by overturning laws criminalizing homosexuality and using existing civil rights laws to minimize or eliminate discrimination based on one's sexual orientation.

Many Americans supported the expansive demands for civil rights, but many did not. Granting greater civil rights to millions of Americans meant that some others, often working-class white families, lost the privileges they had long held simply as a result of their preferred status in American society. This tension would become even more apparent as time progressed. As you will see in the next unit, the Vietnam War and the anti-war and counterculture movements also contributed to this fatigue. Over time, larger numbers of white, middle, and working-class Americans—tired of the constant upheaval and confrontation—looked for new political options. Unit 12 (The Triumph of Conservatism) will focus on how one of the nation's most significant periods of liberal activism and reform was followed up by a shift in a profoundly conservative direction by the 1980s.

11.1: Vietnam and Counterculture

Overview

Military conflict in Vietnam began in the earliest days of the Cold War. Vietnam, which was then part of French Indochina, immediately began fighting its French colonizers when World War II ended, in an effort to secure independence. As early as 1919, Vietnamese nationalists—including Ho Chi Minh—looked to the United States to support Vietnam's independence claim. (Colonized people around the world hoped President Woodrow Wilson would support their claims of self-determination. These hopes were generally ignored.) Ho had embraced communism in the 1920s, but even as late as 1945, when he was authoring the Vietnamese Declaration of Independence, he still modeled it on the U.S. Declaration of Independence. The United States, though, was still unwilling to help Vietnam. By the end of World War II, it was becoming increasingly clear that the Cold War was taking hold. In this context, the United States would not support an avowed communist or anyone they believed was backed by the Soviet Union. War broke out between France and independence fighters in Vietnam in 1946. Fighting continued for years.

Finally, in 1954 the French suffered a massive military defeat at Dien Bien Phu that drove them to the bargaining table. Ho Chi Minh, leader of the insurgent Viet Minh forces, met with French officials at the International Geneva Conference on July 21, 1954. At this meeting the parties essentially agreed to divide the country at the Seventeenth Parallel, giving the Viet Minh control of the North. The former French-backed government currently in power in Saigon, in the southern part of Vietnam, and the United States both rejected the agreement. The Geneva Accords called for national elections in 1956 to determine a national government for Vietnam. The United States and the Vietnamese ruler in the South, Ngo Dinh Diem, did not sign the accords.

The United States believed that U.S. interests and safety could only be achieved through the "containment" of socialism and communism around the world. Beginning in 1954, then, the United States began funneling money and military advisors to South Vietnam in an attempt to prevent the nation from falling to the communists. At first U.S. investment remained somewhat limited. But as the Cold War escalated in the 1960s, U.S. involvement dramatically increased. President John F. Kennedy slowly increased the U.S. presence in Vietnam, but it really exploded under his successor, Lyndon B. Johnson. By the mid-1960s, President Johnson and his advisors felt they had already invested too much in Vietnam to pull out, so they opted to increase involvement in the hopes of helping South Vietnam win the conflict. When Johnson took over the presidency in 1963 (following Kennedy's assassination), there were approximately 17,000 U.S. military "advisors" in Vietnam (U.S. military personnel who worked with the South Vietnamese military and who participated in combat operations). By the time he left office in 1968, there were more than 500,000 U.S. troops on the ground. As the readings in this unit will demonstrate, American attitudes diverged significantly as the war progressed and American involvement escalated.

Martin Luther King Jr., known for his civil rights activism, came out against the war in 1967. He felt the nation was at a crossroads and that the war in Vietnam blocked its movement forward. King began focusing more on economic inequality, arguing that the nation needed to address this problem if it hoped to eliminate discrimination and remaining barriers to opportunity. He joined a growing group of Americans unhappy with U.S. involvement in Vietnam. Changing attitudes towards the war were most apparent with men like John Kerry—soldiers who had served in Vietnam but returned home demanding peace. Likewise, many young people around the country also expressed discontent. Some were ideologically opposed to the conflict; others feared the draft (i.e., mandatory military service). Whatever their reasons were, their protests were growing louder.

The American counterculture movement was most popular among young, middle-class, predominantly white, often college-educated men and women. These young people generally opposed racial segregation, protested against the Vietnam War, advocated for women's and minority rights, and often rejected the consumerism that had defined their parents' generation. "Hippies" became the most recognizable group within the counterculture. These young people were not the first to reject the conformity and social expectations and status quo of their parents' generation.

In the 1950s, a small contingent of young people, called the Beatniks, rejected their sheltered suburban middle-class upbringings, looking for more "authentic" experiences. While they constituted a very small portion of the population, the Beats helped usher in a future generation of young people who very openly rejected the status quo—the hippies of the 1960s counterculture movement. By the 1960s more people were also interested in overturning the status quo, including many African Americans, women, Native Americans, Latinos, gay Americans, environmentalists, and anti-war protestors, just to name a few. Although each of the movements was unique, they are sometimes collectively referred to as the "counterculture movement."

Four of the five primary sources in this unit explicitly relate to the Vietnam War. The fifth, however, focuses on the emerging environmental movement. Many anti-war activists were concerned about the environmental impacts of the war due to the United States' intense use of chemicals such as Napalm and Agent Orange. At home, Rachel Carson's book *Silent Spring,* published in 1962, shocked readers into thinking more about human impact on the environment and the virtually unregulated use of toxic chemicals.

Read in conjunction with the previous two units on 1960s and 1970s civil rights movements in the United States, this unit should further illustrate the issues challenging the nation at home and abroad.

Reading Tip: Take your time in reading and understanding this introduction. The 1950s, 1960s, and 1970s are exciting but challenging periods to explore because so many things were happening at the same time. For example, the Cold War began immediately after World War II and gained strength throughout this period. Similarly, so did the black civil rights movement in America. As that movement progressed, new ones emerged as well, like the women's movement, gay liberation, and more. Keep all of these various developments in mind as you read, since they influenced one another. As the title indicates, this unit focuses on Vietnam and the counterculture movement. The next unit (Unit 12) will examine the conservative response to the social and political upheaval of the period discussed in this unit.

Unit Questions

1. How did Vietnam and counterculture/anti-war movements cause significant divisions within U.S. society? In other words, how may have many Americans felt that they needed to align themselves with either the counterculture/anti-war movement or their (usually conservative) opponents?

2. Synthesize information. Based on what you read in the last two units (on civil rights) and this unit on Vietnam and the counterculture movement, why do many scholars describe the late 1960s and early 1970s as one of the most turbulent periods in American history?

3. Make a prediction. How will conservative political leaders capitalize on some citizens' frustrations with anti-war protests and the counterculture movement to shift the balance of power in favor of conservative politicians?

11.2: Bob Dylan: "Blowin' in the Wind" (1963)

Historical Context

Singer-songwriter Bob Dylan was born in 1941 and came of age in the turbulent 1960s. Dylan quickly became one of the most influential folk musicians in American history. Although Dylan never claimed "Blowin' in the Wind" was a protest song, it was adopted by protesters around the country as an anthem for their causes, which ranged from civil rights to anti-war protests.

Guiding Questions

1. Symbolism is using things or words to represent other ideas, and it often leaves significant room for individual interpretation. What kinds of symbolism do you hear Dylan using in this song? Select three examples and explain what you think they might represent.

2. Why do you think protesters throughout the nation adopted "Blowin' in the Wind" as an anthem for their various causes? Listen to the lyrics and select lines you think some protesters would have found compelling. Make a list of three or four lines that apply. Annotate these with your own ideas.

3. Make a contemporary connection. Why do you think Dylan remains one of the most revered folk musicians in American History today? How could this song be applied to the world today? What sort of people would be able to relate to this song today?

Primary Source

https://www.youtube.com/watch?v=vWwgrjjIMXA

Note: If it is easier for you to read the lyrics instead of listening to them, you may want to search them on the internet.

11.3: Martin Luther King Jr.: "Beyond Vietnam: A Time to Break Silence" (1967)

Historical Context

Martin Luther King Jr. was both deeply loved and hated for his activism in the 1950s and 1960s. He focused on the black civil rights movement in the early part of his career, but as he explains in this speech, by 1967 he felt he could no longer remain silent on the issue of Vietnam. Many civil rights activists feared that by weighing in on Vietnam, King would lose the support of moderate white audiences that had supported his earlier civil rights work. By 1967, however, King felt strongly that in order to fully address the nation's remaining civil rights issues, the country had to deal with issues like income inequality and the Vietnam War.

King's beliefs about civil rights and access to equal opportunity in America evolved significantly over the course of his career. Initially the movement he helped lead focused mainly on desegregation and voting rights in the South, and its most successful moments came with the passage of the Civil Rights Act of 1964 and the Voting Rights Act of 1965. These laws profoundly changed America by reducing discrimination and providing black southerners with improved access to voting, but they did not solve the nation's racial problems or economic inequalities. As black urban residents outside the South could attest to, discrimination remained prevalent even after the passage of the 1964 and 1965 acts.

Witnessing the struggle of black urban residents, King increasingly realized that America had to do more to eliminate poverty if it hoped to end discrimination. He also realized that Vietnam was a major obstacle standing in that path. The following excerpts are from a speech that some consider King's most controversial, because in this speech he clearly and unequivocally states his opposition to the Vietnam War. Many feared a public anti-war stand by King would undermine the civil rights movement.

Guiding Questions

1. Make a list of the reasons why King opposed the Vietnam War. (He says there are seven reasons but only clearly identifies six in the speech.) Explain each of his reasons in your own words. Write these out!

2. Why did some people fear that if King took a public stand against the war, he would undermine the civil rights movement?

3. What does King recommend the United States do to end the war but continue the fight against communism?

181

. . . The recent statements of your executive committee are the sentiments of my own heart and I found myself in full accord when I read its opening lines: "A time comes when silence is betrayal." That time has come for us in relation to Vietnam.

. . . Over the past two years . . . as I have called for radical departures from the destruction of Vietnam, many persons have questioned me about the wisdom of my path. . . . Why are you speaking about war, Dr. King? . . . Aren't you hurting the cause [civil rights] of your people, they ask? . . .

. . . I have seven [six] major reasons for bringing Vietnam into the field of my moral vision. There is . . . [a] connection between the war in Vietnam and . . . [civil rights] in America. A few years . . . [i]t seemed as if there was a real promise of hope for the poor—both black and white—through the poverty program. . . . Then came the buildup in Vietnam . . . and I knew that America would never invest the necessary funds or energies in rehabilitation of its poor so long as adventures like Vietnam continued to draw men and skills and money. . . .

. . . Perhaps the more tragic recognition of reality took place when it became clear to me that the war . . . was sending their [poor black people's] sons and their brothers and their husbands to fight and to die in extraordinarily high proportions relative to the rest of the population. We were taking the black young men who had been crippled by our society and sending them eight thousand miles away to guarantee liberties in Southeast Asia which they had not found in southwest Georgia and East Harlem. . . .

My third reason . . . grows out of my experience in the ghettoes of the North over the last three years . . . As I have walked among the desperate, rejected and angry young men I have told them that Molotov cocktails and rifles would not solve their problems. . . . But they asked—and rightly so—what about Vietnam? They asked if our own nation wasn't using massive doses of violence to solve its problems, to bring about the changes it wanted. Their questions hit home, and I knew that I could never again raise my voice against the violence of the oppressed in the ghettos without having first spoken clearly to the greatest purveyor of violence in the world today—my own government. . . .

For those who ask the question, "Aren't you a civil rights leader?" and thereby mean to exclude me from the movement for peace . . . when a group of us formed the Southern Christian Leadership Conference, we chose as our motto: "To save the soul of America." . . . If America's soul becomes totally poisoned, part of the autopsy must read Vietnam. . . .

. . . [A]nother burden of responsibility was placed upon me in 1964. . . . [T]he Nobel Prize for Peace was . . . a commission to work harder than I had ever worked before for "the brotherhood of man."

Finally . . . I believe that the Father [God] is deeply concerned especially for his suffering and helpless and outcast children, I come tonight to speak for them.

. . . The world now demands a maturity of America that we may not be able to achieve. It demands that we admit that we have been wrong from the beginning of our adventure in Vietnam, that we have been detrimental to the life of the Vietnamese people. . . .

In order to atone for our sins and errors in Vietnam, we should take the initiative in bringing a halt to this tragic war. . . .

. . . Meanwhile we in the churches and synagogues . . . must continue to raise our voices if our nation persists in its perverse ways in Vietnam. . . .

. . . Communism will never be defeated by the use of atomic bombs or nuclear weapons. . . . We must not engage in a negative anti-communism, but rather in a positive thrust for democracy, realizing that our greatest defense against communism is to take offensive action in behalf of justice. We must with positive action seek to remove those conditions of poverty, insecurity and injustice which are the fertile soil in which the seed of communism grows and develops. . . .

11.4: Richard M. Nixon: Address to the Nation on the Situation in Southeast Asia (1970)

Historical Context

Republican Richard M. Nixon won the U.S. presidential election in 1968. The Democratic incumbent, President Lyndon B. Johnson, had decided not to seek reelection due to intense national discontent over the Vietnam War. Troop levels peaked under Johnson in 1968, with more than a half million Americans serving in the war. By 1970 Nixon had cut the number almost in half, but that did not mean he was successfully bringing the war to a close.

Early in his presidency, Nixon introduced a strategy known as "Vietnamization," which entailed withdrawing American troops and replacing them with South Vietnamese soldiers. While this strategy appealed to many American voters, it failed to address a deep, ongoing, underlying problem—for more than a decade American military leaders had failed to inspire or force South Vietnamese soldiers to take over the fight, hence the U.S.'s prolonged engagement in the area. At the same time Nixon was withdrawing American troops, in 1969, he was also secretly expanding the war into Cambodia with bombing raids designed to target North Vietnamese soldiers and supplies in the area. By 1970 Nixon was forced to tell the American public about the war's expansion into Cambodia, since he was planning a ground invasion.

Guiding Questions

1. According to this address, what are Nixon's plans for ending American involvement in the Vietnam War? What goals does he pursue? Under what conditions does he want to end the war? Read the document excerpt carefully and identify all facets of his proposed plan.

2. How does Nixon justify expanding the ground war into Cambodia, while also claiming he is sticking to his promise to end the war quickly?

3. Why would Nixon choose to expand the war into Cambodia, even though it means prolonging the conflict?

Good evening my fellow Americans:

Ten days ago . . . I announced a decision to withdraw an additional 150,000 Americans from Vietnam over the next year. I said then that I was making that decision despite our concern over increased enemy activity in Laos, in Cambodia, and in South Vietnam.

At that time, I warned that if I concluded that increased enemy activity in any of these areas endangered the lives of Americans remaining in Vietnam, I would not hesitate to take strong and effective measures to deal with that situation.

Despite that warning, North Vietnam has increased its military aggression in all these areas, and particularly in Cambodia.

. . . In cooperation with the armed forces of South Vietnam, attacks are being launched this week to clean out major enemy sanctuaries on the Cambodian-Vietnam border.

A major responsibility for the ground operations is being assumed by South Vietnamese forces. . . .

. . . Now let me give you the reasons for my decision.

A majority of the American people . . . are for the withdrawal of our forces from Vietnam. . . .

. . . want to end this war rather than to have it drag on interminably . . .

. . . want to keep the casualties of our brave men in Vietnam at an absolute minimum. . . .

We take this action not for the purpose of expanding the war into Cambodia but for the purpose of ending the war in Vietnam and winning the just peace we all desire. . . .

. . . We have offered to withdraw all of our men if they will withdraw theirs. We have offered to negotiate all issues with only one condition and that is that the future of South Vietnam be determined not by North Vietnam, and not by the United States, but by the people of South Vietnam themselves.

The answer of the enemy has been intransigence at the conference table, belligerence in Hanoi, massive military aggression in Laos and Cambodia, and stepped-up attacks in South Vietnam, designed to increase American casualties.

. . . It is not our power but our will and character that is being tested tonight. . . .

If we fail to meet this challenge, all other nations will be on notice that despite its overwhelming power the United States, when a real crisis comes, will be found wanting.

During my campaign for the Presidency, I pledged to bring Americans home from Vietnam. They are coming home.

I promised to end this war. I shall keep that promise.

I promised to win a just peace. I shall keep that promise.

We shall avoid a wider war. But we are also determined to put an end to this war. . .

.. . . No one is more aware than I am of the political consequences of the action I have taken. It is tempting to take the easy political path: to blame this war on previous administrations and to bring all of our men home immediately, regardless of the consequences, even though that would mean defeat for the United States . . .

I have rejected all political considerations in making this decision.

. . . I would rather be a one-term President and do what I believe is right than to be a two-term President at the cost of seeing America become a second-rate power and to see this Nation accept the first defeat in its proud 190-year history. . . .

11.5: John Kerry: Testimony of the Vietnam Veterans against the War (1971)

Historical Context

John Kerry had a long and distinguished public service career. Kerry was a U.S. Senator (Democrat) from Massachusetts from 1985 to 2013. He ran for president in 2004 but lost to George W. Bush. Kerry later served as Secretary of State under President Barack Obama, from 2013 to 2017.

Kerry began his public service career in the U.S. Naval Reserve. In this capacity he served a four-month tour in Vietnam between 1968 and 1969, where he earned three combat medals (Silver Star, Bronze Star, and the Purple Heart). Upon returning from Vietnam, Kerry joined the Vietnam Veterans against the War organization, and he testified before the U.S. Senate Committee on Foreign Affairs in 1971. The following is an excerpt from his testimony.

Kerry testified before Congress a year after President Richard M. Nixon gave his "Address to the Nation on the Situation in Southeast Asia" in 1970. Recall in that speech that Nixon talked about his plans to withdraw American troops from Vietnam while beginning what he called "Vietnamization" of the conflict. By 1971 the United States was still deeply involved in Vietnam, and the conflict had expanded to neighboring countries Laos and Cambodia. The war would not end until 1975.

Guiding Questions

1. Why, according to Kerry, were Vietnam veterans like himself angry with the U.S. government and President Nixon specifically? Read the document and make a list of the grievances he identifies in this excerpt. Explain why each item listed was problematic.

2. Kerry begins his testimony by explaining how honorably discharged veterans met at a meeting of the Vietnam Veterans against the War (in Detroit) to talk about the war crimes they committed while serving in the Vietnam conflict. Why would soldiers want to talk about or even admit to these crimes? Why do you think Kerry is implying that the government is partly responsible for the actions of these men?

3. What were some of the challenges facing returning veterans, according to Kerry?

. . . I would like to talk, representing all those veterans, and say that several months ago in Detroit, we had an investigation at which over 150 honorably discharged and many very highly decorated veterans testified to war crimes committed in Southeast Asia, not isolated incidents but crimes committed on a day-to-day basis with the full awareness of officers at all levels of command.

. . . They told the stories at times they had personally raped, cut off ears, cut off heads, tape wires from portable telephones to human genitals and turned up the power, cut off limbs, blown up bodies, randomly shot at civilians, razed villages in fashion reminiscent of Genghis Khan, shot cattle and dogs for fun, poisoned food stocks, and generally ravaged the country side of South Vietnam in addition to the normal ravage of war, and the normal and very particular ravaging which is done by the applied bombing power of this country.

We who have come here to Washington have come here because . . . we have to speak out. . . .

. . . We are angry because we feel we have been used in the worst fashion by the administration of this country.

. . . In our opinion, and from our experience, there is nothing in South Vietnam, nothing which could happen that realistically threatens the United States of America. . . .

. . . [W]e are probably angriest about all that we were told about Vietnam and about the mystical war against communism.

We found that not only was it a civil war, an effort by a people who had for years been seeking their liberation from any colonial influence whatsoever, but also we found . . .

. . . most people didn't even know the difference between communism and democracy. They only wanted to work in rice paddies without helicopters strafing them and bombs with napalm burning their villages and tearing their country apart. . . .

. . . We rationalized destroying villages in order to save them. We saw America lose her sense of morality as she accepted very coolly a My Lai [massacre]. . . .

. . . Now we are told that the men who fought there must watch quietly while

American lives are lost so that we can exercise the incredible arrogance of Vietnamizing the Vietnamese. Each day to facilitate the process by which the United States washes her hands of Vietnam someone has to give up his life so that the United States doesn't have to admit something that the entire world already knows, so that we can't say that we have made a mistake. Someone has to die so that President Nixon won't be, and these are his words, "the first President to lose a war."

We are asking Americans to think about that because how do you ask a man to be the last man to die in Vietnam? How do [you] ask a man to be the last man to die for a mistake? . . .

. . . [W]e cannot fight communism all over the world, and I think we should have learned that lesson by now.

. . . [W]hen he [a soldier] gets back to this country he finds that he isn't really wanted, because the largest unemployment figure in the country—it varies depending on who you get it from, the VA Administration 15 percent, various other sources 22 percent. But the largest corps of unemployed in this country are veterans of this war, and of those veterans 33 percent of the unemployed are black. That means 1 out of every 10 of the Nation's unemployed is a veteran of Vietnam.

The hospitals across the country won't, or can't meet their demands. It is not a question of not trying. They don't have the appropriations [money]. . . .

. . . I understand 57 percent of all those entering the VA hospitals talk about suicide. Some 27 percent have tried, and they try because they come back to this country and they have to face what they did in Vietnam, and then they come back and find the indifference of a country that doesn't really care, that doesn't really care.

. . . We wish that a merciful God could wipe away our own memories of that service as easily as this administration has wiped their memories of us. But all that they have done and all that they can do by this denial is to make more clear than ever our own determination to undertake one last mission, to search out and destroy the last vestige of this barbarous war, to pacify our own hearts, to conquer the hate and the fear that have driven this country these last 10 years. . . .

11.6: Richard M. Nixon: Special Message to Congress about Establishing the EPA and NOAA (1970)

Historical Context

Many people in America, including those in the counterculture movements and the broader public, took an unprecedented interest in the environment in the late 1960s and early 1970s. Chemical compounds moved into the mainstream market after World War II. Companies that had developed toxic chemicals for the war effort began looking for commercial uses of these products, especially in agriculture. Government regulation was quite limited during this era, because there were very few research studies that specifically examined the health impacts of exposure to these chemicals. DDT was one of these wartime chemicals that moved into the mainstream in the 1950s.

Many Americans learned about the impacts that chemicals like DDT could have on both the environment and animal species, including humans, in Rachel Carson's 1962 book, *Silent Spring*. Shocked by what they learned, Americans from different parts of the political spectrum began calling for increased regulation and environmental protections.

Graphic Images of the United States using toxic chemical compounds such as Agent Orange and Napalm to defoliate and destroy the Vietnamese countryside also disturbed many people. Anti-war protestors expressed both humanitarian and environmental concerns over the use of such harsh chemicals.

In this broader international and domestic context, President Richard M. Nixon, a conservative Republican, worked with a Democratically controlled Congress to pass a host of environmentally focused measures, including creation of the Environmental Protection Agency (EPA) and the National Oceanic and Atmospheric Administration (NOAA) (1970); the Clean Air Act (1970); the Clean Water Act (1972); and the Endangered Species Act (1973). During this era, concern for the environment was a bipartisan issue that politicians could agree on because they believed that taking care of the environment would help protect American interests.

Vocabulary Tip: "Bipartisan" means that something (e.g., a law, policy, job appointment, and so forth) is supported by both Republicans and Democrats. "Partisan" means that only one side supports the topic under discussion.

Guiding Questions

1. Why did Nixon think it was important to create a new agency—the EPA—tasked with protecting the environment as a whole?

2. Why did Nixon want to create an agency to specifically study the oceans?

3. Make some connections to the present. In the 1970s Republicans and Democrats worked together to pass legislation designed to protect the environment. Why do you think environmental protection has become a highly partisan topic today?

Document Text

To the Congress of the United States:

. . . [I]t has become increasingly clear that we need to know more about the total environment—land, water and air. It also has become increasingly clear that only by reorganizing our Federal efforts can we develop that knowledge, and effectively ensure the protection, development and enhancement of the total environment itself.

. . . As a major step in this direction, I am transmitting today two reorganization plans: one to establish an Environmental Protection Agency, and one to establish, within the Department of Commerce, a National Oceanic and Atmospheric Administration.

ENVIRONMENTAL PROTECTION AGENCY (EPA)

Our national government today is not structured to make a coordinated attack on the pollutants which debase the air we breathe, the water we drink, and the land that grows our food. Indeed, the present governmental structure for dealing with environmental pollution often defies effective and concerted action. . . .

. . . The EPA would have the capacity to do research on important pollutants irrespective of the media in which they appear, and on the impact of these pollutants on the total environment. . . .

. . . This consolidation of pollution control authorities would help assure that we do not create new environmental problems in the process of controlling existing ones. Industries seeking to minimize the adverse impact of their activities on the environment would be assured of consistent standards covering the full range of their waste disposal problems. As the States develop and expand their own pollution control programs, they would be able to look to one agency to support their efforts with financial and technical assistance and training.

NATIONAL OCEANIC AND ATMOSPHERIC ADMINISTRATION (NOAA)

The oceans and the atmosphere are interacting parts of the total environmental system upon which we depend not only for the quality of our lives, but for life itself.

We face immediate and compelling needs for better protection of life and property from natural hazards, and for a better understanding of the total environment—an understanding which will enable us more effectively to monitor and predict its actions, and ultimately, perhaps to exercise some degree of control over them.

We also face a compelling need for exploration and development leading to the intelligent use of our marine resources. The global oceans, which constitute nearly three-fourths of the surface of our planet, are today the least-understood, the least developed, and the least-protected part of our earth. . . . We must understand the nature of these resources, and assure their development without either contaminating the marine environment or upsetting its balance.

. . . Drawing these activities together into a single agency would make possible a balanced Federal program to improve our understanding of the resources of the sea, and permit their development and use while guarding against the sort of thoughtless exploitation that in the past laid waste to so many of our precious natural assets. . . .

11.7: Unit 11 Review

The questions in the unit introduction asked you to think about how the Vietnam War, similar to the civil rights movements of the era, fractured the nation. In order to understand what happened and predict the impact it would all have on the nation, you had to bring together existing knowledge from past units and layer on new knowledge from this unit. Keep reviewing your old notes for previous units. Compare how you have been taking notes and how helpful these have been for taking quizzes and exams. At this point, you should have developed a very effective note-taking system for this course.

Let's review the unit questions that you saw at the beginning of this chapter:

> 1. How did Vietnam and counterculture/anti-war movements cause significant divisions within U.S. society?

> 2. Synthesize information. Based on what you read in the last two units (on civil rights) and this unit on Vietnam and the counterculture movement, why do many scholars describe the late 1960s and early 1970s as one of the most turbulent periods in American history?

> 3. Make a prediction. How will conservative political leaders capitalize on some citizens' frustrations with anti-war protests and the counterculture movement to shift the balance of power in favor of conservative politicians?

The American public partly elected Richard M. Nixon in 1968 because of his promise to bring troops home from Vietnam and end the conflict. While he did begin withdrawing large numbers of ground troops upon taking office, he also expanded the conflict into Laos and Cambodia. For many Americans, this created a credibility gap, as they compared what the president said he would do to what he actually did. (Nixon's credibility dipped even further in public opinion polls when news of the Watergate scandal broke in 1972.) Facing increasing public opposition at home and a congressional threat to quit funding the U.S. war effort, the president moved to bring the war to a close. In 1973 the United States, South Vietnam, and the Vietcong (the North) finally signed the Paris Peace Accords, formally ending U.S. combat. In many ways, the peace agreement was simply a way for the Americans to end involvement without admitting defeat. After the accords were signed, the North continued expanding its hold in the South, and the U.S. did not stop them. In 1975 communist forces from the North overtook the southern capital, Saigon. They unified the country as an independent, communist nation, which it remains today.

The Vietnam era brought to a close one of the most turbulent periods in American history. During the 1950s and 1960s, Americans had grappled with complex social and political issues. Civil rights activists had worked to stamp out injustice in all its forms: white supremacy, misogyny (anti-women attitudes), homophobia, poverty, and more; however, that did not mean the nation agreed on the best path forward. Similarly, the Vietnam War came to a close in the mid-1970s, but many were angry that after years of spending blood and treasure, the country essentially lost the war. As Unit 12 will demonstrate, a new conservative movement in America would give voice to this discontent with the country's direction, and it would fundamentally reshape American politics.

12.1: The Triumph of Conservatism

Overview

In Units 9, 10, and 11, you read about the upheaval sweeping the nation from the mid-1950s through the 1970s, as minorities fought for civil rights and Americans grew more entrenched in Vietnam. At the same time that the United States increased its involvement in Vietnam, larger numbers of Americans, including returning veterans, began to publicly question America's role in that conflict. Americans responded differently to the turbulence of the period.

Some Americans believed that the nation needed to continue working to end discrimination, secure equal rights for everyone, and end the war in Vietnam and poverty in America. Other Americans believed the country should stay the course in Vietnam so that the United States could leave once it had won the conflict and successfully contained communism. Many people, particularly white Americans, also believed that with the passage of the Civil Rights Act of 1964 and the Voting Rights Act of 1965, the nation had secured civil rights for African Americans and therefore the movement was over. Following Martin Luther King Jr.'s assassination in 1968, the black civil rights movement fragmented even further. The rise of Black Power, coupled with the race riots that broke out across the United States after King's assassination in April 1968, left many white Americans questioning the movement. Furthermore, the women's movement and other minority groups' struggle for civil rights also led more conservative Americans to question the direction the nation was heading. Many felt that the anti-war movement, increased gay rights activism, and the campaign to legalize abortion (which would culminate in the 1973 Supreme Court decision *Roe v. Wade*) were leading to moral decay within the nation. These individuals were looking for a political home, since they did not feel their interests aligned with the Democratic Party. Many conservative Americans began gravitating to the new brand of Republicanism that began to emerge in the 1950s and culminated in the election of Ronald Reagan as president in 1980.

In the late 1960s, then, the political winds began to shift. While the Democratic Party retained control of the legislative branch (the House of Representatives and the Senate), the Republican Party won the presidency in 1968 with the election of Richard Nixon. In order to understand Nixon's ascendancy, we need to look at the rise of the modern Republican Party, which began to take shape in the 1950s and early 1960s. Nixon's victory marked a shift in U.S. politics as the nation moved towards electing more conservative presidents, culminating in the election of Reagan. (The legislative branch, however, remained more divided between Republicans and Democrats. Control of the House of Representatives shifted back and forth between the two parties from the 1980s through the 2010s. Democrats controlled the Senate throughout the 1980s and early 1990s. Republicans then took control for most of the late-1990s through the 2010s.)

Unit Questions

1. What ideas did the new Republican Party promote, beginning in the 1960s? As you read the documents, make a list.

2. What ideas did the new Republican Party explicitly reject? As you read the documents, make a list of these. How did the Republicans (successfully) link these ideas they deemed undesirable to the Democratic Party?

3. What role did religion play in the Republican Party during this era? Identify evidence from the different readings to support your argument.

12.2: Barry Goldwater: Acceptance Speech for the Presidential Nomination of the Republican Party (1964)

Historical Context

In 1958 a staunch anti-communist organization called the John Birch Society emerged. It was a far-right organization promoting conspiracy theories (like claiming President Dwight Eisenhower and the U.S. Supreme Court were influenced by communists), but it also attracted Americans who resented some of the recent social changes occurring in the country. For example, Birchers (members of the society) attacked the Supreme Court because they disliked the Court's *Brown v. Board of Education* ruling in 1954 that racial segregation in schools was unconstitutional. While the John Birch Society always remained on the political fringe, it gained some legitimacy in the eyes of Americans when a candidate by the name of Barry Goldwater defended it during his 1964 campaign for president.

Goldwater was a senator from Arizona who believed in principles promoted by President Dwight Eisenhower in the 1950s, and in his vision of "Modern Republicanism," which included limited government, balancing the budget, and cutting government spending, even on national defense. Goldwater, however, believed that Eisenhower did not go far enough in cutting public expenditures. Goldwater became the voice of the new conservative movement in America. He was tolerant in his personal relationships and even joined one of the leading civil rights organizations, the National Association for the Advancement of Colored People (NAACP). As a politician, however, he was a political reactionary. In 1964 Goldwater joined southerners, and a few other senators around the nation, in voting against the Civil Rights Act. His firm belief in limited government meant that he did not support federal intervention in social policies, like civil rights legislation. He also interpreted "freedom" in economic terms. For example, he rejected the idea of a federal income tax as an infringement on personal liberty. He was also a staunch anti-communist who refused to disavow the extremist John Birch Society.

Goldwater's positions appealed to upper-middle-class conservatives, who successfully persuaded him to run for president in 1964 against incumbent Democrat Lyndon B. Johnson. Goldwater refused to run a campaign based explicitly on race, but his ideological positions created space for white supremacy to exist in the new party. By advocating against federal intervention in civil rights issues, Goldwater gave tacit permission for white supremacy and discrimination to continue. Many white southerners recognized this and threw their support behind Goldwater, setting the nation up for a regional and racial political divide. The excerpt below from his acceptance speech at the 1964 Republican National Convention highlights the ideological divide growing between Democrats and Republicans in the 1960s.

197

1. What does Goldwater see as the greatest threat to America from overseas? Make a list of all of the evidence he provides in the excerpt to support this claim.

2. According to Goldwater, how had Democrats failed America? Use the reading to identify specific examples. (Also use this question to help you answer the next one by identifying what policies and ideas he thought the Republican Party must pursue.)

3. What were the main principles the Republican Party stood for in 1964, according to Goldwater? Make a list of each item or idea he mentions, and in your own words explain what each means.

Document Text

. . . I accept your nomination with a deep sense of humility. . . .

. . . The good Lord raised this mighty Republic to be a home for the brave and to flourish as the land of the free—not to stagnate in the swampland of collectivism, not to cringe before the bullying of communism.

. . . During four futile years, the administration which we shall replace has . . . talked the words of freedom, but it has failed. . . .

Now, failures cement the wall of shame in Berlin. Failures blot the sands of shame at the Bay of Pigs. Failures mark the slow death of freedom in Laos. Failures infest the jungles of Vietnam. And failures haunt the houses of our once great alliances and undermine the greatest bulwark ever erected by free nations—the NATO community. . . .

. . . Tonight, there is violence in our streets, corruption in our highest offices, aimlessness amongst our youth, anxiety among our elders, and there's a virtual despair among the many who look beyond material success for the inner meaning of their lives. . . .

. . . Security from domestic violence, no less than from foreign aggression, is the most elementary and fundamental purpose of any government. . . .

History shows us—it demonstrates that . . . nothing prepares the way for tyranny more than the failure of public officials to keep the streets safe from bullies and marauders.

. . . It has been during Democratic years that we have weakly stumbled into conflict. . . .

Yesterday, it was Korea. Tonight, it is Vietnam. Make no bones of this. Don't try to sweep this under the rug. We are at war in Vietnam. And yet the President . . . refuses to say, mind you, whether or not the objective over there is victory. And his Secretary of Defense continues to mislead and misinform the American people. . . .

. . . And during Republican years, this again will be a nation of men and women . . . where all who can will be self-reliant. . . .

We Republicans seek a government that attends to its inherent responsibilities of maintaining a stable monetary and fiscal climate, encouraging a free and a competitive economy and enforcing law and order. . . . we Republicans define government's role where needed at many, many levels—preferably, though, the one closest to the people involved.

Our towns and our cities, then our counties, then our states, then our regional compacts—and only then, the national government. That . . . is the ladder of liberty, built by decentralized power. On it also we must have balance between the branches of government at every level.

. . . This Republican Party is a Party for free men, not for blind followers, and not for conformists.

. . . Today . . . the task of preserving and enlarging freedom at home and of safeguarding it from the forces of tyranny abroad is great enough to challenge all our resources and to require all our strength.

. . . I would remind you that extremism in the defense of liberty is no vice. . . .

And let me remind you also that moderation in the pursuit of justice is no virtue. . . .

12.3: Ronald Reagan: "A Time for Choosing" (1964)

Historical Context

In 1947, when the House Committee on Un-American Activities (HUAC) began investigating communist activity in Hollywood, Ronald Reagan was president of the Screen Actors Guild. He agreed to testify before Congress and proved to be a friendly witness. As time progressed, Reagan shifted further to the political right and began supporting the blacklisting of actors accused of being communists. As the Cold War progressed throughout the 1950s and 1960s, Reagan's anti-communist attitude intensified. In 1962 he changed his party affiliation from Democrat to Republican, and in 1964 he joined Republican presidential candidate Barry Goldwater's campaign. Given Reagan's charisma and exceptional public speaking abilities, he was asked by the campaign to start stumping (traveling around giving political speeches) on behalf of Goldwater. Although Goldwater's 1964 bid for the presidency failed, involvement in the campaign helped launch Reagan's own political career. The following speech is one he gave on behalf of Goldwater in 1964.

Guiding Questions

1. In this speech Reagan repudiates the federal government that President Franklin D. Roosevelt established during the Great Depression and that continued to grow in the 1960s. Specifically, Reagan argues against having a strong central government and welfare. Pick one or two specific examples that Reagan talks about and use them to explain his perspective on American politics. Based on what you know, how did this differ from Democrats' view of government?

2. According to Reagan, what were the major challenges facing the country, including those undermining American freedom, in 1964? Make a list and in your own words explain why Reagan believes each of these issues is causing problems for the nation.

3. The most famous line from this speech is when Reagan tells the audience, "You and I have a rendezvous with destiny." What did he mean when he said this? Identify the major issues Reagan addresses in the speech and explain why he thinks it is Americans' destiny to fight these challenges head-on.

. . . I believe that the issues confronting us cross party lines. Now, one side in this campaign has been telling us that the issues of this election are the maintenance of peace and prosperity. . . .

. . . I have an uncomfortable feeling that this prosperity isn't something on which we can base our hopes for the future. No nation in history has ever survived a tax burden that reached a third of its national income. . . . our government continues to spend 17 million dollars a day more than the government takes in. We haven't balanced our budget 28 out of the last 34 years. . . .

. . . "The full power of centralized government"—this was the very thing the Founding Fathers sought to minimize. . . . A government can't control the economy without controlling people. And they knew when a government sets out to do that, it must use force and coercion to achieve its purpose.

. . . We have so many people who can't see a fat man standing beside a thin one without coming to the conclusion the fat man got that way by taking advantage of the thin one. So they're going to solve all the problems of human misery through government and government planning. Well, now, if government planning and welfare had the answer—and they've had almost 30 years of it—shouldn't we expect government to read the score to us once in a while? Shouldn't they be telling us about the decline each year in the number of people needing help? The reduction in the need for public housing? . . .

. . . Those who would trade our freedom for the soup kitchen of the welfare state have told us they have a utopian solution of peace without victory. . . . they say if we'll only avoid any direct confrontation with the enemy, he'll forget his evil ways and learn to love us. All who oppose them are indicted as warmongers. They say we offer simple answers to complex problems. Well, perhaps there is a simple answer . . . If you and I have the courage to tell our elected officials that we want our national policy based on what we know in our hearts is morally right.

We cannot buy our security, our freedom from the threat of the bomb, by committing an immorality so great as saying to a billion human beings now enslaved behind the Iron Curtain, "Give up your dreams of freedom because to save our own skins, we're willing to make a deal with your slave masters." . . .

. . . You and I have the courage to say to our enemies, "There is a price we will not pay." "There is a point beyond which they must not advance." And this—this is the meaning in the phrase of Barry Goldwater's "peace through strength." . . .

You and I have a rendezvous with destiny.

We'll preserve for our children this, the last best hope of man on earth, or we'll sentence them to take the last step into a thousand years of darkness.

12.4: Richard M. Nixon: "Silent Majority" Speech (1969)

Historical Context

Although Barry Goldwater lost the 1964 election by a landslide to incumbent President Lyndon B. Johnson, many of the ideas that Goldwater promoted gained traction in the years that followed. Republicans worked on refining their messaging, and by the late 1960s they had crafted a platform that appealed to many Americans, especially white working- and middle-class Americans.

The Democratic Party struggled in the late 1960s and 1970s. Johnson, deeply associated with the Vietnam War, had largely lost the support of the American electorate and decided not to run for a second term in the 1968 presidential election. This was an unusual move by an incumbent president who had won the preceding election by a landslide. Shortly after Johnson's announcement, civil rights icon Martin Luther King Jr. was slain by an assassin's bullet, and riots broke out in cities around the United States. Black residents were protesting not only King's assassination but also expressing deep frustration with the state of affairs in 1968. Many African Americans were starting to believe that only violent resistance could truly end white supremacy, bigotry, and discrimination in America. Many black urbanites were also frustrated that the civil rights movement had done little to address persistent economic inequality, and they felt that with King's death, this was even less likely to happen. The 1968 riots further rocked the Democratic Party, then, since white Americans expressed mixed reactions. Many white people began to feel less sympathetic to the interests of black Americans. This sentiment began after the passage of the 1964 Civil Rights Act and the 1965 Voting Rights Act, since many white Americans felt the country had sufficiently addressed black Americans' needs. The rise of Black Power and the increased militancy in the civil rights movement alienated more moderate whites. By the time the riots broke out in 1968, white Americans were more concerned about the war and their own interests than about systemic inequality.

As the nation, and specifically the Democratic Party, grappled with intense anti-war protests, Johnson's decision not to run again, King's assassination, and the subsequent riots, it faced another shocking event only a few months later. In June 1968, following a campaign event in California, an assassin murdered Robert "Bobby" Kennedy, the leading Democratic presidential candidate and the younger brother of John F. Kennedy. The political atmosphere grew more violent in August of that year, when the Democratic National Convention met in the city of Chicago to nominate Hubert Humphrey as their candidate. Demonstrators from various leftist organizations converged on the city to express their discontent, and a riot broke out as protestors clashed with police.

Many white Americans who sat more towards the political middle (somewhere between the Republican and Democratic Parties) increasingly saw civil rights activists, rioters, anti-war protesters, feminists, hippies, and other young people engaged in the counterculture movement as un-American, causing a moral decay in the country, or threatening to undermine their personal peace and prosperity. The turbulent 1960s, then, created a climate ripe for political change.

Nixon won the presidential election with a solid majority in the Electoral College, though the popular vote was much closer. (Southern white supremacist George Wallace, running as an independent candidate, carried the Deep South. Had Wallace not run, Nixon would have won by an even greater majority, as demonstrated in the 1972 election, since southern white voters were shifting to the Republican Party.) Nixon had been elected by promoting law and order, limited government, and on his campaign promise to bring the Vietnam War to a close.

Law and order and limited government are two core Republican principles that can be interpreted and applied in different ways at different points in time. In the late 1960s these principles were sometimes used as racially coded language signaling that a politician would not support federal civil rights initiatives. Rather, such politicians vowed to enforce law and order, which meant preventing civil rights activism through protests and rallies. "Limited government," in the traditional sense, simply meant less federal government involvement in people's lives. Some politicians, however, used it to signal to politicians at the state and local levels that, if elected, they would not use the power of the federal government to actively enforce civil rights legislation. Rather, they would let states pursue their own preferred course of action. Many Americans responded positively to Nixon's goals of ending the war. Nixon, however, wanted to make sure the United States exited the war with honor. To accomplish this, he explicitly asked for the American public's on-going support. The following excerpts are from a televised address Nixon gave to the American public after nearly a year as president.

Guiding Questions

1. Why did some people advocate an immediate withdrawal of U.S. troops from Vietnam? Why did Nixon refuse to simply withdraw American troops from the country? List and explain, in your own words, each of the reasons Nixon provides against immediate withdrawal.

2. What was Nixon's proposed plan for bringing the Vietnam conflict to an end? How did he try to sell this plan to the American people in this televised address?

3. At the end of the speech, Nixon appeals to America's "silent majority." Who made up the silent majority, and what kind of support does he want from these people? If you are not sure, make an educated guess, based on what you know about American society and politics in the late 1960s.

Good evening, my fellow Americans:

I believe that one of the reasons for the deep division about Vietnam is that many Americans have lost confidence in what their Government has told them about our policy. The American people cannot and should not be asked to support a policy which involves the overriding issues of war and peace unless they know the truth about that policy. . . .

. . . [L]et me begin by describing the situation I found when I was inaugurated on January 20.

—The war had been going on for 4 years.

—31,000 Americans had been killed in action.

—The training program for the South Vietnamese was behind schedule.

—540,000 Americans were in Vietnam with no plans to reduce the number.

—No progress had been made at the negotiations in Paris and the United States had not put forth a comprehensive peace proposal.

—The war was causing deep division at home and criticism from many of our friends as well as our enemies abroad.

In view of these circumstances there were some who urged that I end the war at once by ordering the immediate withdrawal of all American forces.

From a political standpoint this would have been a popular and easy course to follow. I could blame the defeat . . . on him [former President Lyndon B. Johnson] and come out as a peacemaker. . . .

But I had a greater obligation than to think only of the years of my administration and of the next election. I had to think of the effect of my decision on the next generation and on the future of peace and freedom in America and in the world.

. . . The great question is: How can we win America's peace?

. . . For the South Vietnamese, our precipitate withdrawal would inevitably allow the Communists to repeat the massacres which followed their takeover in the North 15 years before. . . .

. . . For the United States, this first defeat in our Nation's history would result in a collapse of confidence in American leadership, not only in Asia but throughout the world. . . .

. . . I rejected the recommendation that I should end the war by immediately withdrawing all of our forces. I chose instead to change American policy on both the negotiating front and battlefront. . . .

. . . In the previous administration, we Americanized the war in Vietnam. In this administration, we are Vietnamizing the search for peace.

. . . We have adopted a plan . . . for the complete withdrawal of all U.S. combat ground forces, and their replacement by South Vietnamese forces on an orderly scheduled timetable. . . . As South Vietnamese forces become stronger, the rate of American withdrawal can become greater. . . .

. . . And so tonight—to you, the great silent majority of my fellow Americans—I ask for your support.

I pledged in my campaign for the Presidency to end the war in a way that we could win the peace. I have initiated a plan of action which will enable me to keep that pledge.

. . .

12.5: Jerry Falwell: *Listen America* (1980)

Historical Context

In the late 1970s Christian evangelists like Pat Robertson and Jim Bakker took their message to the airwaves. They began the televangelist movement, and millions of Americans tuned in. Jerry Falwell, a Southern Baptist pastor, televangelist, and conservative activist, soon found his niche in Lynchburg, Virginia. In addition to his TV programing, Falwell founded Liberty University in 1971 and the Moral Majority in 1979.

Falwell recognized that after a decade of turbulent social and political upheaval, many Americans were looking for a spiritual and political home. In the late 1970s the federal government sought to end public support through tax exemptions for "Christian academies," many of which were started in the South in response the Supreme Court's requirement that public schools desegregate in *Brown v. Board of Education* in 1954. Falwell and others saw this as an attack on religion and people of faith. Concerned about the direction of the country, Falwell formed the Moral Majority. The Moral Majority was a political lobbying group, which helped to re-brand the new conservative Republican movement. Falwell's message of traditional religion, values, and conservative politics appealed to millions of evangelicals across the nation. Through the Moral Majority and his televangelism, Falwell helped rally evangelical support behind conservative politicians. Most notably, evangelicals overwhelmingly supported Ronald Reagan in the 1980 presidential election.

Guiding Questions

1. Falwell published the book *Listen America* in 1980 just after founding the Moral Majority. In this excerpt, what does Falwell see as the major problems facing America, and who is to blame? Read the first paragraph carefully. Identify and explain the various issues he addresses.

2. What does Falwell believe are the solutions to America's problems? Paraphrase Falwell's message in your own words.

3. How does Falwell successfully intertwine religion and politics in his messaging? Find specific examples.

We must reverse the trend America finds herself in today. Young people between the ages of twenty-five and forty have been born and reared in a different world than Americans of years past. The television set has been their primary baby-sitter. From the television set they have learned situation ethics and immorality—they have learned a loss of respect for human life. They have learned to disrespect the family as God has established it. They have been educated in a public-school system that is permeated with secular humanism. They have been taught that the Bible is just another book of literature. They have been taught that there are no absolutes in our world today. They have been introduced to the drug culture. They have been reared by the family and the public school in a society that is greatly void of discipline and character-building. These same young people have been reared under the influence of a government that has taught them socialism and welfarism. They have been taught to believe that the world owes them a living whether they work or not.

I believe that America was built on integrity, on faith in God, and on hard work. . . . We now have second-and third-generation welfare recipients. Welfare is not always wrong. There are those who do need welfare, but we have reared a generation that understands neither the dignity nor the importance of work.

. . . I believe that Americans want to see this country come back to basics, back to values, back to biblical morality, back to sensibility, and back to patriotism. Americans are looking for leadership and guidance. . . . But Americans have been lax in voting in and out of office the right and the wrong people.

. . . Through the ballot box Americans must provide for strong moral leadership at every level. . . .

It is now time to take a stand on certain moral issues, and we can only stand if we have leaders. We must stand against the Equal Rights Amendment, the feminist revolution, and the homosexual revolution. . . .

. . . The hope of reversing the trends of decay in our republic now lies with the Christian public in America. We cannot expect help from the liberals. They certainly are not going to call our nation back to righteousness and neither are the pornographers, the smut peddlers, and those who are corrupting our youth. Moral Americans must be willing to put their reputations, their fortunes, and their very lives on the line for this great nation of ours. . . .

Americans must no longer linger in ignorance and apathy. . . . I have listened to God's admonitions and His direction—the only hopes of saving America.

12.6: Ronald Reagan: First Inaugural Address (1981)

Historical Context

Ronald Reagan began his political career as a spokesman for Barry Goldwater's campaign in 1964. This experience propelled Reagan to the forefront of California's Republican Party, and in 1966 he ran for governor and won. Reagan served as governor of California from 1967 to 1975. He challenged incumbent President Gerald Ford in the 1976 Republican primary and lost. President Ford lost the 1976 election to Democrat Jimmy Carter, largely because Americans were disgusted with the Nixon-Ford Administration following the Watergate scandal and Nixon's resignation. President Carter, however, only served one term. He failed to be reelected due to a struggling economy, a massive energy (oil-gasoline) shortage, and the Iran Hostage Crisis. Reagan ran for president in 1980 and won the electoral college by a landslide. The popular vote was closer, but Reagan still carried it by a wide margin.

One of the reasons Reagan won the presidency in 1980 was because he continued a process that had begun under Nixon—he peeled away many moderate middle- and working-class Democrats, getting them to vote Republican. Eventually, this group of voters would come to be known as Reagan Democrats. As noted earlier, by 1968, when Nixon won the presidential election, the Democratic Party was struggling at a national level. This continued in the 1970s, as the 1930s New Deal Coalition (unionized labor, African Americans, and Jews and Catholics of Eastern European origin) fragmented. As you'll read about in the next unit, the nation was undergoing profound economic and demographic changes in the 1970s and 1980s. These changes also reshaped American politics. Many middle- and working-class white Americans throughout the country believed the Democratic Party was only interested in raising taxes, handing out welfare, and representing minority interests. Reagan's conservative message of God, country, anti-communism, morality, family, low taxes, and economic prosperity resonated with voters. The following excerpts are from Reagan's first inaugural address.

Guiding Questions

1. What, according to Reagan, are the challenges facing the nation in 1981? Make a three-column chart in your notes. As you read through the speech, fill in the left and middle columns. In the left column, make a list of the various issues you see. In the middle column, explain each issue in your own words.

2. What are the Republican solutions to the issues you identified? Explain these solutions in your own words in the third column of your chart.

3. What is the tone of this speech? What is the message Reagan is trying to send to the American people and the world? Identify specific words or phrases that illustrate what you mean.

Document Text

. . . These United States are confronted with an economic affliction of great proportions. We suffer from the longest and one of the worst sustained inflations in our national history. It distorts our economic decisions, penalizes thrift, and crushes the struggling young and the fixed-income elderly alike. It threatens to shatter the lives of millions of our people.

Idle industries have cast workers into unemployment, human misery, and personal indignity. Those who do work are denied a fair return for their labor by a tax system which penalizes successful achievement and keeps us from maintaining full productivity.

But great as our tax burden is, it has not kept pace with public spending. For decades we have piled deficit upon deficit, mortgaging our future and our children's future for the temporary convenience of the present. To continue this long trend is to guarantee tremendous social, cultural, political, and economic upheavals. . . .

. . . In this present crisis, government is not the solution to our problem; government is the problem. .. . .

. . . It is my intention to curb the size and influence of the Federal establishment and to demand recognition of the distinction between the powers granted to the Federal Government and those reserved to the States or to the people. . . .

It's not my intention to do away with government. It is rather to make it work—work with us, not over us; to stand by our side, not ride on our back. Government can and must provide opportunity, not smother it; foster productivity, not stifle it.

It is no coincidence that our present troubles parallel and are proportionate to the intervention and intrusion in our lives that result from unnecessary and excessive growth of government. . . .

. . . In the days ahead I will propose removing the roadblocks that have slowed our economy and reduced productivity. . . .

As we renew ourselves here in our own land, we will be seen as having greater strength throughout the world. We will again be the exemplar of freedom and a beacon of hope for those who do not now have freedom.

To those neighbors and allies who share our freedom, we will strengthen our historic ties and assure them of our support and firm commitment. . . .

As for the enemies of freedom, those who are potential adversaries, they will be reminded that peace is the highest aspiration of the American people. We will negotiate for it, sacrifice for it; we will not surrender for it, now or ever.

. . . Above all, we must realize that no arsenal or no weapon in the arsenals of the world is so formidable as the will and moral courage of free men and women. It is a weapon our adversaries in today's world do not have. It is a weapon that we as Americans do have. . . .

. . . The crisis we are facing today . . . does require . . . our best effort and . . . that together with God's help we can and will resolve the problems which now confront us.

12.7: Unit 12 Review

The Unit Questions asked you to consider the following as you read:

1. What ideas did the new Republican Party promote, beginning in the 1960s? As you read the documents, make a list.

2. What ideas did the new Republican Party explicitly reject? As you read the documents, make a list of these. How did the Republicans (successfully) link these ideas they deemed undesirable to the Democratic Party?

3. What role did religion play in the emerging Republican Party during this era? Identify evidence from the different readings to support your argument.

After reading the unit, it should be clear that Republicans successfully framed their conservative economic and political agenda as a moral responsibility, and they often used religion to reinforce that idea. Many American voters, usually white working- and middle-class people, responded positively to the new call for fiscal and social conservatism and limited government. Ronald Reagan won a second term in office in 1984, in a landslide victory, but he knew he needed to pursue bipartisan policies, since Democrats controlled the House of Representatives. Reagan passed immigration legislation that provided a path to citizenship for millions of previously undocumented immigrants, he reformed the tax code, and he signed an arms-control treaty with the Soviet Union.

One of Reagan's most significant achievements was ushering in the end of the Cold War. This massive political change was possible due in large part to Reagan's Russian counterpart, Soviet President Mikhail Gorbachev. Gorbachev realized that the existing Soviet system was unsustainable, so he instituted a series of reforms aimed at bolstering and reinventing the Soviet Union as a more prosperous and productive nation. Two of the most important elements were *glasnost* and *perestroika*. Glasnost encouraged an opening of Russian society by reducing censorship, eliminating the secret police, and allowing non-communist political parties to participate in elections. Perestroika was aimed at restructuring the Soviet economy. The government would continue to direct the economy, but private industries would produce goods. The reforms were slow to yield results, and Soviet citizens often suffered shortages of food and consumer goods. Many people also resented the wealth that Communist Party leaders and industrial elites gained during this transition. In the end, many of the reforms unintentionally moved the Soviet Union towards collapse. Gorbachev also recognized that the arms race was costing an exorbitant amount of money, so he sought to reduce tensions with the West (Western Europe, the United States, and other Western-style democracies). Discontent spread within the Soviet Union, and in 1989 Poland revolted and the Berlin Wall fell in East Germany, becoming one of the

most iconic images of the end of the Cold War. By 1991 the Soviet Union had dissolved, bringing the Cold War to a close.

As we'll see in the next unit, some of the so-called Reagan Democrats who had helped
propel the Republican Party to victory in the 1980s found that the economic policies
of the Reagan Administration did little to boost their wealth or status, so they began
looking for alternatives. Deindustrialization and globalization created challenges
and opportunities in the 1970s, 1980s, and 1990s and further reshaped the American
economy and politics.

13.1: Deindustrialization and the Booming Nineties

Overview

America thrived economically in the latter half of the twentieth century, thanks in large part to its emergence as a world power after World War II. Consumerism boomed and legislation like the GI Bill helped many Americans move into the middle class. In industrial cities throughout the Northeast and Midwest, though, economies were beginning to change in profound ways.

Factories began relocating first to northern suburbs, and then in the subsequent years to the American South. This marked the beginning of "deindustrialization," or a decline of economic production. Extremely high inflation and two oil crises further damaged the economy in the 1970s. America also began to lose good-paying, blue-collar jobs to foreign countries.

These economic changes had profound social and political impacts. Throughout the 1970s and 1980s many (white) northerners relocated to the South and West looking for new job opportunities, leaving behind more poor people and people of color. Northern cities began to decline as deindustrialization took hold, and working-class and ethnic white voters often blamed minority populations living in those areas for urban decay, crime, and poverty. Union membership also declined nationally because most southern and western states had "right to work" laws that made unionization difficult. These white working- and middle-class Democrats increasingly gravitated to the new conservative Republican Party. Moderate, socially conservative, and white supremacist Democrats in the South also shifted to the Republican Party after passage of the Voting Rights Act of 1965, which enfranchised millions of African Americans. As you learned in the last unit, Ronald Reagan succeeded in the 1980s by tapping into predominantly white voters' discontent over issues like the size and role of government, reproductive health, religion, and economics.

Reagan offered voters a new economic theory on taxation that broke with past policies. He argued that cutting taxes for wealthier people and businesses would lead to reinvestment and economic growth among the rest of the nation. For many Americans, this approach did not pan out. The poorest Americans slipped further into poverty, the wealthiest Americans got wealthier, and most people in the middle stayed about the same. The economy changed dramatically in the 1990s, however, with the widespread adoption of computers and the advent of the commercial internet. This new global economy created challenges and opportunities for workers and very different political ideas about how best to help people pursue the American dream.

Reagan's vice president, George H.W. Bush, ran for president in 1988 and won but served only one term. He lost his reelection campaign to Bill Clinton in 1992. This unit

214

examines the political and economic environment from deindustrialization in the 1980s to the "Booming Nineties," as they are sometimes referred.

Unit Questions

1. What contributed to deindustrialization and economic hardship in places like Pittsburgh, Detroit, and Milwaukee—cities once known for their significant industrial production? What impact did deindustrialization have on America in general? Make a flowchart or a concept map of the events and their consequences.

2. What created opportunities for a Democrat like Bill Clinton to win the White House in the 1990s, but at the same time for Republicans to win, and then retain, control of Congress?

3. How did the U.S. and global economy change significantly in the 1990s and beyond, and how did this create new challenges and opportunities for the United States? Make a list of the most significant changes in the United States and other parts of the world.

13.2: Bill Tolan: "In Desperate 1983, There Was Nowhere for Pittsburgh's Economy to Go but Up: A Tide of Change" (2012)

Historical Context

Pittsburgh was similar to many other northeastern and midwestern industrial cities in the 1950s through the 1980s. Communities that once were part of America's manufacturing heartland became known as the nation's "Rust Belt." These manufacturing centers boomed during World War II when demand for their products was high, but in the post-war period the economic climate began to change. This document is an article that was published in 2012 in the *Pittsburgh Post-Gazette* about a story published thirty years prior. In your notes, make a timeline of at least the three dates (1982, 2012, and now) to put this into better historical context. Always annotate your timelines with important events that happened during that time. As the document reveals, many cities were hard hit and were generally unprepared to deal with those changes and their consequences.

Guiding Questions

1. What were some of the causes of deindustrialization? Asked another way, what factors affected manufacturing companies in places like Pittsburgh?

2. What impact did deindustrialization have on Pittsburgh and the surrounding areas? Use specific evidence from the reading to support your claims.

3. Make a connection to the present. What were some of the long-term consequences of deindustrialization? How could that history continue to impact those communities today?

Document Text

December 23, 2012

Town by town, factory by factory, job by job. A tide of change.

—A story from the Dec. 5, 1982 *Pittsburgh Press*, about the death of the century-old foundation of Pittsburgh's regional economy.

He was just 29, and already a 10-year veteran of the mills and the mines. That's what rugged young men living in this stretch of steel country did in those days. They left high school, got a job at the mill, married, fathered two kids and bought a house before the age of 30.

His name was Denny Bambino. . . .

. . . Mr. Bambino had seen the writing on the wall many times over, in the form of transfers and layoff notices. . . .

. . . By December 1982, he was perpetually unemployed, his wife was gone, his home was up for sale, and he'd moved back in with his parents. His unemployment benefits ran out the week before Christmas. . . .

It couldn't get any worse. But it did, for one more month.

In January 1983, the regional economy officially—that is, numerically—bottomed out. Unemployment in Allegheny County hit 13.9 percent, a rosy figure compared to the rest of the Pittsburgh metropolitan statistical area, where the adjusted unemployment rate hit an astonishing 17.1 percent (unadjusted, the number was actually higher, 18.2 percent). . . . Regionally, the number of unemployed hit 212,000.

In Armstrong County . . . unemployment peaked at 19.5 percent. In industrialized Beaver County, the rate hit 27.1 percent in January 1983—greater than the peak U.S. unemployment rate during the Great Depression. In Johnstown's Cambria County, the rate topped 23 percent. . . .

. . . This was a region hanging on by its fingernails.

. . . The city could not have realized it in the early 1970s, not as the region was still employing close to 300,000 in manufacturing trades. Few were that prescient—and those few who saw what was coming were ignored.

But Jimmy Carter's malaise became Ronald Reagan's recession. As 1981 bled into a gory 1982, the headlines spoke to a permanent, shattering change to the regional economy. . . .

. . . [F]or the region, January 1983 stands alone as the nadir.

. . . So much was lost—not just jobs, but people. Pittsburgh had been shrinking since the 1950s, but between 1970 and 1990, the city proper lost a full 30 percent of its population. People left to find work. . . .

. . . The unemployment rate came down after January 1983 . . . not because people were returning to work here but because the young and able-bodied left the region, and thus its labor force. . . .

. . . In an eight-year span, from 1979 to 1987, the Pittsburgh region lost 133,000 manufacturing jobs. Some of those jobs vanished into obsolescence because new technologies led to improved productivity, and many more drifted overseas and into non-union mini-mills.

. . . Deindustrialization was happening across the country, but in few places were the forces of globalization felt so acutely—and so abruptly—as in Pittsburgh, 1982 and 1983. . . .

13.3: George H.W. Bush: "Read My Lips" Speech (1988)

Historical Context

George Herbert Walker Bush had a long and prestigious career in public service. He served in World War II, became a U.S. Congressman for the state of Texas, worked as the U.S. Ambassador to the United Nations, was an envoy to China, and directed the CIA. Bush ran against Ronald Reagan in the Republican Party primary for the 1980 election and lost. He served as Reagan's vice president for the full eight years, and then ran for president in the 1988 election. The following text is from Bush's speech at the Republican Presidential Convention. Bush won the election in 1988 but then lost to Bill Clinton in 1992.

Bush was a pragmatic politician. He was more moderate than his predecessor, President Reagan, and knew that sometimes politicians had to compromise in order to best serve the needs of the country. Bush fiercely defended his political ideas but was largely regarded as a kind, dignified, and thoughtful man by friends and political opponents alike. During the 1988 campaign, however, Bush used some language that would later cause him problems both in terms of his political career and his legacy. He suffered politically when he promised in this speech not to raise taxes and later reversed course as president. Many political pundits and scholars argued this led to his defeat in the 1992 presidential election. Other language that damaged his legacy, particularly among minority voters, was his talk about being tough on crime.

In this speech, you'll see Bush say it is a "scandal to give a weekend furlough to a hardened first degree killer." He was referencing a man by the name of Willie Horton, who had been incarcerated in a Massachusetts prison and was given several weekend passes to leave the prison. This type of program was common throughout the fifty states as prisons looked for ways to rehabilitate prisoners. Horton became notorious because while on a furlough, he committed another brutal crime. An outside organization created a campaign advertisement highlighting Horton and emphasizing Bush's "tough on crime" position and his opponent, Michael Dukakis's "weaker" stance (since Dukakis was the governor of Massachusetts, where Horton was imprisoned.) The advertisement did not air long because many people expressed deep concerns that it had severe racial overtones. Scholars are still debating the role race played in the advertisement and its impact on voters, but most agree that the use of racially coded language and the "tough on crime" stance it promoted both had lasting impacts on America.

Guiding Questions

1. What did Bush see as the successes of the Reagan administration? What were the areas that needed attention and improvement according to Bush? Make a two-column chart identifying "successes" on the left and "needs improvement" on the right.

2. Read the text carefully. What are the values, ideas, and actions Bush believes the country must embrace in order to stay strong and secure?

3. At the end of the speech, Bush says "Read my lips: no new taxes." Make a prediction. Why do you think this line became one of the most famous, and politically damaging, lines of the speech for President Bush?

Document Text

. . . I accept your nomination for President. . . .

. . . Eight years ago I stood here with Ronald Reagan. . . . Eight years later look at what the American people have produced: the highest level of economic growth in our entire history—and the lowest level of world tensions in more than fifty years. . . .

. . . But let's be frank. Things aren't perfect in this country. There are people who haven't tasted the fruits of the expansion. I've talked to farmers about the bills they can't pay. I've been to the factories that feel the strain of change. I've seen the urban children who play amidst the shattered glass and shattered lives. And there are the homeless. . . . We have to help them.

. . . I want [economic] growth that stays, that broadens, and that touches, finally, all Americans. . . .

. . . We will do it—by maintaining our commitment to free and fair trade, by keeping government spending down, and by keeping taxes down. . . .

. . . I do not hate government. A government that remembers that the people are its master is a good and needed thing.

I respect old fashioned common sense. . . .

For instance:

Should public school teachers be required to lead our children in the pledge of allegiance? . . . I say yes.

Should society be allowed to impose the death penalty on those who commit crimes of extraordinary cruelty and violence? . . . I say yes.

Should our children have the right to say a voluntary prayer, or even observe a moment of silence in the schools? . . . I say yes.

Should free men and women have the right to own a gun to protect their home? . . . I say yes.

Is it right to believe in the sanctity of life and protect the lives of innocent children? I say yes. We must change from abortion—to adoption. . . .

. . . [I]t is a scandal to give a weekend furlough to a hardened first degree killer who hasn't even served enough time to be eligible for parole. . . .

I'm the one who won't raise taxes. . . . The Congress will push me to raise taxes, and I'll say no, and they'll push, and I'll say no, and they'll push again, and I'll say to them, "Read my lips: no new taxes."

Let me tell you more about the mission. . . .

. . . I want a drug-free America. . . .

. . . I am going to do whatever it takes to make sure the disabled are included in the mainstream. . . .

I am going to stop ocean dumping. . . . And we must clean the air.

. . . In foreign affairs I will . . . move toward further cuts in the strategic and conventional arsenals of both the United States and the Soviet Union. I will modernize and preserve our technological edge. I will ban chemical and biological weapons from the face of the earth. . . .

. . . We've come far, but I think we need a new harmony among the races in our country. . . . we've got to leave the tired old baggage of bigotry behind. . . .

. . . I will keep America moving forward, always forward—for a better America, for an endless enduring dream and a thousand points of light. . . .

221

13.4: Bill Clinton: Remarks on Signing the North American Free Trade Agreement (1993)

Historical Context

During the 1988 presidential campaign, the Soviet Union was on the verge of collapsing and the Cold War was coming to an end. Although President George H.W. Bush was less charismatic than Ronald Reagan, many people (both at home and abroad) who worked with him liked him because he was a pragmatist. He recognized the need for political compromise and building political coalitions. Bush was also seen as very qualified leader in 1988 because of his significant foreign policy experience. Many Americans and foreign leaders thought Bush would provide a steady hand to help bring peace to the world in the post-Cold War period. In general Bush did this well. The Cold War ended, and foreign affairs remained relatively quiet. The United States did fight one war—the First Gulf War—in which it formed a broad coalition to push Saddam Hussein and his Iraqi forces out of Kuwait. The war ended, and peace was restored to the area relatively quickly. The region was largely stable, as were U.S. interests around the world. Domestically, however, the United States entered a recession around the same time. This did not bode well for President Bush.

With a stable world, Bush's foreign policy expertise seemed less relevant to American voters. They wanted a president who would shore up the U.S. economy. President Bush vowed in 1988, "Read my lips: no new taxes." But in 1990 he violated that pledge and worked with Democrats, who controlled both houses of Congress, to pass a funding bill. It generally raised taxes on the wealthiest Americans and cut spending on government programs. Members of Bush's conservative base were angry, and even his success in the Gulf War did not heal the party. As a result, Bill Clinton (Democrat) won the 1992 presidential election against the incumbent Bush (Republican). Clinton appealed to many American voters, especially "Reagan Democrats" (white, suburban, working-class Americans who had voted for Ronald Reagan.) Clinton grew up in poverty and worked to put himself through school. He was young, charismatic, and spoke vaguely about having an economic plan. Clinton, a Democratic governor of Arkansas, also garnered strong support among African Americans.

Shortly after taking office, Clinton signed into law the North American Free Trade Agreement (NAFTA), which had been negotiated by outgoing President Bush. (Congress was held by Democrats at the time.) The following text is from the speech he gave when signing NAFTA into law.

Guiding Questions

1. What is a "free trade" law supposed to accomplish? Read the text carefully and identify how NAFTA creates "free trade." Explain each proposed element in your own words.

2. What risks or challenges, for the United States, might arise as a result of free trade? Look for specific examples from the reading.

3. Why did Bill Clinton promote the United States signing a free trade agreement, even if there were some significant risks? Find textual support for your findings.

Document Text

In a few moments, I will sign the North American free trade act into law. NAFTA will tear down trade barriers between our three nations. It will create the world's largest trade zone and create 200,000 jobs in this country by 1995 alone. The environmental and labor side agreements negotiated by our administration will make this agreement a force for social progress as well as economic growth. . . .

Today we have the chance . . . to remake the world. For this new era, our national security we now know will be determined as much by our ability to pull down foreign trade barriers as by our ability to breach distant ramparts. Once again, we are leading. And in so doing, we are rediscovering a fundamental truth about ourselves: When we lead, we build security, we build prosperity for our own people.

We've learned this lesson the hard way. Twice before in this century, we have been forced to define our role in the world. After World War I we turned inward, building walls of protectionism around our Nation. The result was a Great Depression and ultimately another horrible World War. After the Second World War, we took a different course: We reached outward. Gifted leaders of both political parties built a new order based on collective security and expanded trade. They created a foundation of stability and created in the process the conditions which led to the explosion of the great American middle class. . . .

. . . The cold war is over. The grim certitude of the contest with communism has been replaced by the exuberant uncertainty of international economic competition. And the great question of this day is how to ensure security for our people at a time when change is the only constant.

Make no mistake, the global economy with all of its promise and perils is now the central fact of life for hard-working Americans. It has enriched the lives of millions of Americans. But for too many those same winds of change have worn away at the basis of their security. For two decades, most people have worked harder for less. Seemingly secure jobs have been lost. And while America once again is the most productive nation on Earth, this productivity itself holds the seeds of further insecurity. After all, productivity means the same people can produce more or, very often, that fewer people can produce more. This is the world we face.

We cannot stop global change. We cannot repeal the international economic competition that is everywhere. We can only harness the energy to our benefit. Now we must recognize that the only way for a wealthy nation to grow richer is to export, to simply find new customers for the products and services it makes. That, my fellow Americans, is the decision the Congress made when they voted to ratify NAFTA.

13.5: Republican Contract with America (1994)

Historical Context

President Bill Clinton, a Democrat, served two terms as president between Republican presidents George H.W. Bush and Bush's son, George W. Bush. Clinton won the 1992 election handily in the Electoral College, but the popular vote was much closer, in part because an independent candidate named Ross Perot further split the electorate. As a result, Clinton often embraced more conservative positions and policies than some liberal Democrats would have preferred. This was particularly true following the 1994 midterm elections.

Slow economic recovery from the 1990-91 recession left many Americans discontented, and they liked some of Democratic presidential candidate Bill Clinton's ideas. Clinton proposed a fairly moderate agenda, and his message resonated with voters. Although Clinton won the 1992 presidential election, his victory somewhat masked America's continuing shift to the political right. By 1994 Republicans were looking for new ways to reinvigorate voters. They did this by successfully tapping into their traditional base of support among evangelical Christians, talking about "culture wars" and the decline in American religion and morality, and linking this decline to the Democratic Party. Led by Newt Gingrich, who would become Speaker of the House of Representatives, Republicans named their agenda the "Contract with America" in the 1994 midterm elections. This alone, however, did not lead to Republican success.

In the first two years in office, President Clinton attempted to create a universal health care system for all Americans. This effort was led by First Lady Hillary Rodham Clinton. While the idea garnered support from some Americans, others felt it was a significant government overreach. Republicans capitalized on voters' concerns in the 1994 midterm elections in what some call the "Republican Revolution," when Republicans won control of both houses of Congress.

Guiding Questions

1. Read through the list of proposed laws. Under what various themes, or categories, can they be grouped together? Identify a main theme (e.g. "family values") and then list relevant proposals under each them. You may consider making a concept map to help organize your ideas.

2. Make an educated guess. Why did proposed laws, like the ten listed here, appeal to many conservative American voters in 1994? Explain your answer.

3. Apply your knowledge. How do the ideas promoted in the Contract with America compare to policies promoted by Ronald Reagan in the 1980s? Do

you think the ideas presented in the Contract with America would resonate with Republican voters today? Why or why not?

Document Text

As Republican Members of the House of Representatives and as citizens seeking to join that body . . . we offer . . . a detailed agenda for national renewal. . . .

. . . [W]ithin the first 100 days of the 104th Congress, we shall bring to the House Floor the following bills. . . .

1. THE FISCAL RESPONSIBILITY ACT: A balanced budget/tax limitation amendment and a legislative line-item veto to restore fiscal responsibility to an out- of-control Congress, requiring them to live under the same budget constraints as families and businesses.

2. THE TAKING BACK OUR STREETS ACT: An anti-crime package including stronger truth-in- sentencing, "good faith" exclusionary rule exemptions, effective death penalty provisions, and cuts in social spending from this summer's "crime" bill to fund prison construction and additional law enforcement to keep people secure in their neighborhoods and kids safe in their schools.

3. THE PERSONAL RESPONSIBILITY ACT: Discourage illegitimacy and teen pregnancy by prohibiting welfare to minor mothers and denying increased AFDC for additional children while on welfare, cut spending for welfare programs, and enact a tough two-years-and-out provision with work requirements to promote individual responsibility.

4. THE FAMILY REINFORCEMENT ACT: Child support enforcement, tax incentives for adoption, strengthening rights of parents in their children's education, stronger child pornography laws, and an elderly dependent care tax credit to reinforce the central role of families in American society.

5. THE AMERICAN DREAM RESTORATION ACT: A $500 per child tax credit, begin repeal of the marriage tax penalty, and creation of American Dream Savings Accounts to provide middle class tax relief.

6. THE NATIONAL SECURITY RESTORATION ACT: No U.S. troops under U.N. command and restoration of the essential parts of our national security funding to strengthen our national defense and maintain our credibility around the world.

7. THE SENIOR CITIZENS FAIRNESS ACT: Raise the Social Security earnings limit which currently forces seniors out of the workforce, repeal the 1993 tax hikes on Social Security benefits and provide tax incentives for private long-term care insurance to let Older Americans keep more of what they have earned over the years.

8. THE JOB CREATION AND WAGE ENHANCEMENT ACT: Small business incentives, capital gains cut and indexation, neutral cost recovery, risk assessment/cost-benefit analysis, strengthening the Regulatory Flexibility Act and unfunded mandate reform to create jobs and raise worker wages.

9. THE COMMON SENSE LEGAL REFORM ACT: "Loser pays" laws, reasonable limits on punitive damages and reform of product liability laws to stem the endless tide of litigation.

10. THE CITIZEN LEGISLATURE ACT: A first-ever vote on term limits to replace career politicians with citizen legislators.

Further, we will ... work to enact additional budget savings, beyond the budget cuts specifically included in the legislation described above, to ensure that the Federal budget deficit will be less than it would have been without the enactment of these bills.

Respecting the judgment of our fellow citizens as we seek their mandate for reform, we hereby pledge our names to this Contract with America.

13.6: Bill Clinton: Farewell Address (2001)

Historical Context

While Bill Clinton was campaigning for president, questions emerged over the Clintons' investment in the Whitewater Development Corporation in Arkansas. This plagued the Clinton administration for the first two years in office, and in 1994 the Justice Department opened an investigation with a special counsel to investigate the issue. The investigation found no proof of criminal activity by the Clintons. The special counsel did, however, uncover evidence that Clinton engaged in an extramarital affair with a young intern. In 1998 the special counsel released its report listing several possible grounds for impeachment. The Judiciary Committee for the House of Representatives focused on two charges, lying under oath and attempting to obstruct justice, and the Republican-controlled House impeached Clinton. Impeachment means to formally charge with a high crime or misdemeanor. The Senate conducted the president's impeachment trial, and in early 1999 it found him not guilty on both charges. He thus remained in office.

Over the years several women had accused Clinton of sexual harassment and assaults that happened between the 1970s and 1990s. In 2017 the social media #MeToo movement shined a spotlight on the pervasive sexual harassment and assault of women on all parts of the racial and socioeconomic spectrum in America. In the wake of this movement, historians and other scholars began to reevaluate Clinton's legacy.

By the time Clinton reached the end of his presidency in 2001, he had weathered significant political turmoil but also presided over unprecedented economic prosperity. Clinton had spent the majority of his presidency working with a Republican-controlled Congress. That meant that in order to pass any legislation, he had to garner significant support among conservatives. Keep this in mind as you read his Farewell Address.

Guiding Questions

1. What policies or practices does President Clinton highlight in his speech that sound like they could be ideas championed by the Republican Party? Read the text carefully and make a list of specific examples.

2. What, according to Clinton, are the *international* challenges facing America moving forward? What are his proposed solutions? Read the text carefully and make a list of specific examples.

3. What, according to Clinton, are the *domestic* challenges facing America in the twenty-first century? What are his proposed solutions? Read the text carefully and make a list of specific examples.

My fellow citizens, tonight is my last opportunity to speak to you from the Oval Office as your President....

...I have sought to give America a new kind of Government, smaller, more modern, more effective, full of ideas and policies appropriate to this new time, always putting people first, always focusing on the future.

Working together, America has done well. Our economy is breaking records with more than 22 million new jobs, the lowest unemployment in 30 years, the highest homeownership ever, the longest expansion in history. Our families and communities are stronger. Thirty-five million Americans have used the family leave law; 8 million have moved off welfare. Crime is at a 25-year low. Over 10 million Americans receive more college aid, and more people than ever are going to college. Our schools are better.... More than 3 million children have health insurance now, and more than 7 million Americans have been lifted out of poverty. Incomes are rising across the board. Our air and water are cleaner. Our food and drinking water are safer. And more of our precious land has been preserved in the continental United States than at any time in 100 years.

...Tonight I want to leave you with three thoughts about our future. First, America must maintain our record of fiscal responsibility....

Second, because the world is more connected every day, in every way, America's security and prosperity require us to continue to lead in the world....

The global economy is giving more of our own people and billions around the world the chance to work and live and raise their families with dignity. But the forces of integration that have created these good opportunities also make us more subject to global forces of destruction, to terrorism, organized crime and narcotrafficking, the spread of deadly weapons and disease, the degradation of the global environment.

The expansion of trade hasn't fully closed the gap between those of us who live on the cutting edge of the global economy and the billions around the world who live on the knife's edge of survival. This global gap requires more than compassion; it requires action. Global poverty is a powder keg that could be ignited by our indifference.

...If we want the world to embody our shared values, then we must assume a shared responsibility....

Third, we must remember that America cannot lead in the world unless here at home we weave the threads of our coat of many colors into the fabric of one America. As we become ever more diverse, we must work harder to unite around our common values and our common humanity. We must work harder to overcome our differences, in our hearts and in our laws. We must treat all our people with fairness and dignity, regardless of their race, religion, gender, or sexual orientation, and regardless of when they arrived in our country—always moving toward the more perfect Union of our Founders' dreams.

13.7: Unit 13 Review

Many people like to say the past does not change. While it is true the events of the past have occurred and cannot change, our interpretation of those events can change significantly as time passes and we gain access to new information. Historians, then, are still grappling with our nation's more modern "history." As time passes and more documents are declassified, more interviews conducted, and more books and articles written, historians engage in rigorous scholarship seeking to understand how decisions were made and the impact those choices had on nations and individuals.

We can draw some basic conclusions about our most recent history, but our understanding of American history in the last thirty years is less nuanced than it will be in another thirty years when we have the benefit of more information and hindsight. Our goal now, then, is two-fold. First we want to draw the conclusions we can by analyzing the materials we have available—documents like the ones in this unit. Second, we want to ask questions that will help us draw those conclusions and determine what we need to learn more about to better understand the world we live in. This unit helps us achieve those two goals. It provides a doorway for us to walk through, walk back in time and study what happened. But it also opens a window to the present and the future. This allows us to ask thoughtful questions about how the most recent past influences our current state of affairs.

The unit questions asked you to consider the following:

1. What contributed to deindustrialization and economic hardship in places like Pittsburgh, Detroit, and Milwaukee—cities once known for their significant industrial production? What impact did deindustrialization have on America?

2. What created opportunities for a Democrat like Bill Clinton to win the White House in the 1990s, but at the same time for Republicans to win, and then retain, control of Congress?

3. How did the U.S. and global economy change significantly in the 1990s and beyond, and how did this create new challenges and opportunities for the United States?

After reading the unit, it should be clear that the global economy changed dramatically from the 1970s to the 1990s. New technologies like computers and the internet fundamentally changed workers' productivity and created a more integrated global economy. Goods could be made and traded around the world. This created many opportunities for consumers to purchase goods at lower prices, but it also increased job competition. Politicians looked for new ways to take advantage of these changes through trade agreements like NAFTA, but the outcomes were not always clear or advantageous to everyone.

Although this unit focused on the political and economic changes during this era, it also noted an increase in cultural tensions, particularly in the 1990s, sometimes referred to as an era of "culture wars." Many of the divisions over social issues emerged in the 1960s and 1970s and increased throughout the latter half of the twentieth century. In the twenty-first century Democrats and Republicans have moved further apart, with each advocating more strongly for its own party's social and economic perspectives.

The final unit in this document reader is Unit 14: Twenty-First Century America. It is designed to help you identify and understand some current trends in America and to draw connections between what is happening in more modern times and what has happened in the past.

14.1: Twenty-First Century America

Overview

The last unit concluded by noting that the 1990s saw an increase in "culture wars" and a polarization of our politics. In many ways this trend has continued into the twenty-first century. Our goal is to understand how and why that occurred and when and why we see breaks with the past. The readings in this unit are aimed at highlighting some of the major events and ideas that have shaped the modern century.

The terrorist attacks on September 11, 2001, altered the course of the nation and Americans' attitudes and perceptions. The attacks on the Twin Towers in New York, the Pentagon in Virginia, and the plane that passengers took down in Pennsylvania before it could strike its target combined to form the largest coordinated terrorist attack on U.S. soil, and the first major attack of any kind by foreigners since the Japanese attack on Pearl Harbor in 1941. The first reading in the unit shines a spotlight on 9/11 to illustrate how Americans were feeling that day and how President George W. Bush sought to comfort them. It is no surprise that these events left Americans feeling vulnerable and ready to fight those responsible for the death and destruction. In the subsequent days, the United States would engage in war in Afghanistan in an attempt to bring the perpetrators of the 9/11 attacks to justice. It would prove to be a more complicated war than anyone anticipated. The subsequent reading, by Senator Robert C. Byrd, expresses concerns over a second war that America engaged in within a two-year period, the war in Iraq.

In that speech Byrd provides numerous reasons as to why he could not support the war in Iraq. Among those reasons is his rejection of the "doctrine of preemption." The notion of preemptive war would later be called the "Bush Doctrine," since it was a break with past policy, and some argued it was a violation of Article 51 of the Charter of the United Nations. Article 51 provides nations with the right to militarily defend themselves from an attack, but it does not specify at what point that can legally occur. President Bush's administration published a paper in September 2002 that claimed countries could preemptively defend themselves through the use of military force against potential attacks by enemies employing weapons of mass destruction (WMDs). Much of the international community believed that was an inappropriate reading of the UN charter and that the Bush administration developed that interpretation in order to lay the groundwork for the Iraq invasion of 2003, since up to that point there had been no new evidence or intelligence that justified an armed military intervention by the United States. Senator Byrd took to the Senate floor a few months after the United States invaded Iraq to lay out all of the reasons he could not support the president or the war.

In 2008 Barack Obama inherited both the wars in Afghanistan and Iraq when he was elected president of the United States. Before winning the election, however, he delivered a candid assessment of the role of race in American society and politics. Obama was uniquely situated to address the issue of race as the most popular candidate of color in a presidential election to date. Obama was of mixed ancestry. His mother was a white woman from Kansas and his father a black man from Kenya. Some people described him as "too black" and others as "not black enough," since his family did not bear the legacy of American slavery as many African American families do. (His wife, Michelle, however, is the descendent of formerly enslaved people and, therefore, their two daughters are as well.) Obama's election offered a real moment of hope for the country. It signaled the possibility that the nation could move beyond the racial and ethnic divides that had long torn at the fabric of American society. However, during Obama's presidency the partisan divide in America grew stronger.

The last two speeches in this unit illustrate that divide but also reflect a shift in partisan loyalty among some Americans. In 2010 the Tea Party movement helped Republicans regain control of Congress during the midterm elections. Obama retained control of the presidency for a second term, but Republicans held the Congress throughout that time. In 2016 Republican Donald J. Trump won the presidency, in part with the help of one-time Obama voters in key midwestern states. This shift in voter loyalty recalled the rise of Reagan Democrats in the 1980s.

The 2016 presidential election and its aftermath intensified partisan divisions and saw a renewal of racial and ethnic hostility. In particular, those who espoused white nationalist and white supremacist views gained new visibility, particularly through social media platforms such as Twitter, Facebook, and YouTube. This visibility also led to events such as the violent confrontations surrounding a 2017 neo-Nazi march in Charlottesville, Virginia, and the 2018 Tree of Life synagogue attack in Pittsburgh, Pennsylvania. In Charlottesville a man intentionally crashed his car into those protesting the white nationalist rally, killing a woman. In Pittsburgh a man murdered eleven people at the synagogue after making statements that he wanted to "kill Jews."

As you read the following documents, think about how the ideas and events they articulate have impacted your experience in America. Consider how your own political perspectives may affect the way you analyze and understand contemporary issues and our current state of affairs.

1. How has America's war on terror impacted or defined your life and/or the world around you? Come up with two or more specific examples.

2. What issues do you think are most pressing in contemporary America? How do these compare to the issues facing the nation historically? Give specific examples where you see history informing or affecting the present.

3. How can we learn from our history so that we can make informed decisions moving forward? What can we do as a nation to become a stronger, more unified community where all people thrive?

14.2: George W. Bush: Address to the Nation on September 11, 2001

Historical Context

On the evening of September 11, 2001, President George W. Bush spoke to the nation about the terrorist attacks perpetrated on the nation earlier that day by members of al-Qaeda, under the direction of its leader, the Saudi-born Osama bin Laden. The 9/11 attacks fundamentally reshaped American attitudes, perceptions, and foreign policy in the twenty-first century. Terrorist attacks had occurred in the past, but the magnitude of the 9/11 attacks and the methods used led Americans to view terrorism through a new lens. On this day, nearly 3,000 people were killed, most of whom were civilians. On the day of the attacks, when Bush gave the following speech, no one knew how terrorism would come to define the early decades of the new century.

In response to 9/11, America began fighting a war against al-Qaeda in Afghanistan. That country had been under the control of a radical Islamic group known as the Taliban since 1996. The Taliban had refused to hand over bin Laden and had allowed al-Qaeda terrorist cells to use the country as a safe haven. (Al-Qaeda had cells throughout the region, including places like Pakistan where Osama bin Laden was later killed by U.S. Special Forces in 2011.) The war in Afghanistan began with a joint coalition of British and American forces. Working together, the two nations and their Afghan allies overthrew the restrictive Taliban regime in 2001, shortly after the American-British invasion. Since that time, however, the war in Afghanistan has become the United States' longest war. (At the time of publication, 2019, the United States was still fighting this war.)

The 9/11 attacks deeply affected American attitudes and perceptions, particularly about American safety, Muslims, and immigrants. Within six weeks of the attacks, Congress passed the USA PATRIOT Act: Preserving Life and Liberty in an effort to better fight terrorism. (The law's official title is "Uniting and Strengthening America by Providing Appropriate Tools Required to Intercept and Obstruct Terrorism.") The law was revised in 2005 when many people realized that it was quite expansive and violated Americans' civil liberties. Some controversial provisions remain in effect today, but law enforcement agencies highlight the law as an important tool in combating terrorism.

The 9/11 attacks also initiated America's war on terror, which resembles the Cold War of the twentieth century. It is not a formal conflict but rather a set of ideals, convictions, attitudes, policies, and practices aimed at combating terrorism at home and abroad. Similar to the Cold War, the war on terror has played on people's fears and in many cases increased Americans' wariness of certain groups of people, in particular Muslims and immigrants. There were increased physical and verbal assaults on Muslims, both citizens and foreigners, in the United States following the 9/11 attacks, and anti-Muslim rhetoric increased as well. This legacy is one that America is still grappling with, especially as white nationalism has surged throughout the United States and Europe.

Guiding Questions

1. Read the following speech by George W. Bush and consider the tone. What message was he trying to send to the American people? Why?

2. What steps did the president plan to take following the attacks to get the country back to normal? Identify specific examples from the text.

3. Based on the speech, what do you learn about many foreign nations' responses to the attacks?

Document Text

Good evening. Today, our fellow citizens, our way of life, our very freedom came under attack in a series of deliberate and deadly terrorist acts. The victims were in airplanes, or in their offices; secretaries, businessmen and women, military and federal workers; moms and dads, friends and neighbors. Thousands of lives were suddenly ended by evil, despicable acts of terror.

The pictures of airplanes flying into buildings, fires burning, huge structures collapsing, have filled us with disbelief, terrible sadness, and a quiet, unyielding anger. These acts of mass murder were intended to frighten our nation into chaos and retreat. But they have failed; our country is strong.

A great people has been moved to defend a great nation. Terrorist attacks can shake the foundations of our biggest buildings, but they cannot touch the foundation of America. These acts shattered steel, but they cannot dent the steel of American resolve.

America was targeted for attack because we're the brightest beacon for freedom and opportunity in the world. And no one will keep that light from shining.

Today, our nation saw evil, the very worst of human nature. And we responded with the best of America—with the daring of our rescue workers, with the caring for strangers and neighbors who came to give blood and help in any way they could.

Immediately following the first attack, I implemented our government's emergency response plans. Our military is powerful, and it's prepared. Our emergency teams are working in New York City and Washington, D.C. to help with local rescue efforts.

Our first priority is to get help to those who have been injured, and to take every precaution to protect our citizens at home and around the world from further attacks.

The functions of our government continue without interruption. Federal agencies in Washington which had to be evacuated today are reopening for essential personnel tonight, and will be open for business tomorrow. Our financial institutions remain strong, and the American economy will be open for business, as well.

The search is underway for those who are behind these evil acts. I've directed the full resources of our intelligence and law enforcement communities to find those responsible and to bring them to justice. We will make no distinction between the terrorists who committed these acts and those who harbor them.

I appreciate so very much the members of Congress who have joined me in strongly condemning these attacks. And on behalf of the American people, I thank the many world leaders who have called to offer their condolences and assistance. . . .

14.3: Robert C. Byrd: "The Emperor Has No Clothes" Speech (2003)

Historical Context

Robert C. Byrd was a Democratic senator from West Virginia who held that position from 1959 until his death in 2010. Byrd was generally considered a war hawk, meaning someone who supported the military and government intervention in foreign affairs. But by 2003 he was concerned about the president having too much power and taking over responsibilities constitutionally delegated to Congress. In particular, Byrd was a strong critic of President Bush's proposed war in Iraq.

President Bush's administration tried to establish connections between al-Qaeda and Iraqi leader Saddam Hussein shortly after the 9/11 terrorist attacks. No viable links were established, but raising the question put enough doubt in some Americans' minds that they were willing to entertain the possibility of a war in Iraq. This idea, coupled with false claims that the Iraqi regime was developing weapons of mass destruction (WMDs)—chemical or nuclear—eventually paved the way for war. In 2003 the United States engaged in a ground invasion to remove Hussein from power. Six months after that ground invasion and the removal of Hussein, the United States had not found any evidence of WMDs or nuclear facilities.

Political leaders around the world had long agreed that Saddam Hussein was a terrible dictator who severely abused certain members of his population. Up to that point, however, American and world leaders did not believe that the situation was problematic enough to warrant military intervention. What changed? If the United States genuinely believed that Hussein was developing WMDs that he planned to use on the United States, some people argued that such actions would justify armed intervention. Evidence that proved he was developing WMDs, however, remained spotty and even at the time was never proved to be highly credible. Critics of the Bush administration argued that the real reason the administration wanted to invade Iraq was likely two-fold. First, it would bring a final close to the Gulf War that occurred under President George H.W. Bush in the 1990s. Many of the senior White House officials in the younger Bush's administration had also been members of his father's administration and were not satisfied that they had left Hussein in power at the end of that conflict. Second, Iraq possessed significant oil reserves, and some analysts and political pundits believed that motivated U.S. action in Iraq.

The United States invaded Iraq in March 2003, and in October, Senator Byrd—a fierce critic of the war—gave the following speech. He used Hans Christian Andersen's fairy tale, "The Emperor's New Clothes," to illustrate his feelings towards the war. In that tale, two traveling men convince the emperor they are weavers and can weave him the finest robes in the land—robes that were magical. They were visible only to those who were bright, capable, and fit for office. The greedy emperor who loved new clothes ordered the cloth to be made. He sent his aids to check on the weavers and make sure they were producing the cloth. All of the aids he sent feared they would lose credibility if they said they could not see the cloth, so they lied and commented on its beauty. When presented with the new "robes" the emperor could not see them either. Rather than admit this, he pretended he could see them. He got dressed and headed out to a procession through the town wearing his new finery. At first everyone cheered. . . . Keep this story in mind as you begin reading the document.

Guiding Questions

1. How does Byrd use the story of "The Emperor's New Clothes" to make his point about the war in Iraq?

2. What, according to Byrd, are the falsehoods or misrepresentations President Bush told the nation to get people to support the war? List them.

3. What reasons does Byrd give as to why he cannot support the war or the president? Make a numbered list explaining these reasons in your own words.

Document Text

. . . But, the bubble burst when an innocent child loudly exclaimed, for the whole kingdom to hear, that the Emperor had nothing on at all. He had no clothes.

That tale seems to me very like the way this nation was led to war.

We were told that we were threatened by weapons of mass destruction in Iraq, but they have not been seen.

We were told that the throngs of Iraqi's would welcome our troops with flowers, but no throngs or flowers appeared.

We were led to believe that Saddam Hussein was connected to the attack on the Twin Towers and the Pentagon, but no evidence has ever been produced.

We were told in 16 words that Saddam Hussein tried to buy "yellow cake" from Africa for the production of nuclear weapons, but the story has turned into empty air.

We were frightened with visions of mushroom clouds, but they turned out to be only vapors of the mind.

We were told that major combat was over but 101 [as of October 17] Americans have died in combat since that proclamation from the deck of an aircraft carrier by our very own Emperor in his new clothes.

Our emperor says that we are not occupiers, yet we show no inclination to relinquish the country of Iraq to its people.

Those who have dared to expose the nakedness of the Administration's policies in Iraq have been subjected to scorn. Those who have noticed the elephant in the room—that is, the fact that this war was based on falsehoods—have had our patriotism questioned. . . .

The Emperor has no clothes. This entire adventure in Iraq has been based on propaganda and manipulation. . . .

Taking the nation to war based on misleading rhetoric and hyped intelligence is a travesty and a tragedy. . . . It is dangerous to manipulate the truth. It is dangerous because once having lied, it is difficult to ever be believed again. . . .

I cannot support the continuation of a policy that unwisely ties down 150,000 American troops for the foreseeable future, with no end in sight.

I cannot support a President who refuses to authorize the reasonable change in course that would bring traditional allies to our side in Iraq.

I cannot support the politics of zeal and "might makes right" that created the new American arrogance and unilateralism which passes for foreign policy in this Administration.

I cannot support this foolish manifestation of the dangerous and destabilizing doctrine of preemption that changes the image of America into that of a reckless bully.

The emperor has no clothes. And our former allies around the world were the first to loudly observe it. . . .

14.4: Barack Obama: "A More Perfect Union" (2008)

Historical Context

In 2008 Democratic presidential candidate Barack Obama gave a speech entitled "A More Perfect Union" that explicitly addressed the role of race in historical and contemporary America. The title of the speech comes from the opening line of the U.S. Constitution, "We the people, in order to form a more perfect union . . ." Obama wove the concept of a "more perfect union" into the speech to illustrate how the nation can live up to its creed by addressing its racial legacy head-on and looking for common ground that would benefit all Americans, regardless of their racial or ethnic identity.

As a black man running for president, Obama had largely avoided directly addressing the issue of race during most of the campaign season. However, he chose to engage with it directly following the public release of videos of his friend and former pastor Jeremiah Wright speaking angrily from the pulpit about race and expressing anti-white sentiments. Obama did not excuse Wright's position and language or disown him as a friend and confidant, but he did use the issue as a tool to help America think more deeply about the legacy of the nation's racial past and how it impacts people today. Throughout the speech Obama focused on how America could take steps to move beyond its racial heritage and create "a more perfect union."

Guiding Questions

1. In the full text of the speech, Obama addressed the importance of understanding the history of the black experience in America. He elaborated on a few examples of issues from the nation's past that have negatively affected African Americans' access to equal opportunities and economic security. Based on what you have learned in the previous units, identify some of the topics you think would be on Obama's list and explain their impact on America.

2. What frustrations and fears, legitimate or not, do some white Americans harbor that could lead to anger and frustration and increase racial tensions? Identify specific examples from the text and explain why each could cause frustration and tension?

3. What are Obama's proposed solutions to binding up the nation's racial wounds and becoming "a more perfect union"? Identify specific examples from the text.

. . . For the men and women of Reverend Wright's generation [African Americans who lived during segregation], the memories of humiliation and doubt and fear have not gone away; nor has the anger and the bitterness of those years. That anger may not get expressed in public, in front of white co-workers or white friends. But it does find voice in the barbershop or around the kitchen table. . . .

. . . In fact, a similar anger exists within segments of the white community. Most working- and middle-class white Americans don't feel that they have been particularly privileged by their race. . . . as far as they're concerned, no one's handed them anything, they've built it from scratch. They've worked hard all their lives, many times only to see their jobs shipped overseas or their pension dumped after a lifetime of labor. They are anxious about their futures, and feel their dreams slipping away; in an era of stagnant wages and global competition, opportunity comes to be seen as a zero sum game, in which your dreams come at my expense. So when they are told to bus their children to a school across town; when they hear that an African American is getting an advantage in landing a good job or a spot in a good college because of an injustice that they themselves never committed; when they're told that their fears about crime in urban neighborhoods are somehow prejudiced, resentment builds over time.

Like the anger within the black community, these resentments aren't always expressed in polite company. But they have helped shape the political landscape for at least a generation. Anger over welfare and affirmative action helped forge the Reagan Coalition. Politicians routinely exploited fears of crime for their own electoral ends. Talk show hosts and conservative commentators built entire careers unmasking bogus claims of racism while dismissing legitimate discussions of racial injustice and inequality as mere political correctness or reverse racism.

. . . And yet, to wish away the resentments of white Americans, to label them as misguided or even racist, without recognizing they are grounded in legitimate concerns—this too widens the racial divide, and blocks the path to understanding.

. . . But I have asserted a firm conviction . . . that working together we can move beyond some of our old racial wounds, and that in fact we have no choice if we are to continue on the path of a more perfect union.

For the African-American community, that path means embracing the burdens of our past without becoming victims of our past. It means continuing to insist on a full measure of justice in every aspect of American life. But it also means binding our particular grievances—for better health care, and better schools, and better jobs—to the larger aspirations of all Americans—the white woman struggling to break the glass ceiling, the white man whose been laid off, the immigrant trying to feed his family....

... In the white community, the path to a more perfect union means acknowledging that what ails the African-American community does not just exist in the minds of black people; that the legacy of discrimination—and current incidents of discrimination, while less overt than in the past—are real and must be addressed.... It requires all Americans to realize that your dreams do not have to come at the expense of my dreams; that investing in the health, welfare, and education of black and brown and white children will ultimately help all of America prosper....

... I would not be running for President if I didn't believe with all my heart that this is what the vast majority of Americans want for this country. This union may never be perfect, but generation after generation has shown that it can always be perfected....

14.5: Sarah Palin: Keynote Speech at the Inaugural Tea Party Convention (2010)

Historical Context

Sarah Palin, the governor of Alaska, skyrocketed to fame when Republican John Mc-Cain chose her as his running mate during the 2008 presidential election. McCain and Palin lost the election to Democrat Barack Obama (and Vice President Joe Biden), but the ideas they campaigned on resonated with many American voters. Palin returned to those issues in her 2010 speech, in an effort to energize the electorate. Her efforts and those of other Tea Party activists proved successful.

The Tea Party was not a political party. Rather, it was a new vein emerging among conservative Americans. Individuals who identified with the Tea Party movement came from various political backgrounds and included Libertarians, independents, and traditional Republicans, to name a few. Many of the ideas promoted by the Tea Party would eventually be adopted by Republicans who leaned further to the right on the party's political spectrum, and starting in the 2010 midterm elections these members helped push the Republican Party as a whole even further to the right. There is no singular definition of what the Tea Party platform entailed, but as Palin noted in this speech, it revolved around conservative ideas like lower taxes, limited government, and national security. Some Tea Party candidates and activists also played off Americans' racial and ethnic fears by promoting false narratives about President Obama's citizenship and religion. (He is an American and a Christian, not a foreign-born Muslim as some politicians claimed.) Many Tea Party members also adopted a firm anti-immigrant stance, arguing the nation needed to secure its borders and deport undocumented people in the country. As you read the following excerpt of Palin's speech, you will learn more about Tea Party views.

Tea Party activists were extremely successful in changing the political landscape in 2010. It is not unusual for the party in power (in this case the Democrats) to lose control of Congress when they also hold the presidency. The shift in power in 2010, however, was noteworthy since Republicans won 63 seats in congressional elections. (They only needed 39 to regain control of Congress.) This monumental midterm political shift happened as Republicans, many of whom identified as Tea Party candidates, tapped into the hopes, dreams, and fears of conservative Americans.

Guiding Questions

1. Read through the excerpt of Palin's speech and list attributes associated with the Tea Party. When necessary, include a brief definition so that you know what a term means.

2. Review your notes from Unit 12 and explain who Barry Goldwater was and why he was important to the Republican Party. Next, explain why Palin quotes Goldwater and how she thinks that America's current course of action could lead to its demise as Goldwater predicted.

3. How, according to Palin, have the Democrats failed America, and what solutions do Palin and the Tea Party offer to save the country?

Document Text

. . . The Tea Party movement is not a top-down operation. It's a ground-up call to action. . . .

The soul of this movement is the people —everyday Americans who grow our food and run our small businesses, teach our kids, and fight our wars. They're folks in small towns and cities across this great nation who saw what was happening—and they saw and were concerned, and they got involved. Like you, they go to town hall meetings, and they write op-eds. They run for local office. You all have the courage to stand up and speak out. You have a vision for the future, one that values conservative principles and common sense solutions. . . .

. . . The problems that we face in the real world require real solutions. . . . However, as Barry Goldwater said: "We can be conquered by bombs . . . but we can also be conquered by neglect by ignoring our constitution and disregarding the principles of limited government."

And in the past year, his words rang true. Washington has now replaced private irresponsibility with public irresponsibility. The list of companies and industries that the government is . . . bailing out and taking over, it continues to grow. First it was the banks, mortgage companies, financial institutions, then automakers. Soon, if they had their way, health care, student loans. . . .

. . . When Washington passed a 787 billion dollar "stimulus bill," we were nervous because they just spent 700 billion dollars to bailout Wall Street. . . .

. . . [T]he White House can't even tell us how many jobs were actually created [by the "stimulus bill"]. . . .

But one number we are sure of is the unemployment number. And that's at 9.7, which is well above the 8 percent mark that we were promised our stimulus package would go to avoid. And unemployment now is — underemployment now is 16.5 percent. . . .

. . . We're drowning in national debt and many of us have had enough.

. . . Our government needs to adopt a pro-market agenda. . . . Washington
has got to . . . lower taxes for small businesses so that our mom and pops can
reinvest and hire people so that our businesses can thrive. . . .

. . . And while we're at it, let's expedite the regulatory and permitting and legal
processes for on and offshore [oil] drilling. . . .

. . . And finally, if we're going to get serious about fiscal restraint . . . cut spending. . . .

. . . We are the loyal opposition. And we have a vision for the future of our
country . . . anchored in time tested-truths: that the government that governs least, governs best. And that the Constitution . . . provides the best road
map towards a more perfect union. And that only a limited government can
expand prosperity and opportunity for all. And that freedom is a God-given
right and it is worth fighting for. . . .

. . . Tea Party nation, we know that there is nothing wrong with America that
together we can't fix as Americans.

14.6: Donald J. Trump: Inaugural Address (2017)

Historical Context

Republican Donald J. Trump won the 2016 presidential election against Democrat Hillary Clinton. Trump carried rural America and won the support of blue-collar workers throughout the nation, including miners and other factor workers, both current and former. Even though Trump himself was a wealthy man, he spoke to voters' frustrations about income inequality and declining job and economic opportunities and their fears about national security. He promised to bring back mining and manufacturing jobs, restrict immigration, and shore up the nation's borders. Trump promoted a populist ideology, one that advocated getting rid of career politicians and bureaucrats in order to give voice to Americans who felt their interests had been overlooked by mainstream politicians.

Guiding Questions

1. In the following excerpts from President Trump's inaugural address, he states that "a new vision will govern our land, from this day forward, it's going to be only America first." What does "America first" mean according to Trump, both ideologically and practically? Identify and explain specific examples to support your response.

2. What role does "patriotism" play in Trump's vision of America? How might people interpret the concept of patriotism differently?

3. The tagline of Trump's campaign, "Make America great again," appears in this speech. Why did some Americans express support for this sentiment and why did some express concern? Use what you have learned over the course of the semester as evidence to support your explanation. Be specific.

Document Text

...For too long a small group in our nation's capital has reaped the rewards of government while the people have borne the cost.

...That all changes—starting right here, and right now....

...January 20th 2017, will be remembered as the day the people became the rulers of this nation again.

The forgotten men and women of our country will be forgotten no longer.

Americans want great schools for their children, safe neighborhoods for their families, and good jobs for themselves.

. . . But for too many of our citizens, a different reality exists . . . poverty in our inner cities; rusted-out factories . . . across the landscape of our nation; an education system, flush with cash, but which leaves our young and beautiful students deprived of all knowledge; and . . . crime and gangs and drugs. . . .

. . . For many decades, we've enriched foreign industry at the expense of American industry; Subsidized the armies of other countries, while allowing the sad depletion of our own military; We've defended other nation's borders while refusing to defend our own. . . .

. . . One by one, the factories shuttered and left our shores, with not even a thought about the millions upon millions of American workers left behind.

The wealth of our middle class has been ripped from their homes and then redistributed all across the world.

But that is the past and now we are looking only to the future.

. . . From this day on a new vision will govern our land. From this day forward, it's only going to be America First. . . .

Every decision on trade, on taxes, on immigration, on foreign affairs will be made to benefit American workers and American families.

. . . We will bring back our jobs, we will bring back our borders, we will bring back our wealth, we will bring back our dreams.

. . . We will follow two simple rules—buy American and hire American.

. . . At the bedrock of our politics will be a total allegiance to the United States of America, and through our loyalty to our country, we will rediscover new allegiance to each other.

. . . It's time to remember that old wisdom our soldiers will never forget: that whether we are black or brown or white, we all bleed the same red blood of patriots, we all enjoy the same glorious freedoms, and we all salute the same great American Flag.

. . . To all Americans, in every city near and far, small and large, from mountain to mountain, and from ocean to ocean, hear these words:

You will never be ignored again.

Your voice, your hopes, and your dreams, will define our American destiny. And your courage and goodness and love will forever guide us along the way.

Together, We Will Make America Strong Again. We Will Make America Wealthy Again. We Will Make America Proud Again. We Will Make America Safe Again. And, Yes, Together, We Will Make America Great Again.

14.7: Unit 14 Review

This unit began by asking you to think about how the ideas and events articulated in the readings have impacted your experience in America and to consider how your own political perspectives may affect the way you analyze and understand contemporary issues and our current state of affairs. Specifically, the unit questions asked you to reflect on your experiences and to draw connections between the past and present:

1. How has America's war on terror impacted or defined your life and/or the world around you?

2. What issues do you think are most pressing in contemporary America? How do these compare to the issues facing the nation historically? Give specific examples where you see history informing or affecting the present.

3. How can we learn from our history so that we can make informed decisions moving forward? What can we do as a nation to become a stronger, more unified community where all people thrive?

We are living in contemporary America and therefore do not have the necessary time, space, distance, or archival material to engage in a full historical analysis of the present day. Nevertheless, we can use our historical knowledge to better understand the world we live in. We can be better informed citizens by watching the news and thinking critically about the information we consume. In order to be more critical consumers, we need to evaluate contemporary sources with the same rigor that we apply to historical sources. For example, we should ask questions like: Who is authoring the piece? Where did they get their information? What is the goal of the piece? What does the author, or the author's affiliations, have to gain by promoting a certain perspective? Do you feel that you have enough background knowledge to effectively analyze and evaluate a document? Do you feel that your own political preferences may influence how you read, analyze, and evaluate a document? What should members of your own generation do to better understand history and make good decisions for the future?

CPSIA information can be obtained
at www.ICGtesting.com
Printed in the USA
LVHW061452210122
709062LV00014B/827